TM 9-705

M3 / M3A1 SCOUT CAR AND M2 MORTAR MOTOR CARRIAGE

TECHNICAL MANUAL

Originally published
February 19, 1941

by WAR DEPARTMENT

©2012 Periscope Film LLC
All Rights Reserved
ISBN#978-1-937684-71-6

TM 9-705

WAR DEPARTMENT

TECHNICAL MANUAL

SCOUT CARS, M3, M3A1, AND 4.2
MORTAR MOTOR CARRIAGE, M2

February 19, 1941

TM 9-705

TECHNICAL MANUAL
No. 9-705

WAR DEPARTMENT,
Washington, *February 19, 1941*.

SCOUT CARS, M3, M3A1, AND 4.2 MORTAR MOTOR CARRIAGE, M2

Prepared under direction of the
Chief of Ordnance

	Paragraphs
Section I. General	1-2
II. Description and characteristics	3-4
III. Engine group	5-11
IV. Fuel system	12-16
V. Ignition system	17-23
VI. Cooling system	24-27
VII. Clutch	28-31
VIII. Transmission	32-35
IX. Transfer case	36-39
X. Propeller shafts	40-43
XI. Axle assemblies and steering gear	44-52
XII. Electrical equipment; instruments	53-60
XIII. Operating instructions	61-76
XIV. Field expedients	77-82
XV. Maintenance	83-88
XVI. Lubrication	89-93
XVII. Inspections	94-97
XVIII. General care; preservation; records	98-102
XIX. Spare parts and accessories	103-104
XX. Armament and mounts	105-115

	Page
Appendix. List of references	147
Index	219

Section I

GENERAL

	Paragraph
Purpose and scope	1
References	2

1. Purpose and scope.—The instructions and principles set forth in this manual are published for the information and guidance of

285994°—41——1　　　　1

the using arms and all personnel charged with the operation, inspection, and maintenance of the vehicles. Included are descriptions of the major units and instructions for their operation, inspection, and minor repair.

2. References.—All Standard Nomenclature Lists, Technical Manuals, Field Manuals, Army Regulations, and other publications for the matériel described herein are listed in the appendix.

Section II

DESCRIPTION AND CHARACTERISTICS

	Paragraph
General description	3
Tabulation of characteristics	4

3. General description.—The vehicles described in this manual are intended for military use in the theater of operations as combat vehicles by the Calvary and Field Artillery, involving the transportation of personnel and battery details, and operation for messenger service, reconnaissance, and combat purposes. While basically of similar construction, the various models are grouped together to include scout car, M3, and 4.2 mortar motor carriage, M2 (T5E1), in one category and scout car, M3A1, in another for purposes of description and comparison.

a. Construction.—As manufactured by the White Motor Company, Cleveland, Ohio, these vehicles consist of a specially designed, commercial type, four wheel, four-wheel drive, truck chassis powered with a conventional six-cylinder gasoline engine and surmounted by a special armored hull. Armored sections of the hull, including the engine hood, radiator cover, and body (tonneau or personnel compartment) are fabricated by the Diebold Safe and Lock Co. from ¼-inch armor plate, assembled with nickel-steel, American standard, ⅜-24 oval countersunk head screws and elastic stop nuts, and mounted on a double drop type, channel section frame.

b. Scout car, M3.—This vehicle (fig. 1, 2, 3, and 4) can be identified by the square rear corners of the body and the circular steel track for machine-gun mounts which encircles the body interior flush with the top of the armor plates.

(1) *Hood.*—Top and side protection is afforded the engine by the hood which is made of two double panels hinged together to facilitate opening. Two latches on each side secure the hood when closed. A four-blade, armor plate shutter is provided for radiator protection and is operated manually from the driver's compartment; stops are pro-

vided to hold the shutters open in three intermediate positions between the fully opened and closed positions.

(2) *Windshield.*—The full width shatterproof ¼-inch glass windshield is provided with glass wings on each side and is hinged at the bottom to the cowl. Provision is afforded to fold the glass windshield forward onto the hood where it can be secured. With the glass windshield out of the way, a protective shield of ½-inch armor plate, hinged at the top to the shield supporting frame, may be lowered in place after releasing its outer prop. For observation purposes, two vision slots are provided in the armor shield; each opening may be covered by a sliding panel of armor which is held in position by a thumbscrew.

(3) *Body.*—The body, with one rear and two side doors, is protected by armor plate at the sides and rear. Each side door is provided with a quadrant to hold the door open at various positions up to the extreme width of the vehicle, and a folding armor shield to heighten the armor protection for the driver's compartment. The side shields are hinged to the respective doors and held in an upright position by vertical rods which extend up from and are latched to the doors. Observation openings are provided in the side shields similar to the vision slots in the front shield. All flooring is fabricated from checkered aluminum alloy plates. A seat is provided in the driver's compartment at the front for the driver (left) and observation commander (right); additional seats in the personnel compartment to the rear provide for a crew of six.

(4) *Top.*—Two removable metal bows connected with web strips form a support together with the windshield frame for the detachable canvas top. Removable curtains having pyrolin windows are also provided at the sides and rear and secured in place by a row of fasteners all around the upper, outside edge of the body. Top and side curtains may be stowed in the bag provided on the right front fender.

(5) *Equipment.*—Ammunition racks are located over the rear wheel housings at both sides of the vehicle. Provision is made for locating a radio set, when used, on the left side in place of the respective ammunition rack; the radio mast is then mounted outside the body on the left side. Other equipment is distributed and mounted as indicated in the figures. Canvas-covered rubber pads are provided for attachment to the gun rail at front and rear to protect personnel while traveling.

c. 4.2 mortar motor carriage, M2 (T5E1).—This vehicle (figs. 5 and 6) is a modification of scout car, M3, involving the elimination of the gun rail and rearrangement of the interior body installations to facilitate emplacement of the mortar. Equipment is distributed and mounted as indicated in the figures. A large ammunition rack is installed behind the driver's compartment (capacity three men for this vehicle) and in rear of that, for the gun crew, are two seats which must be removed to permit access to the ammunition. A pedestal mount for a machine gun is provided on the running board in rear of the right front fender.

d. Scout car, M3A1.—This vehicle, Ordnance Serial Nos. 106 to 417 inclusive, and shown in figures 7, 8, 9, and 10, is essentially the same as scout car, M3, as to general construction and purpose. The main divergence of this model, for identification purposes, concerns the wider body with its square corners and overhung top, lowered gun rail and reduced silhouette, seating arrangement, bumper top plate extension at the rear, and roller bumper at the front. Armament is such that it can be used for barrage and antiaircraft fire. The tourelle gun mount has been provided with a cross-leveling device for firing from that part of the gun rail which is sloped as a ramp, or when the vehicle is not level.

(1) *Hood.*—The hood arrangement is similar to that of scout car, M3.

(2) *Windshield.*—The shatterproof glass windshield, in two sections, is clamped into and flush with the weather stripped frame structure. It is necessary to loosen the clamps and remove the glass sections manually, however, before lowering in place the protective shield of ½-inch armor plate, hinged at the top to the windshield supporting frame, and held normally in a raised position by three cowl props. For observation purposes, vision slots are provided similar to those employed in scout car, M3.

(3) *Body.*—The body is similar in construction to that of scout car, M3, except that there is no rear door; external side shelves are eliminated to permit widening the body; fuel tanks are placed under the seats in the driver's compartment and protected underneath by a steel plate; the circular steel track for the gun mounts is lower in the body. Each side door is provided with a quadrant and armor shield as in the case of scout car, M3. Vents are provided for conducting fresh air from beneath the hood into the driver's compartment for ventilation purposes. The arrangement of the rear seats for the crew of six and the foot wells is different but the personnel capacity remains unchanged. Seat cushions consist of a folded blanket, furnished by the occupant, inserted in a canvas case lined with sponge rubber.

(4) *Top.*—Three removable metal bows connected with web strips form a support together with the windshield frame for the detach-

SCOUT CARS AND MORTAR MOTOR CARRIAGE

able waterproofed duck top. The bows have each end set into two brackets which are secured inside the body. Integral side and rear curtains, without windows, are secured by zipper fastenings to facilitate opening, and roll and fasten on the inside. The top and its curtains overlap the body and windshield frame and are secured by straps which extend through loops riveted to the plates. Separate curtains and rods are provided for the side doors. The top and side curtains, when not in use, are stowed in the bag provided and carried inside the vehicle. A wet top should not be permitted to dry in a lowered or folded position as a top thus dried will usually shrink to such an extent that the fit is seriously impaired. A wet top should be dried while in the raised position, under tension if possible, before being lowered or stored. It should be possible to restore a top, which has shrunk due to atmospheric conditions or improper handling, to the original dimensions by wetting thoroughly and allowing to dry while held under tension.

(5) *Equipment*.—Ammunition racks are located over the rear wheel housings at both sides of the vehicle and another large compartment is provided between the front seats for ammunition or a radio set. Smaller sections for ammunition and water chests are provided to the rear of the front seats and the tool box is directly behind the right front seat. The radio mast is mounted inside the body. Provision is made for storing the waterbucket and crosscut saw at the rear of the body. Other equipment is distributed and mounted as indicated in the figures. Sponge rubber pads are provided for the gun rail at the front seats and along the rear section; these pads may be shifted a short distance laterally along the rail or track but must be unstrapped and removed if full travel of the rolling gun mount is required.

(6) *Radios*.—Various combinations of radio sets installed in scout car, M3A1, include type SCR–193 and 193–D (transmitter and receiver) for the large cabinet; type SCR–209 and 209–D, or type SCR–245–G (transmitter and receiver) for the small cabinet; and type SCR–210 and 210–D (receiver only) for the small cabinet.

4. Tabulation of characteristics.—Data indicating comparative size and performance of the vehicles are tabulated in *a* below. Characteristic armament and mounts for these vehicles are tabulated in *b* below.

a. Vehicles.

Characteristics	Scout cars		Carrier
	*M3A1	M3	M2
Wheel base_____inches__	131	131	131
Length, overall_____do____	221.25	202.50	202.50
Width, overall_____do____	71.25	80.37	80.37
Height, overall_____do____	79.25	81	81
Tread {front_____do____	63.25	63.75	63.75
{rear_____do____	65.25	63.75	63.75
Weight (approximate):			
Net, equipped_____pounds__	8,810	8,135	7,670
Gross, with load_____do____	11,660	----------	----------
Shipping_____do____	8,635	----------	----------
Capacity {payload_____do____	2,850	1,850	1,800
{crew_____	8	8	5
Center of gravity above ground inches__	30.25	25.50	25.50
Bridging limit:			
Approach angle_____degrees_	37	----------	----------
Departure angle_____do___	35	----------	----------
Minimum turning circle diameter feet__	57	29.25	29.25
Ground clearance_____inches_	15.75	9.75	9.75
Limiting factor_____	(1)	(2)	(2)
Fording depth_____inches__	24	22.50	22.50
Limiting factor_____	(3)	(4)	(4)
Ground pressure pounds per square inch__	----------	57	57
Towing facilities {front_____	(5)	(5)	(5)
{rear_____	(6)	(6)	(6)
Drawbar or pintle height__inches__	28.25	29.50	29.50
Speed (transmission case low or high):	L. H.	L. H.	L. H.
{Reverse_____	5.05 9.5	5.5 10.0	5.5 10.0
{First_____	6.0 11.1	6.03 11.7	6.03 11.7
M. p. h. {Second_____	9.5 17.6	9.85 19.1	9.85 19.1
{Third_____	17.0 32.3	17.68 34.3	17.68 34.3
{Fourth_____	29.5 55.5	30.20 58.6	30.20 58.6
Maximum allowable speed_____	45	55	55

[1] Transfer case.
[2] Spring clip.
[3] Muffler.
[4] Exhaust pipe.
[5] Hooks.
[6] Pintle.
*Vehicles manufactured prior to fiscal year 1941.

SCOUT CARS AND MORTAR MOTOR CARRIAGE

b. Weapons and mounts.

Vehicle	Weapons per vehicle	Weapons	Figure	Mounts per vehicle	Mounts	Figure
M2	1	Gun, machine, Browning, cal. .30, M1919A4, flexible.	47, 57	1	Mount, tripod, cal. .30, M2.	46, 47
				1	Mount, pedestal, cal. .30, T34.	53
M3	1	Mortar, chemical, 4.2 inch, M1A1.	55			
	2	Gun, machine, Browning, cal. .30, M1919A4, flexible.	47, 57	2	Mount, tripod, cal. .30, M2.	46, 47
				2	Mount, gun, cal. .30, M22.	56
	1	Gun, machine, Browning, cal. .50, M2, HB, flexible.	49	1	Mount, tripod, cal. .50, M3.	48, 49
				1	Mount, gun, cal. .50, M21.	59
	1	Gun, submachine, Thompson, cal. .45, M1928A1.				
M3A1	2	Gun, machine, Browning, cal. .30, M1917A1.	52	2	Mount, tripod, cal. .30, M1917A1.	51, 52
				2	Mount, gun, cal. .30, D36956.	60
	1	Gun, machine, Browning, cal. .50, M2, HB, flexible.	49	1	Mount, tripod, cal. .50, M3.	48, 49
				1	Mount, gun, cal. .50, D36958.	61
	1	Gun, submachine, Thompson, cal. .45, M1928A1.				

Section III

ENGINE GROUP

	Paragraph
General	5
Characteristics	6
Mechanical components	7
Electrical components	8
Timing	9
Lubrication	10
Troubles and remedies	11

5. General.—The Hercules model JXD engine (fig. 11) is of the four cycle, six cylinder in line, L-head type, with characteristics as described in paragraph 6. The cylinders and crankcase are cast in block with a detachable cylinder head. The inlet and exhaust manifold, carburetor, fuel pump, and starting motor are mounted on the right side; the water pump, distributor, generator, oil filter pipe, and oil level gage are mounted on the left side. The fan is driven by dual V-type belts from a pulley keyed to an extension on the crankshaft and held in place by the starting crank dog.

6. Characteristics.—*a. Identification.*—Each engine's serial number is stamped on a name plate on the right side of the engine. Cylinders and connecting rods are numbered from front to rear, the engine front (fan and timing gear end) being toward the front of the vehicle. As viewed from the front end, engine crankshaft rotation is clockwise.

b. Ratings.—While the model designation and general construction are the same for all engines of this group, the engine employed in scout car M3A1, develops more horsepower by reason of its higher compression ratio and different manifold. There is also a variation in some accessories applied to the engines for scout car, M3A1, and those used for other vehicles; the tabulation of data in *c* below, therefore, classifies information under M3 and M3A1 for reference purposes. If necessary, engines may be interchanged as assemblies complete with accessories. In lieu of parts lists, Hercules engine parts are ordered with reference to engine model and serial number.

c. Tabulation of engine data.

Model	Hercules JXD.
Cylinders	6.
Bore and stroke	4″ x 4¼″.
Piston displacement, cubic inches	320.
Firing order	1-5-3-6-2-4.
Compression ratio	M3, 5.78; M3A1, 5.88.

SCOUT CARS AND MORTAR MOTOR CARRIAGE

Maximum torque, pounds feet at 1,100 r. p. m	M3, 224; M3A1, 241.
Maximum b. h. p. at 3,000 r. p. m	M3, 95; M3A1, 110.
*Weight in pounds (less accessories)	M3, 590; M3A1, 650.
Crated displacement	48″ x 28″ x 28″.
Lubrication	Forced feed.
Crankcase oil capacity, quarts	6.
Oil filler location	Front upper left side.
Oil drain location	Bottom of oil pan.
Oil pressure regulation	Spring regulated valve.
Cooling system capacity, quarts	M3, 18; M3A1, 19.
Water drain locations	Bottom of water pump. / Rear lower left side.

*Includes engine, flywheel, timing drive, oil and water pumps.

d. *Tabulation of accessories.*

Component	Description	Model or part
Fuel pump	A. C., diaphragm type	M3, Series "B" (AC–1522226).
Fuel pump	A. C., with vacuum pump	M3A1, Series "AV" (AC–1537105).
Carburetor	Zenith, downdraft type	M3, 20-B-10; M3A1, IN-167SJ.
Air cleaner	United, oil bath type	M3, T165-8239; M3A1, T175-9497.
Ignition coil	Auto-Lite, radio shielded	All, CF-4001.
Shielding	Breeze	M3, E532-21A-1A.
Shielding	Titeflex	M3A1, C-26219.
Distributor	Auto-Lite, semiautomatic	M3, IGW-4005A; M3A1, IGW-4940B.
Spark plugs	Champion (6)	M3, #1 Commercial; M3A1, #J8 or #J10.
Generator	Delco-Remy, belt driven	M3, 950.
Generator	Auto-Lite, belt driven	M3A1, GDJ-4802A.
Starter	Auto-Lite, Bendix drive	All, MAU-4006.
Fan	Schwitzer-Cummins	All, A105005.
Fan belts	Gates, ¾″, V-type (2)	All, 10R44.
Oil filter	Purolator, bypass type	All, EAN-294.

7. Mechanical components.—*a. Cylinder block and crankcase.*— The cylinder block and crankcase are cast in one piece to permit more efficient cooling by water jacketing the cylinders the full length of the bore and to supply a rigid unit for the support of the crankshaft in its seven main bearings.

b. Crankshaft.—The crankshaft is a drop forging of heat-treated steel, statically and dynamically balanced, and Tocco hardened in the case of scout car M3A1. The use of seven large main bearings provides ample bearing surface and permits the use of a main bearing support on each side of the connecting rods. The crankshaft gear is keyed to the crankshaft extension at the front end and held in place by a press fit. The fan drive pulley is keyed to the crankshaft and secured by the starting crank jaw. End float or thrust of the crankshaft of .002 inch to .004 inch is taken by a flange at the rear main bearing.

c. Main bearings.—The bearing caps are all drop forgings, but two types of bearings are employed. In the case of engines for the scout car, M3, group, the bearing metal (babbitt) is poured directly into the tinned cap and the upper half of the main bearing not subjected to the power stroke pressures is of the bronze backed shell type lined with bearing metal. The engines of scout cars, M3A1, have bearing caps fitted with removable precision bearing shells of harder composition (cadmium nickel) and a higher melting point for use with the hardened crankshaft. Upper and lower halves of the latter shells are interchangeable with each other but not with the shells of the babbitted caps. Main bearing studs are tightened uniformly at initial assembly to the following stresses:

	Bolt diameter (inch)	Pound-inches
Main bearings, center and rear	$7/16$	714
Main bearings, front and intermediate	$1/2$	840

d. Cylinder head.—The detachable cast head has the major part of the combustion space over the valves and is completely water jacketed. A gas and watertight seal is maintained by means of a copper and asbestos gasket which should be renewed when the head is removed. Cylinder head cap screws should be tightened in rotation, a few turns at a time, starting with the center and working out toward the sides and ends of the head. These cap screws are to be given a final tightening after the engine has warmed up. A tension indicating wrench should be used to tighten the cap screws by stressing to the equivalent of 630 pound-inches.

e. Pistons and rings.—The pistons are of aluminum alloy and mount three $1/8$-inch compression (upper) rings and one $3/16$-inch oil control (lower) ring with piston ring gap .015-inch to .020-inch. Pistons are marked to indicate the side toward the front of the engine when properly assembled.

f. Connecting rods and rod bearings.—The connecting rods are of drop forged, heat-treated steel with poured babbitt bearing metal in the case of engines for scout car, M3, group and cadmium shells in the case of later engines. The bearings are not interchangeable. The piston pin is clamped rigidly in the upper end of the rod by means of a clamp screw which passes through a notch in the pin

SCOUT CARS AND MORTAR MOTOR CARRIAGE

and is locked in place with a lock washer. Connecting rod bolts are tightened uniformly at initial assembly to the following stresses:

	Bolt diameter (inch)	Pound-inches
Connecting rod bolt	7/16	630

g. Valves and tappets.—Valves are of the poppet type with a 45° angle seat. The inlet valves are of chrome nickel steel, and the exhaust valves are of silchrome steel. The valves are actuated by the cams through the valve tappets which are of the mushroom type and provided with a suitable screw and lock nut to facilitate adjustment of valve stem clearance. The valve and tappet guides are removable bushings pressed into special webs in the cylinder block.

(1) *Clearance.*—Valve tappet adjustment or clearance should be made with the engine HOT, in the amount of .006 inch for both intake and exhaust. When checking or setting the valve clearance, crank the engine to the firing position for each cylinder before setting the valves on that cylinder.

(2) *Timing.*—The proper timing of the valves depends upon the proper meshing of the camshaft gear with the crankshaft gear, the positions of the gears on their respective shafts being established by Woodruff keys. At assembly, proper correlation is obtained by meshing the gears so that the marked tooth of the crankshaft gear matches the marked tooth space of the camshaft gear. Punch marks are on the front face of the gears. The timing cycle is as follows:

Inlet opens 1 degree 52½ minutes after top dead center.

Inlet closes 46 degrees 52½ minutes after bottom dead center.

Exhaust opens 43 degrees 7½ minutes before bottom dead center.

Exhaust closes 1 degree 52½ minutes after top dead center.

NOTE.—When checking valve timing in degrees and minutes of crankshaft or flywheel travel, the clearance of the valves used for checking purposes is set at .010 inch for the intake and .016 inch for the the exhaust, although neither value is the proper running clearance. The flywheel is marked "DC" indicating top dead center for No. 1 piston, and is visible through the flywheel timing hole which is located on the left side of the engine in the flywheel housing.

h. Camshaft.—The high lift camshaft is of the cast alloy type and supported on four steel backed, removable, babbit lined bearings of the continuous ring type, enclosed in the upper half of the crankcase. The camshaft helical gear is keyed to the shaft and held in place with a nut; the special lock washer originally employed is not used for the later engine model. Integral with the camshaft are twelve cams for the valves, a cam for the fuel pump, and a spiral gear in the center which drives the oil pump. A thrust washer is placed between the camshaft gear and the crankcase.

i. Accessory gears.—The gear cover or timing gear case of the automotive trunnion type is secured to the front of the crankcase. As shown in figure 12 ②, the accessory or water pump drive is located on the side (left) opposite that on which the camshaft and valves are located and consists of a sleeve casting bolted to the front part of the crankcase. The idler gear is mounted on a shaft which is pressed into the gear and supported by a babbitt lined bushing pressed into the crankcase. The idler gear is also provided with a thrust washer between it and the case. The end play of the camshaft, idler shaft, and accessory shaft can be adjusted through the respective set screws located in the front face of the timing gear case. At long intervals or after the engine has been disassembled for repairs, it may be necessary to check the end play of these shafts. As shown in figure 12 ③, each of the special screws had a hard fibre button C inserted in its inner end which bears against a hardened steel plug E in the end of the shaft. To make the adjustment, loosen the lock nut B for each screw in turn and with a screw driver or wrench, tighen the screw A with a light pressure and then back it up $1/8$ turn before tightening the lock nut. The respective gear retaining nut and lock washer are represented by F and G, and the gear cover by D.

j. Flywheel.—The flywheel in the No. 3 SAE bellhousing is bolted and doweled to the flange at the rear end of the crankshaft. The starter ring gear is shrunk on the flywheel.

k. Lubricating oil pump.—The oil pump is of the gear type, bolted to the center main bearing web (fig. 12 ④), and driven from the camshaft. The suction tube extends into the oil reservoir in the oil pan and needs no priming but its oil strainer must not become clogged.

(1) *Oil pressure.*—The oil pressure is automatically regulated by a compression spring which controls a relief or bypass valve incorporated in the fuel pump. The oil pressure should not be changed until it is known that the proper oil is being used and the engine is warmed up to normal operating temperature. As the bearings become worn, more oil will escape around them into the crankcase and cause a slight reduction in pressure. It is not advisable to attempt to correct a slight loss of pressure by an adjustment of the oil pressure regulator because the extra amount of oil being thrown off by the worn bearings is already over oiling the cylinder walls. The oil pressure should be 26 pounds at normal engine speed (1,600 r. p. m.); between 5 and 10 pounds at idling speed; about 35 pounds at high speed (3,500 r. p. m.).

TM 9-705

SCOUT CARS AND MORTAR MOTOR CARRIAGE 7–10

(2) *Oil pressure adjustment.*—If it is necessary to change the oil pressure, the adjusting cap screw for the spring loaded plunger in the cylindrical regulator extension on the oil pump body may be reached through a plug aperture in the left side of the oil pan (fig. 12②). Using the crowfoot wrench, loosen lock nut *A* (fig. 12①) and with the T-handled socket turn screw *B* IN to increase pressure and OUT to decrease pressure. After the adjustment, the lock nut must be tightened securely, the tools removed, and the pipe plug replaced. Engine oil pressure should then be checked under conditions similar to those which appeared initially to justify a pressure change.

l. Fan.—See paragraph 25.

m. Water pump.—See paragraph 26.

n. Fuel pump.—See paragraph 13.

o. Carburetor.—See paragraph 14.

p. Air cleaner.—See paragraph 15.

q. Manifold.—The intake and exhaust manifold is cast in one piece, the intake having a "hot spot" incorporated to provide for a shorter warm-up period with increased power and economy by delivering to the engine at all times a highly vaporized charge of fuel.

r. Muffler.—The center tube type, 6-inch Oldberg or Maremont muffler is located on the right side of the chassis to the rear of the transfer case. The improved design of the unit (White part No. 304039) for scout car, M3A1, is interchangeable with the other type.

8. Electrical components.—*a. Starter.*—See paragraph 55.

b. Generator.—See paragraph 56.

c. Ignition.—See section V.

9. Timing.—*a. Valves.*—See paragraph 7*g*(2).

b. Ignition.—See paragraph 22.

10. Lubrication.—*a. System.*—Lubricating oil under pressure is delivered from the oil pump through suitable connections to a drilled passage in the crankcase which extends from front to rear of the engine on the side opposite the camshaft and is closed at either end by suitable threaded plugs. Radial holes are drilled from the crankshaft bearings to meet this horizontal oil passage so that continuous pressure lubrication is supplied to the main bearings and through drilled holes in the crankshaft to the connecting rod bearings. The cylinder walls, camshaft, and valve mechanism are lubricated by means of the mist of oil thrown off around the connecting rod bearings. The camshaft bearings are supplied with oil by gravity feed from oil collected in pockets. The idler shaft and gear are oiled by pressure to the bearing housing and through drilled holes in the shaft and gear, from which the timing gears receive lubrication.

ORDNANCE DEPARTMENT

b. Capacity and grade.—The oil level is measured with a bayonet type gage on the left side of the crankcase. The oil level should be checked daily and maintained at or near the 4/4 or "Full" mark on the gage, the capacity being 6 quarts. In checking the oil level, the gage blade should be cleaned carefully before reinserting in the reservoir to determine the level accurately. For breaking in a new engine during the initial period of 2,000 miles or 50 hours of operation, use SAE 20 (light) oil for normal conditions and a lighter oil if cold weather or cold climate conditions prevail. After the breaking-in period, SAE 30 (medium) is suggested for normal conditions of climate. For warm weather with temperatures averaging above 75° F., an SAE 40 (heavy) may be used; for cold weather, an oil should be used whose pour point is at least 10° F. below the temperature to be encountered.

c. Oil filter.—The oil filter is the Motor Improvement Company's "Purolator" bypass type EA-283 or EAN-294. The case containing the filtering element or cartridge is of steel and so constructed as to be leak and tamper proof. The filter cannot starve the bearings since it is connected in a bypass oil line which is taken off the main oil supply gallery. Bypassed oil, however, is not filtered.

d. Servicing.—(1) The crankcase should be drained and refilled with fresh oil frequently, depending on operating conditions, service encountered, and the oil and filter. Oil should be changed more often when the engine is new than after it is well run in since initial wearing of various new parts will result in minute metallic particles in the oil which frequent draining will help to remove. Also in cold weather, choking and cold running tends to dilute the oil with unburned fuel and condensation and justify frequent oil changes to remove such harmful impurities. Fine dust which is not removed by the air cleaner or filler cap will accumulate in the crankcase irrespective of the type or condition of the engine oil filter used. The responsibility for draining engine oil must necessarily rest with the operating personnel.

Caution: Color is not necessarily an indication of the cleanliness of the oil. Field experience indicates that by reason of the peculiar operating conditions encountered by these vehicles, the engine oil pan should be dropped frequently to permit an examination for oil contamination by dirt, dust, metal particles, and sludge. The degree of contamination from sediment can only be ascertained by inspecting the bottom of the oil pan where such an accumulation will settle and remain undisturbed by flushing. All parts, including the screen, must be cleaned thoroughly. For the worst conditions, the intervals may be 300 to 500 miles, and the frequency of oil changes will be affected accordingly. For favorable operations on improved roads or during prolonged marches, the intervals may be lengthened to several thousand miles.

Oil should be drained when the engine is hot, as after a day's run, the oil will be agitated, flow more freely, and carry off more sediment. *Kerosene will not be used for flushing.*

Care should be exercised in replacing the screen in the pan section or on the suction line to the pump to secure proper fits of washers and tubing, as the case may be, to prevent entrance of dirty oil and sludge into the system. A tight joint must be secured between the oil pan, crankcase, and flywheel housing, especially at the corners or angles. After all cap screws are started, draw up gradually and progressively on vertical and horizontal screws alike.

(2) *Oil filter.*—The average effective life of the absorption type cartridge filter is approximately 5,000 miles in commercial applications, varying with operating conditions, and manufacturers' recommendations develop accordingly. In connection with combat vehicles and more frequent oil changes as indicated above, the filter cartridges should be replaced every 2,000 miles or in such a manner that not more than two fillings of fresh oil will pass through a used filter element.

e. Frozen oil.—(1) *Test.*—Whenever it is suspected that the oil in an engine has become frozen, the bayonet oil level gage should be removed and examined to see whether or not the adhering oil is in a solid, plastic, or liquid state.

(2) *Procedure.*—If a heated building is not available or if the vehicle is needed for immediate operation, the oil may be thawed by pouring boiling water in the oil filler cap and draining the oil and water emulsion from the crankcase. This oil should never be used again and the crankcase should be filled with new oil.

Caution: Under no circumstances should an attempt be made to start an engine when the oil is frozen. Because of fire hazard, an attempt to thaw frozen oil by applying a blow torch or open flame to the oil pan should never be made. Electrical immersion heaters are useful if sufficient current is available.

11. Troubles and remedies.—In order to locate and correct a malfunction or fault in an engine, operating personnel should understand the fundamental principles of engine operation, recognize and identify fundamental trouble symptoms, and be prepared to follow a systematic procedure of diagnosis to eliminate the tedious guesswork of a hit-or-miss search for the difficulty.

a. Essentials.—The essential factors necessary for an engine to operate comprise cranking; fuel and air, compression, ignition, and exhaust; proper lubrication and cooling; correct adjustments.

b. Symptoms.—The following are the basic faults which may develop ordinarily in an engine:

(1) Starter will not crank the engine.
(2) Engine will not start when cranked.
(3) Engine starts, runs, and stops.
(4) Engine runs but lacks power, misses or backfires.
(5) Overheating.
(6) Low oil pressure.
(7) Operating knocks.

c. Systems.—The engine may be considered as comprising a group of interrelated units or systems, each one of which should be checked thoroughly in turn after determining from the engine performance the factors which appear to be functioning correctly and those which are not. The several systems involved in the study of the engine symptoms listed and their cross references are indicated as follows:

(1) *Starter.*—For $b(1)$ above, refer to sections XII and XIII.

(2) *Air-fuel system.*—For $b(2)$, (3), and (4) above, refer to section IV.

(3) *Ignition system.*—For $b(2)$, (4), and (5) above, refer to section V.

(4) *Mechanical system.*—For $b(5)$, (6), and (7) above, refer to sections III and XIII.

(5) *Lubrication system.*—For $b(1)$, (5), (6) above, refer to sections III and XVI.

(6) *Cooling system.*—For $b(4)$, and (5) above, refer to section VI.

Section IV

FUEL SYSTEM

	Paragraph
General	12
Fuel pump	13
Carburetors	14
Air cleaner	15
Troubles and remedies	16

12. General.—The air-fuel system (fig. 13) comprises two rectangular terne-plated gasoline tanks, double seamed with soldered joints; a transfer and shut-off valve; a mechanical fuel pump; a carburetor; an air cleaner; and a manifold.

a. Operation.—The fuel take-off is through the transfer and shut-off valve in the driver's compartment where one tank or the other

TM 9-705
SCOUT CARS AND MORTAR MOTOR CARRIAGE   12-13

may be selected for the supply of fuel. The system continues through the fuel pump to the carburetor, where air through the air cleaner is mixed with the fuel and the resulting explosive mixture is distributed through the manifold to the cylinders.

b. Capacity.—Each fuel tank of scout car, M3, and mortar motor carriage, M2, has a capacity of 13¼ gallons; each tank of scout car, M3A1, has a capacity of 15 gallons. An electrical fuel gage unit is installed in each tank to indicate fuel level. A drain plug is provided in the bottom of each tank.

13. Fuel pump.—Fuel is drawn from the supply tank and pumped to the carburetor by a mechanical diaphragm type fuel pump which is attached to the crankcase and operated by an eccentric on the engine camshaft. The pumps (fig. 14) are manufactured by the A. C. Spark Plug Division of the General Motors Corporation. Series "B" represents the fuel pump employed for the scout car, M3, group and series "AV" represents the fuel pump, combined with a vacuum pump for the windshield wipers, as employed for scout car, M3A1.

a. Series "B"; operation.—The pump rocker arm on the suction stroke is actuated by a revolving eccentric on the camshaft to pull the diaphragm downward and create a vacuum in the pump chamber (fig. 14 ①). Fuel is drawn from the strainer bowl through the strainer screen and suction valve into the pump chamber. On the return stroke of the rocker arm, the diaphragm spring expands to push the diaphragm upward and force fuel through the pressure valve to the carburetor. When the carburetor bowl is filled, the inlet needle valve closes and creates a back pressure in the pump chamber sufficient to hold the diaphragm down against its spring where it remains inoperative until the carburetor requires more fuel and the needle valve reopens; a slot in the pull rod permits the rocker arm to move up and down without engaging the diaphragm during such a period. The rocker arm spring serves to hold the rocker arm in contact with the eccentric. The working parts of the fuel pump are lubricated from the engine oil which comes through the opening in the crankcase.

b. Series "AV".—(1) *Operation.*—Operation of the fuel supply section is similar to series "B" except that the rocker arm pulls the diaphragm upward to begin the operating cycle and movement thereafter is in the opposite direction. The air dome relieves the diaphragm and carburetor valve of excess pressure when the carburetor needle valve is closed and utilizes this pressure to increase the delivery rate.

(2) *Vacuum section.*—The vacuum section of this fuel pump supplies a constant vacuum for the windshield wiper operation. Actuation of the rocker arm pushes the vacuum link and diaphragm upward to expel the air from the upper chamber through the air exhaust valve into the intake manifold. On the return stroke of the rocker arm, the diaphragm spring moves the diaphragm downward to create a suction in the chamber, open the air intake valve, and draw air through the inlet passage from the windshield wipers. When the windshield wiper is not being used, the manifold vacuum holds the diaphragm upward against spring pressure so that it does not make a complete stroke for every stroke of the rocker arm. When the manifold vacuum is greater than the vacuum created by the pump, air will flow from the windshield wiper through both valves of the pump, and the operation of the wiper will be the same as if the pump were not installed.

14. Carburetors.—There are two types of the Zenith, down draft, double venturi carburetors as shown in figures 15 and 16.

a. Model 20-B-10.—This model is employed for the engine in scout car, M3. The removable primary venturi (1) (fig. 16 ①) adjusts the air capacity to the size of the engine. The delivery end of the secondary venturi (12) is located near the throat of the primary venturi, at the point of greatest suction, so the suction at the throat of the secondary venturi, where the fuel is discharged, will be as great as possible to effect atomization and improve distribution.

(1) *Fuel system.*—The main jet (2) exerts its principal influence at the higher engine speeds; its fuel is discharged into the air stream through the slot in the secondary venturi (12). The compensator (3) discharges its fuel through channels (A) and (B) into the well (13) and through holes in the cap jet base (9) into the annulus (14) between the cap jet base and the main jet. As the throttle is opened, this fuel is discharged into the air stream after passing through the cap jet calibration (7) and the cap jet top (8). The cap jet calibration, by means of the size and shape of its opening, determines the rate of fuel discharge when progressing from an idling speed to higher engine speeds. Air is admitted through the ventilating hole (14) into the well, to mix with fuel from the compensator so that the effect of the engine suction will be reduced. The compensator, therefore, exerts its principal effect at low speeds.

(2) *Idling system.*—The idling jet (4) measures the fuel and the idling adjusting needle (16) regulates the air; the idling jet receives its fuel through channels (A), (B), and (C) from the compensator at idling and speeds below 25 m. p. h. when the throttle plate is almost

TM 9–705

SCOUT CARS AND MORTAR MOTOR CARRIAGE   **14**

closed and there is a very strong suction past the edge. The priming plug (10) leaves an opening of suitable shape near the edge of the throttle where the idling emulsion is discharged.

(*a*) *Function.*—The idling system acts as a priming device because when the engine is at rest the idling jet passageway is submerged in the fuel that fills the well. When starting, the throttle should be opened slightly to create a strong suction on the idling jet. Fuel passing at high velocity over the edge of the throttle is finely atomized and the high vacuum instantly vaporizes and mixes it with air to assure the first few explosions.

(*b*) *Adjustment.*—A new or rebuilt engine that is too stiff to "rock" on compression, when stopped, will not idle well at low speed. For normal adjustment, however, set the stop screw on the throttle lever so that the engine will run sufficiently fast to keep it from stalling. Turn in or out on the idling needle valve adjusting screw until the engine hits evenly and without rolling or skipping. Back off on the stop screw until desired engine speed is obtained after which it may be possible to open the needle valve a trifle. For this carburetor, the correct idling adjustment is usually between $3/4$ and 2 turns open of the idling needle valve.

(3) *Power jet system.*—Channel (D) connects the power jet vacuum piston (17) with the carburetor barrel below the throttle plate. At normal driving speeds, the manifold vacuum is sufficient to overcome the spring tension and hold up the vacuum piston but at low speed lugging with wide open throttle or at sustained high speeds, the piston drops in its cylinder to open the power jet valve (18) and fuel from the bowl is measured through the power jet (5) to augment the normal supply and furnish the extra fuel for full power development.

(4) *Accelerating system.*—The accelerating pump piston is forced downward in its cylinder when the throttle is opened, by the downward stroke of the pump lever (19) which actuates the accelerating pump rod (21) through the link (20). Fuel from the carburetor bowl has previously entered the cylinder through the check valve (22) and as the pump piston starts its downward stroke, it applies pressure upon the fuel to close the check valve and displace the fuel through the needle valve (23). Check valve (24) is closed causing the fuel to be discharged into the air stream through the accelerating jet (6). When the fuel has been discharged from the pump cylinder, there is no longer any pressure against the needle valve (23) or the check valve (24) so the former drops on its seat and the latter opens. Air is admitted to eliminate any direct suction on the fuel

and no further fuel discharge takes place from the accelerating jet until the accelerating procedure is repeated.

(5) *Strangler.*—Manual control (choke) is provided for the strangler which is mounted off center on a spring loaded shaft so that the engine suction tends to pull it open while a spring tends to pull the strangler shut except at cranking speeds where the spring is the weaker of the two forces. Overchoking, with corresponding crankcase dilution, is prevented by the strangler automatically opening and closing as the engine speeds up or slows down. The strangler control is pulled out as usual for starting, and left alone or pushed in slightly until the engine warms up, and then pushed in to the open position for running.

(6) *Maintenance.*—The carburetor should be cleaned and blown out periodically to eliminate dirt and water, the main factors that can disturb the normal functioning. Before making any changes in carburetor jets, check the air-fuel system elsewhere, and the ignition. The fuel level is 45/64-inch to 55/64-inch below the top edge of the fuel bowl and the float hinge should not be bent to change this level. The fuel valve and seat assemblies are replaceable and new ones can be installed without the use of the level test gage.

b. Model IN1675J.—This model is employed for the engine in scout car, M3A1.

(1) *Main jet system.*—All fuel for part throttle operation of model IN1675J (fig. 16 ②) is supplied through the main jet orifice, its influence being greatest at speeds from 25 miles per hour and up. When manifold depression drops, the power jet system comes into operation to supply the additional fuel for maximum power. The main jet fuel passes through the main discharge jet (1) and into the air stream through the secondary venturi (2). The main jet (3) is located in the fuel bowl.

(2) *Compensating system.*—The compensating system consists of the main discharge jet and the well vent (4). The flow of fuel from the main jet is controlled by the size of the well vent and the size of the main discharge jet, proper seating of the latter and the well vent being insured by a tapered seat without the use of gaskets.

(3) *Idling system.*—The idling jet (9) receives fuel from the main jet through the main discharge jet and channel (A). The fuel then goes through the small calibration in the side of the idle jet, and through channel (B) to (C) where it mixes with air admitted through the idle adjusting needle (10). The idling system functions only at idling and at speed below 20 miles per hour. At such speeds, the throttle plate (12) is almost closed and there is a very strong suction

SCOUT CARS AND MORTAR MOTOR CARRIAGE

TM 9-705
14-15

past the edge of the throttle plate. The mixture of fuel and air from the idling jet is discharged through the priming plug (11).

(4) *Power and accelerating system.*—This system supplies the extra fuel required for maximum power or acceleration. When the manifold vacuum is low, as in the case of a quickly opened throttle, high engine speeds, or lugging with wide open throttle but low engine speeds, the vacuum piston assembly (6) drops in its cylinder. Check valve (14) closes and fuel is forced through the power jet valve (7) and passes through channels (E) and (F) to the power and accelerating jet (5) through which it is measured into the air stream at a rate determined by the size of the metering orifice. This extra flow of fuel continues only as long as the manifold vacuum is low. As the vacuum increases, the vacuum piston assembly is drawn upward in its cylinder, the power jet closes, shutting off the extra fuel, and normal economical mixture proportions prevail.

15. Air cleaner.—The United air cleaner (fig. 13) is of the oil bath type and mounted under the right side of the hood in an accessible location on the dash. Dust entering through the carburetor or breather and mixing with the lubricating oil forms an abrasive compound which causes excessive wear of engine parts; the air cleaner frees the air drawn through it of such dust and dirt. Air cleaners and connections are not interchangeable between the two scout car groups.

a. Operation.—Dust laden air enters the cleaner at the top and passes downward into the oil chamber where the impact and sudden reversal of flow, created by the baffle, causes most of the dust to be thrown into the oil reservoir. Partially cleaned air passes upward through the oil-wetted filter element where the remaining dust is captured, and thence to the carburetor. The effectiveness of the cleaner can be maintained by proper servicing.

b. Servicing.—The oil level in the cup at the bottom of the cleaner should be checked daily before running the engine, by loosening the clips and dropping the cup to note oil level in reference to the indicating bead. A sufficient quantity of oil should be added to maintain the proper level. The reservoir should be cleaned thoroughly and refilled with fresh oil each time the crankcase is drained and refilled, or at intervals of 2,000 miles; oil similar to engine lubricating oil in season should always be used for refilling or replenishing the air cleaner reservoir. While the filtering element should not be removed from the cleaner, the engine cleaner assembly should be removed from the dash occasionally and cleaned by washing thoroughly in kerosene and blowing out. The instructions covering the care of the air cleaner apply when operating conditions are normal;

when the air is laden with abnormally large quantities of dust and dirt of various kinds, the recommended attention should be given at more frequent intervals.

16. Troubles and remedies.—*a. Fuel.*—(1) *Supply.*—The fuel supply should be checked regularly; in the case of an inaccurate fuel gage, a dip stick will prove useful. If the engine has stopped by reason of lack of fuel resulting from empty tanks, the fuel supply should be replenished and the engine cranked for about 15 seconds (with ignition off, choke out, and throttle shut) to draw fuel into the pump and thence into the carburetor.

(2) *Impurities.*—If the engine does not start, the reason may concern water, ice, or dirt in the fuel system as observed from an examination of the fuel pump sediment bowl. Clean the strainers in the fuel pump and carburetor and empty the bowls; drain the fuel tanks until the fuel flows free of impurities; disconnect the fuel lines and blow them out with air. If ice is found, heat the parts with boiling water before cleaning. Water in the fuel tanks forms from the condensation of the moisture in the air which is drawn into the tank as the fuel is used, and it accumulates more rapidly in cold, damp weather and when the tanks are relatively empty of fuel.

b. Carburetor.—(1) *Flooding.*—Choking too long during cranking floods the cylinders and prevents starting; a noticeable gasoline odor or dripping at the carburetor usually indicates flooded conditions although dirt under the float valve will also cause dripping of the carburetor. Push in the choke, close the ignition switch, open the throttle wide (do not pump); and crank the engine for about 10 seconds. When the engine starts, partly close the throttle and do not use the choke again unless it is necessary to keep the engine from stalling. If the carburetor still drips, tap it sharply or remove the cover of the float chamber and clean out dirt around the float valve.

(2) *Choke valve setting.*—If the engine will not start after cranking for 5 seconds with the choke pulled out and ignition satisfactory, the choke valve may not be closing completely. Examine the choke valve at the carburetor when the choke button is pulled out all the way and if the valve has not closed, change the setting of the choke wire so that the valve closes.

(3) *Gasoline test.*—If a hissing sound is not heard in the carburetor when cranking with the choke out, a lack of gasoline is indicated in the carburetor. Test by disconnecting the fuel supply pipe from the carburetor; if there is not a steady flow from the fuel pipe, the trouble must be traced back through the fuel system, with the engine turning over for the test. If the trouble is in the carburetor, remove

and clean the strainer below the float bowl. If the carburetor strainer, bowl, and jet pockets are free from dirt and water, or ice, the trouble is elsewhere in the carburetor and must be adjusted.

(4) *Mixture.*—If the engine runs irregularly at idling speed or black smoke appears in the exhaust and the muffler backfires, the carburetor mixture is too rich. Dry soot on the shell or porcelain near the points of the spark plugs also indicates this condition. If a warm engine backfires into the carburetor when accelerating or when the vehicle is running downhill in gear, the air-fuel mixture is probably too lean. If the spark plug porcelain is a light straw color, the mixture is extremely lean. Excessive burning of the spark plug points also indicates a lean mixture or an incorrect plug. Adjust the carburetor correctly; summer driving requires an adjustment different from that for winter driving. A dirty air cleaner causes a rich mixture and a loss of power.

c. Fuel pump.—(1) *No fuel.*—Disconnect the fuel pipe at the carburetor, shut off the ignition, and turn engine with the starter. If no fuel appears, the trouble may be in the supply line, pump, or strainers. Examine the tubing for kinks and leaks and check strainer bowl for sediment. If the bowl is dirty, remove and clean it and the strainer screen. Replace the gasket if it is broken and replace bowl if it has a clipped edge, checking for a tight fit and proper gasket installation. Disconnect the fuel pipe from the tank at the fuel pump and apply air to the supply tank to test condition of fuel line and flow. If the line is open and connections are tight, the pump is defective and must be replaced or repaired.

(2) *Valves.*—Examine valve seats to make certain there are no irregularities which prevent proper valve seating. Valve plugs and valves should be cleaned, and if the latter are warped or damaged they should be replaced. Place valve in chamber with the polished side toward its seat, making certain that the valve lies flat on its seat and is not left standing on edge. Reassemble valve plug and spring making certain that spring is around the lower stem of the valve stem properly.

(3) *Leaks.*—In case of leakage at the diaphragm, tighten the cover screws alternately and securely. Sometimes there appears to be a leak at the diaphragm, whereas the leak actually exists at one of the pipe fittings and the fuel runs down around the diaphragm flange. Leakage of fuel through the body venthole, a worn or punctured diaphragm, loose diaphragm nut, or defective pull rod gasket requires replacements or adjustments. Complete disassembly of fuel pumps is not practicable for forward echelons by reason of special fixtures and parts required for reassembly.

(4) *Lubrication.*—All the working parts of the fuel pump should be lubricated automatically from the oil coming through the opening in the crankcase.

d. Manifold.—A steady whistling sound at the manifold indicates a leaky gasket, and irregular engine running at idling speed usually results. While the engine is running, squirt oil around the inlet manifold gasket to locate points where whistling will cease. Examine hose connections at the windshield wiper and check other accessories for air leaks. Replace hose and gaskets if necessary and tighten manifold bolts and hose connections.

Section V

IGNITION SYSTEM

	Paragraph
General	17
Circuits	18
Coil	19
Distributor	20
Spark plugs	21
Timing	22
Troubles and remedies	23

17. General.—The closed circuit, battery and coil ignition system consists of the ignition switch and wiring, ignition coil and coil filter, distributor, spark plugs, and radio shielding conduit (figs. 17, 18, 19, 20, and 42).

18. Circuits.—*a. Wiring.*—It is imperative that all wiring and ground straps be kept in good condition and all connections clean and tight. Connections include a primary (low voltage) cable assembly from the fuze (battery) to the ignition switch; a shielded cable assembly from the switch to the filter; a primary and secondary shielded cable assembly from the ignition coil to the condenser and distributor; a secondary (high tension) shielded conduit assembly from the distributor to the spark plugs. Loose connections will cause hard starting and misfiring of the engine, and if the engine is allowed to operate in this manner for any length of time, burning and pitting of the distributor points will occur. Regular inspections should be accomplished at 6,000-mile intervals.

b. Shielding.—In order that sensitive radio equipment may be operated without interference, the ignition and wiring system of the vehicle are completely shielded. Within the flexible shielded conduit standard unshielded ignition or automotive cable is used.

(1) *Operation.*—The most serious interference is the radiation which results from the high voltage spark plug discharge so elements

and wires of the high tension system are encased in metallic shields which are grounded to prevent radiation of such disturbances. The relay action of the voltage regulator introduces undesirable transients in the low voltage system so filters are provided and the exposed system is also shielded.

(2) *Types.*—The Breeze system (fig. 19) is employed for the scout car, M3, group and the Titeflex system (fig. 20) is used for scout car, M3A1. Parts from one type will not interchange with the other. For the Breeze type ignition harness, the spark plug radio shield cap is held on by a spring clip which is pried off to remove the plug. When removing a plug with the Titeflex harness, loosen the knurled nut which secures the shield and remove insulator and shield to make plug accessible. The Breeze type shield for the distributor is in two parts which are secured together by screws independent of the distributor housing, but the complete assembly must be removed to provide access to the latter. The top half of the Titeflex type shield may be turned slightly counterclockwise and lifted off directly to expose the distributor cap and permit its removal; the bottom slotted section in two parts of the shield is fastened to the distributor housing by the breaker plate screws. Knurled nuts may be turned by hand.

(3) *Precautions.*—The type of shielding employed in these vehicles does not require frequent adjustment or excessive care but does require frequent inspection to insure that it is tight and clean. In order to be effective, the shielding system must be electrically continuous throughout with no breaks or high resistance joints and it is for this reason that all joints must be kept tight and free from oil, grease, or insulating substances. The shielding is oil and water spray proof and if continuous, protects the inclosed wiring from these liquids. If crushed, however, the inside weather proofing conduit spreads, thus opening the shielding to water and oil leaks. Oil, water, and fuel may also enter the conduit if coupling nuts are allowed to work loose. If abrasion takes place in the metal braid applied over the conduit so that gaps appear, the shielding will no longer be effective.

(4) *Maintenance.*—Servicing of the vehicle should include inspection of the shielding for crushed conduit, abrasion of shielding, and looseness of coupling nuts. In cleaning couplings or plug shields, a solution of carbon tetrachloride should be used. In the event that oil or fuel has seeped into the conduit, the latter and its wiring should be disconnected, removed, cleaned, and replaced. In removing a length of wire from a shield, a piece of strong twine should be at-

tached to the end of the wire and pulled through as the wire is removed; the fishline can then be used to pull through cleaning rags and facilitate later replacement of wire. Coupling threads should be cleaned to brightness with a small wire brush to remove high resistance oxidation. If available to shop crews, the use of an insulation or resistance testing instrument (Megger) will be of invaluable service in testing shielding and conduit insulation and resistance very rapidly, and tracing circuit continuity.

19. Coil.—*a.* The Auto-Lite model CF–4001, 12-volt ignition coil is of large size for maximum operating conditions and is mounted in the ignition circuit shielding box on the engine side of the dash. The induction coil consists of two sets of insulated wire windings wound on a common iron core. Terminals must be kept tight, clean, and dry. The center top high tension terminal is for the 7-mm cable connection to the distributor cap. The negative low tension terminal (stud) is for connection to the distributor points. The positive low tension terminal (stud) is for connection to the filter coil.

b. Perfect insulation of the windings and leads thereto must be maintained. Precision testing of the coil while mounted in the vehicle is not practicable and wastes time, besides exposing the shielding to the elements. A weak coil may contribute to more trouble than its retention will do good.

20. Distributor.—The distributor is mounted on the water pump housing and driven from a gear which is keyed to the water pump shaft and held in place by a snap ring. A gear on the end of the distributor shaft, the rotation of which is clockwise as viewed from the top of the unit, engages with the gear on the water pump shaft. The Auto-Lite unit (fig. 18) is a six-cylinder, semiautomatic, single breaker arm type which contains the battery circuit contact points, automatic advance mechanism, and high tension distributor.

a. Construction.—(1) *Breaker mechanism.*—The breaker mechanism consists of a pair of breaker contacts, a breaker cam, and an external condenser. The breaker cam is carried at the upper end of the distributor shaft and operates the contacts or points. The breaker cam and contacts are located on the breaker plate and are accessible when the distributor cap is removed.

(2) *Advance mechanism.*—The manual and automatic advance control operate independently of each other. The centrifugal automatic mechanism, which begins to function at about 600 r. p. m. engine speed, consists of governor weights and springs located in the breaker cup beneath the breaker plate. As the engine speed increases, centrifugal force causes under control of springs to move outward and

actuate the breaker cam in the direction of distributor shaft rotation. The governor mechanism can be checked for free operation by turning the breaker cam in the direction of the driven rotation as far as it will go and releasing it when it should return to its original position without any hesitancy or drag.

(3) *High tension distributor.*—This element consists of the rotor and cap. The former, mounted on the breaker cam, distributes the high tension impulses to the contacts inside the cap. The latter connects with the high tension leads to deliver current to the spark plugs in the proper firing order. The distributor cap is held in place by two flat springs, hinge mounted and located one on either side of the breaker cup.

b. Installation.—Whenever the water pump is removed from the engine, it is also advisable to remove the distributor which can be lifted after removing the clamp hold down screw and spring and disconnecting the electrical connections and manual control cable. After the water pump has been reinstalled, turn the engine over until No. 1 piston is on the compression stroke and bring to top dead center as indicated by the DC mark on the flywheel when lined up in the center of the inspection hole located in the forward wall of the left engine leg. Install the distributor shaft in the opening provided in the water pump housing in such a way as to have the battery terminal on the distributor housing point to the rear of and parallel with the engine block; the rotor should be set so that the contact points are just ready to break. In this position the rotor should be pointing directly toward the No. 1 cylinder.

c. Lubrication.—Every 1,000 miles, add three drops of light engine oil in the oiler on the outside of the housing. Every 6,000 miles, lubricate the breaker cam with a wipe of petrolatum and add one drop only of light engine oil to the breaker arm pivot pin and to the wick in the top of the breaker camshaft to saturate the felt thereat.

d. Maintenance.—The breaker contacts should be inspected every 2,000 miles to see that they are in good condition and properly adjusted. If the contacts are dirty or gummy, they must be cleaned thoroughly; if rough or pitted, they should be resurfaced; if badly worn, they should be replaced by installing a new breaker arm and points. A service set of breaker points including the breaker arm assembly and contact screw is described as Electric Auto-Lite Part No. IGW-3028S. Clean out any oil, dust, or moisture which may have accumulated in the breaker box or on the inside of the distributor cap. Work on contacts should proceed as follows:

(1) Remove distributor cap shielding, cap, and rotor.

(2) Loosen the nut holding the condenser wire and breaker arm spring to the breaker arm and remove the latter. Loosen the lock nut on the contact screw and remove same from the breaker plate.

(3) Resurface the contacts on a moderately coarse oilstone, rounding their faces slightly so that the point of contact will be near the center and not at the edge.

(4) Replace contacts and set breaker arm tension at 17 to 20 ounces as measured by a spring scale. This tension may be obtained by shifting the spring in the slot.

(5) Turn engine over until breaker contacts are fully separated.

(6) Loosen the lock nut on the contact screw and adjust to obtain maximum gap of .020 inch with points fully separated.

(7) Tighten nut on contact screw and recheck gap. Insert narrow strip of soft paper between the contacts and turn the engine until the contacts close. Draw the paper back and forth to remove any oil or grease remaining on the point surfaces and obtain good contact.

(8) Replace the rotor and check the cam setting by rocking back and forth as far as the slack in the distributor gears will permit. If the setting is correct, the points should open and close.

(9) Try out the engine at various speeds after replacing distributor cap. If the engine does not run smoothly and develop its full power, check spark plugs and ignition wiring before retiming.

21. Spark plugs.—The spark at the points of each spark plug must be of full strength at all engine speeds and under all conditions of operation in order to give the maximum initial impetus for the almost instantaneous burning and expansion of the compressed mixture. This action is very definitely dependent upon the efficiency of the spark plugs themselves and upon their operating condition.

a. Operation.—Plugs must operate reasonably hot at lower engine speeds to keep free from oil and fouling matter, and cool at top engine speeds to prevent excessive burning of electrodes and pre-ignition; they must insulate perfectly the high tension current at all speeds and changes in temperature to which they are subjected throughout the range of engine operation. In this connection, the selection of plugs must incorporate the heat range factor, or the relative ability of a plug by reason of its physical size to transfer heat from the firing end to the cooling water or air. The rate of heat flow depends on the length and shape of the cylinder end of the insulator from the tip to the inside gasket, the larger plug being the so-called cooler type.

b. Types.—Champion No. 1 commercial ($7/8''$ x 18; $15/16''$ hex.) plugs were used initially for normal operation of engines in the

SCOUT CARS AND MORTAR MOTOR CARRIAGE

scout car, M3, group. Champion No. J8 (14-mm; $13/16''$ hex.) plugs are being supplied on engines for scout car, M3A1; the two types are not interchangeable.

c. Maintenance.—(1) *Servicing.*—Gaps should be checked carefully with a feeler gage every 500 miles. Plugs should be checked in a tester every 4,000 miles, cleaned if necessary, and regapped to .025 inch.

(2) *Replacement.*—Gaps are burned open by the constant application of spark, heat, pressure, and the chemical action of the fuel mixture. Electrodes become oxidized and corroded, causing increased resistance to the passage of current. The firing end of the core becomes crusted with carbon and other deposits, resulting in missing because of current loss over and through these deposits. Plugs develop a gas leakage between the core and shell or between the center electrode and core. Experience indicates that by reason of all the above, spark plugs literally wear out and should be replaced after 10,000 miles.

d. Troubles and remedies.—The several basic difficulties which can develop in connection with spark plugs and contributing causes are tabulated below.

Conditions	Procedure	Other possibilities
Gap too wide or narrow; electrodes badly worn or burned away.	Set gap; replace plugs in service more than 10,000 miles; replace badly burned plugs with cooler types.	Check ignition system; battery; timing; distributor point gap.
Insulator broken on upper end.	Install new plug; avoid careless handling.	Use proper spark plug socket wrench.
Insulator cracked on lower end.	Install new plug; check specifications; may require cooler plug.	Avoid careless work in regapping; adjust by bending side electrode only.
Upper part of insulator blackened; lower part not sooty.	Install cooler type plugs.	Blow by.
Insulator blistered or glassy; reddish or brownish deposits.	Clean and test; if condition is habitual, change to cooler plugs.	Check timing; carburetor adjustment; leaks in intake manifold and cooling system; fuel.
Insulator covered with dry black soot.	Check type; clean and set gap; if condition is habitual, replace with hot plug.	Too rich mixture; distributor point gap; excessive choking.

Conditions	Procedure	Other Possibilities
Insulator caked with oily carbon or soot.	Check type; clean and set gap; if condition is habitual, replace with hot plug.	Too rich carburetor adjustment; distributor point setting; ignition system; timing; battery; choke; too much oil in crankcase; leaky or stuck valves; loose or worn pistons and rings.
Plug oily but not sooty or carboned.	Dry plug; clean and set gap; examine for cracked insulator; reinstall and test.	

22. Timing.—*a. General.*—By timing of the ignition is meant that the air-fuel mixture is ignited or fired at a moment when an engine piston is in a position in its cylinder where the most power will be obtained from the resulting action. At this position of a piston stroke, the breaker arm must snap away from the stationary contact in the distributor. The exact point of circuit interruption to set up the spark depends on the engine size, speed, and load. By reason of the variable timing requirements set up for any engine under different operating conditions, the terms "advanced" and "retarded" refer respectively to early and late timing obtained through manual, automatic, or a combination control to shift the distributor unit in its mounting.

(1) *Advanced.*—A certain amount of time passes between the moment ignition occurs and the moment when all fuel is burned up, and during this time, much power will be lost unless the loss of time is compensated. A practical solution for load conditions is effected by allowing the spark to occur while the piston is still moving on its compression stroke. The cyclic degrees of piston travel between the point where the spark occurs and the outer dead center is called the "advance." Provision is made for a manual advance (spark control button pushed in against panel) of 6 distributor degrees on both distributors, whereas the automatic advance provides for 10 degrees on the type IGW-4147 for scout cars, M3A1, and 6 degrees on the type IGW-4005-A for the scout car, M3, group. Engine degrees are double these figures. Too much advance will cause a knock in the engine and decreased power.

(2) *Retarded.*—To facilitate starting and prevent the engine from kicking back, provision is made to allow the spark to occur at outer dead center or a little past dead center and the spark control button is pulled out for this purpose. Too retarded a spark with the engine running causes overheating and loss of power due to the fact that the entire charge in the cylinder will not be burned completely before the exhaust valve opens permitting the flame to come in contact with the exhaust manifold and exhaust pipe.

SCOUT CARS AND MORTAR MOTOR CARRIAGE

TM 9-705
22

b. Procedure.—The correct ignition timing is of the utmost importance for the proper operation of the engine. In consequence, the ignition unit should not be disturbed until it is positively known to be inoperative or out of adjustment.

(1) Check the breaker points carefully to make sure that they are in good condition and have the correct gap of .020 inch, maximum, when fully separated.

(2) Turn the engine over by hand in the direction of normal running until the No. 1 piston reaches top dead center on the compression stroke, as indicated by the centering of the flywheel DC mark in the inspection hole.

(3) Pull the spark control button out to the full limit for the manually retarded position.

(4) With the spark plug wires, trace the lead from the No. 1 plug; the rotor contact should have a position opposite the No. 1 terminal in the cap. If this is not the case, loosen the advance arm clamp screw and rotate the body of the distributor around the shaft until the No. 1 terminal is opposite the rotor contact with the points just beginning to break open. The opening can be checked by a feeler of very thin strong paper, or by the ammeter when the ignition switch is turned on. Be sure to tighten the advance arm clamp screw after making the adjustment. On this position, therefore, the No. 1 cylinder will fire at idling speed with fully retarded spark at top dead center. The firing order is 1-5-3-6-2-4.

c. Check.—If a neon timing light is available, a final check should be made.

(1) Make a white chalk mark $\frac{1}{16}$ inch wide on the flywheel so as to coincide with the DC top dead center mark.

(2) Remove the cable from the No. 1 spark plug and connect one lead of the light to the No. 1 spark plug and the other to the No. 1 cable.

(3) Start the engine and let it run at idling speed, directing the light flash on the opening in the flywheel housing to check position of the chalk line in relation to the center of the inspection hole as it should line up exactly in the center. If it fails to do so, loosen the distributor advance arm clamp screw and advance or retard the unit as the case may be.

(4) If the chalk mark blurs or widens out, it is an indication of a worn distributor shaft, sticking governor weights, weak governor weight springs, improper breaker contact adjustment, or excessive wear in the distributor drive gears. The difficulty should be investigated and corrected by the proper parties.

23. Troubles and remedies.—The basis of a systematic analysis of trouble in the ignition circuit is the behavior of the ammeter in the instrument panel. With the ignition switch closed, the ammeter may indicate normal oscillation of between 2 to 5 amperes discharge and zero; constant normal discharge of 2 to 3 amperes; no discharge and zero reading; abnormal discharge of more than 5 amperes. Electrical trouble existing before the engine is started can be localized by noting the action of the ammeter needle. An attempt should be made to start the engine so that running symptoms may be noted also.

a. Normal ammeter oscillation.—Since battery ignition systems work on the principle of electromagnetic induction, current must flow through the primary windings of the coil to build up a magnetic field around the coil, and the circuit must then be interrupted to collapse the magnetic field and by so doing induce a high voltage in the secondary circuit. The condenser across the breaker points accelerates the field collapse and increases the secondary voltage. It is the repeated "making" and "breaking" of the primary circuit that causes normal oscillation of the ammeter needle. If the primary circuit is correct (oscillation normal), the secondary circuit is then traced. The high voltage current produced in the secondary windings of the coil is conducted to the distributor rotor, which transmits its successively through the wires leading to the different spark plugs. When the potential breaks down the resistance of the spark gap, momentary current flows to the grounded electrode of the plug to complete the circuit and produce the spark which fires the cylinder mixture.

(1) *Coil distributor circuit.*—Remove the coil distributor, high tension (secondary) cable and hold it ⅜ inch from ground (any convenient metal part of the engine, free of gasoline, oil, etc.). Make and break the primary circuit with the ignition turned on, either by using the starting motor or by rocking the cam inside the distributor back and forth. A hot, snappy spark should result and if so, proceed to test as given in (2) below.

If no spark occurs, check the coil distributor wire to be sure it can conduct current or substitute a wire known to be good and repeat. If a weak spark is obtained, either the condenser or coil or both are at fault. Turn engine over with starting motor and look for excessive arcing at the breaker points, probably indicative of bad condenser. Replace condenser and repeat original test. If spark is still weak, coil replacement is indicated.

(2) *Distributor cover.*—With the coil distributor wire inserted in the center well of the distributor cover, remove cover and turn engine over to induce current in the secondary circuit. Observe cover in-

terior for cracks and moisture and watch for leakage or a short circuit wherein sparks jump from the center terminal to the spark plug terminals. Carbon paths which resemble cracks will also be apparent in the bakelite of the cover. To test whether the secondary circuit is established through the center brush or terminal inside the distributor cover, hold one end of a high tension cable against this point with its other end 3/8 inch from ground. A spark should jump to ground when a secondary current is induced.

(3) *Distributor rotor.*—A grounded rotor will interrupt the passage of current between the center segment and the spark plug cables. To test the insulation of the rotor, detach at the cover the cable leading from the coil, remove the distributor cover, and hold the coil distributor cable approximately 3/8 inch from the rotor. Induce a secondary voltage by making and breaking the primary circuit and if a spark occurs, the rotor is grounded and must be cleaned or replaced.

(4) *Spark plug cables.*—Having proved that the secondary current reaches the spark plug cables, check the cables by removing each one in turn from its plug, holding it approximately 3/8 inch from ground, and inducing a secondary voltage by means of the starting motor. If a spark does not occur with regularity in any cable, the cable must be replaced.

(5) *Spark plug testing.*—With the secondary current checked as far as the plugs, the latter must be tested to insure that the spark jumps its gap and ignites the charge in the cylinder. There are several ways in which faulty plugs may be detected.

(*a*) A commercial spark plug tester may be used. This instrument requires the plug to fire in a chamber of compressed air whose pressure may be regulated. A mirror arrangement permits observation of sparks occurring at the electrodes, and external sparking or leaking may be noted for faulty plugs.

(*b*) A spark that will jump the point or gap of a spark plug when the plug is out of the cylinder may not have enough strength to jump when the plug is screwed in the cylinder and under compression. The spark should be strong enough to punch a hole through a visiting card held between the points.

(*c*) A running engine has a certain rhythm. If a spark plug of a regularly firing cylinder is shorted out, a different rhythm is produced. By shorting out individual plugs with the bit of a screw driver across the terminal to ground and noting the result on the operation of the engine, faulty cylinders may be checked quickly. If a cylinder is already missing, no change will be noted when its plug is shorted out.

(*d*) If a plug does not fire satisfactorily after it has been cleaned and adjusted for the correct gap setting, replacement is necessary.

b. Ammeter indicates constant normal discharge.—Under such circumstances, the primary circuit is complete but it is not being interrupted to induce a secondary discharge. Several tests can be made for checking troubles of this kind in circuits beyond the ignition coil.

(1) *Distributor.*—Disconnect the primary wire where it enters the distributor and if the ammeter needle returns to zero, the distributor is at fault. Remove the distributor cover and inspect for opening of contact points; presence of foreign matter as a shunt around the points; terminal insulation to insure that movable point is not grounded; condenser. If the condenser is shorted, a spark will occur when the condenser "pig tail" is disconnected from the distributor and touched to the live wire.

(2) *Coil distributor wire.*—If the ammeter needle does not return to zero when the primary circuit is opened at the distributor as above, reconnect the wire to the distributor and disconnect the end at the primary exit of the coil to check for a grounded coil distributor wire. If the needle still does not return to zero, examine the coil terminal for a ground, foreign material, etc. If no ground is found externally, the trouble must be inside the coil where one of the primary windings near the exit may be grounded. Coil replacement is necessary.

c. Ammeter shows no discharge.—A zero reading on the ammeter with the ignition switch closed indicates an open circuit. Ground the terminal where the primary winding enters the distributor, and if a spark results, the trouble is in the distributor. If no flash occurs, the fault lies back toward the source.

(1) *Distributor.*—Check the points for closing and make sure that there is a continuous path for the primary circuit through the stationary point to ground.

(2) *Primary circuit.*—Return to the battery side of the ammeter and flash test the wire. (Hold one end of a test wire at the terminal being checked and strike the other end on a convenient ground.) If the starting motor turned the engine, current must be available and by starting at the ammeter, a logical sequence of tracing can be followed. If a spark is obtained on the battery side of the ammeter, *place this lead on the far side of the ammeter to shunt the ammeter during remainder of test* and protect against excessive test currents. Continue the tests for the fuze, the battery (hot) side of the ignition switch, the dead side with the switch closed, and so on to complete the circuit to the distributor. The break or defect will be found be-

tween the last terminal that showed the presence of current and the next succeeding one that denoted its absence. After satisfactory repair or replacement has been accomplished, the ammeter should be reconnected in the circuit.

d. Ammeter shows abnormal discharge.—Such a discharge may be caused by a ground before the primary current passes through the majority of the primary windings of the coil. The trouble can be localized by observing the ammeter while turning the ignition switch.

(1) *Switch "off".*—If the ammeter registers zero with the switch "off", trouble must be past the switch but short of the coil exit terminal.

(2) *Switch "on" or "off".*—If the discharge exists with the switch either "on" or "off", the trouble lies between the ammeter and switch involving an examination of the generator circuit and lead to the fuze box. Remove the respective wires to note effect on ammeter and localize fault. A large discharge or direct short should burn out a fuze.

Section VI

COOLING SYSTEM

	Paragraph
General	24
Fan	25
Water pump	26
Operation and maintenance	27

24. General.—The water-cooling system incorporates a Modine fin and tubular type radiator, radiator fan, and centrifugal water pump. The capacity of the cooling system is 18 quarts for the scout car, M3, group and 19 quarts for scout car, M3A1. The system may be drained by opening the drain cocks at the bottom of the water pump and in the left rear side of the engine block.

25. Fan.—The air flow through the radiator core is maintained by movement of the vehicle and a six-bladed fan. The Schwitzer-Cummins fan (fig. 21) is fully enclosed by a shroud and mounted on a bracket bolted to the crankcase forward of the cylinder block. The fan is driven off the crankshaft by dual V-type belts which should be replaced at the same time for best results since they are matched in sets. By releasing the spindle jam nut and turning the adjusting screw, the fan hub assembly may be moved up or down in the slot of the supporting bracket to give the belts the desired tension. When the belts are properly adjusted, it should be possible to turn the fan without undue force. Every 1,000 miles, the fan hub roller bearings should be lubricated through the fitting provided or by removing the slotted head screw in the hub and filling the reservoir with engine oil until oil drips from the fan shaft.

26. Water pump.—The water pump of the impeller type is supported by a sleeve flange from the front of the crankcase on the left side and is gear driven from the timing gear train. The pump may be removed without disturbing the gear cover.

a. Servicing.—The packing nuts on pumps of the regular packing type require very little pressure due to the ample width of packing used. When tightening packing nuts to stop a water leak, use very little force, and if the leak does not stop, the pump should be repaired. Split ring type packing is furnished for service so that the pump can be repacked without complete disassembling. Packing should be tightened with the pump shaft revolving.

b. Lubrication.—The front bushing for the pump shaft is automatically lubricated by the oiling system of the engine, while the rear bushing is lubricated by means of a grease cup on the water pump housing. Use water pump grease in this cup and give it one full turn every 500 miles.

27. Operation and maintenance.—The operator must assure himself that there is always a sufficient supply of water in the system. If the engine should run low on water and overheat, it should be stopped and allowed to cool before refilling with clean, soft water. Hose connections should be examined frequently and replaced, if they show signs of disintegration, to prevent leaks and obstructions of the system by particles. If the vehicle is to stand exposed to freezing temperature without sufficient antifreeze protection, the system should be thoroughly drained to prevent a cracked block, frozen pump, etc. It is advisable to run the engine for $\frac{1}{2}$ minute after draining is apparently complete to eliminate water pockets and clear the pump.

a. Cold weather precautions.—(1) In freezing weather, the cooling system should be filled with an antifreeze solution employing either approved alcohol, ethylene glycol or equivalent, based on a careful investigation to determine the effects, if any, on the radiator, hose, or engine. Alcohol is the most commonly used antifreeze but it has the disadvantage of evaporating out of solution. The system should be cleaned thoroughly and tightened before any antifreeze is added. The chart below gives the approximate quantity of antifreeze necessary for various temperature conditions but an antifreeze solution hydrometer should be used as a check.

SCOUT CARS AND MORTAR MOTOR CARRIAGE

ANTIFREEZE CHART

Temperature:	Denatured alcohol Quarts	Ethylene glyco Quarts
+20° F	3½	3
+10° F	5½	4½
Zero	7	6
—10° F	8	7
—20° F	9	8
—30° F	10	8½

(2) To prevent excessive cooling of the engine and poor combustion in cold weather, the radiator shutters should be partly closed or the radiator core partly covered in some manner.

b. Overheating.—Overheating may be caused by a deficiency in the cooling system or a fault in some other part of the engine. In the cooling system, overheating may result from—

(1) A leak in the system causing an insufficiency of water.

(2) Dirt, rust, grease, or hose particles causing a restriction of the flow of water in the radiator, pipes, or engine.

(3) A broken pump or sheared impeller which fails to circulate the water.

(4) A slipping or broken fan belt or bent blades causing a reduction in the fan's circulation of air through the radiator.

(5) Clogged air passages in the radiator or paint on the fins.

(6) Insufficient water.

c. Inspection.—Inspection should be systematic in order to locate trouble and the following sequence is recommended for the cooling system:

(1) Remove filter cap to see that there is sufficient solution in the radiator, overflow pipe is open, and interior clean.

(2) Examine the radiator for leaks, dirty air passages, and feel for cold spots which indicate clogged sections if the engine is warm.

(3) Observe in and under the vehicle for water leaks and around the engine block for rusty lines which indicate loose fittings or leaky cylinder gaskets.

(4) Examine hose connections for tightness and feel them to note whether they are alive or apparently in a collapsed state; test efficiency of the pump by feeling the upper hose connection while accelerating the engine to note a surge if circulation is effected.

(5) Examine the pump shaft and pump gaskets for leaks.

(6) Note action of fan and check blade mounting for pitch and tightness; fan belts should be clean and have about 1 inch play in both directions when pressed.

(7) Check condition of and connection to the hot water heater, when used, in the driver's compartment; this heater accounts for the extra capacity of the cooling system of scout car, M3A1.

d. Servicing.—Cooling systems should be given a systematic servicing every 6,000 miles, or about twice a year (spring and fall). Cooling systems should always be serviced before the introduction of an antifreeze into the system and after its removal.

(1) *Cleaning.*—The servicing of the cooling system consists of dissolving the dirt, rust, scale, and grease in the system and flushing. The operation is initiated by removing 1 gallon of water and adding a solution of 1 pound of washing soda in 1 gallon of clean water. The engine should then be run until the solution boils thoroughly, after which it can be drained from the system by *disconnecting the lower hose connection*, care being taken not to scald the hands; the drain cocks should not be used because their openings are too small and would probably become plugged. The upper hose and any thermostats should then be disconnected and the system flushed thoroughly.

(2) *Flushing.*—Flushing of the system should be effected in the direction opposite the direction of normal flow; the radiator, therefore, should be flushed up and the block down in that order to permit the block to cool. After flushing, thermostats when used should be checked by dipping in hot and cold water.

(3) *Finishing.*—Before reconnecting sections of hose, they and their clamps should be examined carefully for serviceability and replaced if unsatisfactory. Shellac should not be used for connections. System should be made waterproof and refilled.

e. Thawing.—If the water in the cooling system of a vehicle freezes solid, it must be thawed by placing the vehicle in a warm place. Under no circumstances should the engine be run when the water in the system is completely frozen. In the case of mush ice, it is safer to place the vehicle in a warm place but the ice may be thawed by covering the radiator and running the engine slowly. If the engine has been started and the radiator is steaming, stop the engine, cover the radiator and hood and, when the steaming stops, start the engine again and let it run at idling speed, keeping the water below the boiling point until proper circulation is reestablished.

Section VII

CLUTCH

	Paragraph
General	28
Construction	29
Adjustment	30
Lubrication	31

28. General.—The clutch (fig. 22) is manufactured by the Long Manufacturing Company and designated as Model 12–CB–CL. It is of the single plate, dry disk, semicentrifugal type and incorporates a mechanical vibration dampener and a provision for automatic adjustment to compensate for wear. The Long clutch is interchangeable as an assembly with the Rockford (Borg-Warner) Model CLA–1191 used on later production of scout cars, M3A1.

29. Construction.—*a. General.*—(1) The clutch consists of a cover plate assembly and a driven member assembly. The clutch cover plate assembly (C) is secured to the engine flywheel (A) by twelve ⅜-inch cap screws. The flywheel forms a part of the clutch housing and the finished rear face of the flywheel is the forward plate, in effect, of the clutch.

(2) Fabric friction material (B) is riveted to both sides of the clutch disk or driven plate (G) which is secured to the splined hub (M) of the driven member assembly. The hub mounts on the end of the transmission main gear shaft which is supported by the clutch shaft pilot bearing (R) in the flywheel. Between the disk and its rear lining are six crimped spring steel segments which constitute an independent cushioning means for the lining and provide a smooth clutch engagement.

(3) The back or pressure plate (E) is held in contact with the friction material (B) by twelve coil springs (Q) set upon asbestos base washers on the pressure plate. There are six release fingers (F) of hardened, forged steel which are mounted on needle bearings to reduce wear and friction. Application of pressure to the clutch pedal causes the clutch throw-out ball bearing (J) to actuate the release fingers and compress the springs (Q) to release pressure on the clutch disk.

b. Clutch dampener.—The mechanical dampener is of the spring and friction type, and it is installed to eliminate noises occasioned by the synchronizing of vibrations in the drive system. A set of ten coil springs (I) cushions the load both when accelerating or decelerating, and are prevented from overstressing because of a sudden clutch application, by four stop pins (P) which limit the amount of movement. The friction which is necessary to dampen torsional vibrations completely is obtained by eight friction washers (N), four of which are on either side of the hub flange, under an adjustable spring (O) load.

30. Adjustment.—*a. Internal.*—No internal adjustment of the clutch itself should be necessary during the life of any one set of linings. Adjustment of the throw-out fingers (F) for uniform contact with the throw-out bearing (J) is by means of the adjusting nuts (H). Suitable locking is effected to maintain the original factory setting until the clutch is completely disassembled.

b. External.—The spring (K) attached to the clutch throw-out bearing sleeve pulls that sleeve from contact with the clutch fingers and against the clutch release yoke (L). The adjustment for clearance between the clutch throwout bearing and the clutch fingers is made through an adjusting yoke on the rod from the clutch pedal to the lever on the clutch release shaft. Adjustment should be made to provide approximately 1 inch of clutch pedal travel before the clutch throwout bearing contacts the fingers, and must be checked from time to time as the clutch lining wears. The floor will serve as a stop for the pedal in the rear position or with the clutch engaged.

31. Lubrication.—The clutch shaft pilot ball bearing (R) is packed with lubricant at the factory and sealed so that further attention is unnecessary. The clutch throw-out ball bearing (J) is completely enclosed and lubricated, together with the clutch throwout bearing sleeve, with oil from a well in the sleeve. Every 500 miles, seven drops of oil should be added through the oil cup (D) on the clutch housing.

Section VIII

TRANSMISSION

	Paragraph
General	32
Construction	33
Gear ratios and shifts	34
Lubrication	35

32. General.—The transmission shown in figure 23 is manufactured by the Clark Equipment Company and designated as model 230-F. It is conventional in its location and construction and operates as a selective-gear type to provide four speeds forward and one speed reverse. Direct drive is in fourth gear.

33. Construction.—*a.* The cast iron transmission case (A) (fig. 23 ③) is provided with a removable bell housing (B) and both can be removed from the engine as a unit. The front ends of the main

(C) and counter (D) shafts are mounted in straight, solid type, roller bearings, (E) and (F) respectively, and the rear ends in ball bearings, (G) and (H) respectively. The third (I) and second (J) speed mainshaft gears are mounted on straight, solid type, roller bearings while the reverse idler gear shaft is mounted in bronze bushings.

b. The countershaft fixed drive (K) and driven gears (L) and (M), and the main shaft drive (N), third (I) and second (J) speed gears are of the helical type and constant mesh; these gears are shifted by the sliding toothed clutch (O). The countershaft first speed gear (P), the mainshaft first speed and reverse gear (Q), and the reverse gear are of the spur type with the teeth "pointed" to prevent chipping and facilitate shifting.

c. The main drive or clutch gear (N) is driven from the clutch through an integral splined shaft (R); the rear end of the shaft is supported by a ball bearing (S) mounted in the transmission case while the forward end is supported by a ball bearing fitted into the flywheel. (See sec. VI.) The third speed gear (I) and the clutch gear (N) have internal teeth which mesh with the teeth on the sliding clutch (O). The hub of the second speed gear (J) has external teeth which mesh with internal teeth in the first or low speed sliding gear (Q); the latter acts as a clutch when engaging second speed.

d. A yoke (T) mounted on the rear end of the main shaft provides a means of connection for the propeller shaft which extends to the transfer case. The shifter rods (U), with the interlocking devices, and the gear shift lever (V) are mounted in the shift bar housing (W). The hand emergency or parking brake lever, on a notched sector, is mounted to the rear and at the side of the case and the auxiliary shift lever for the transfer case is supported on the top side. The clutch and brake pedals are mounted on a protruding shaft (X) at the left side of the transmission case.

34. Gear ratios and shifts.—*a. General.*—The transmission incorporates the SAE standard four-speed truck gear shift with ratios and arrangement as follows:

	Gear ratios	Ball positions
First	5.00 :1	① } Engine Neutral.
Second	3.07 :1	③
Third	1.71 :1	② ④
Fourth	1.00 :1	
Reverse	5.83 :1	Ⓡ

In the four-speed type, gears should be shifted into the second speed position to facilitate cover removal.

b. Shifting.—Gear shifting should be properly executed by moving the gear shift lever at all times to its extreme position for any particular shift, to insure complete meshing of the gears. Silent shifting is accomplished by establishing gear rotation momentarily of nearly equal speeds; this is a matter of proper declutching and timely shifting in consideration of whether shifting up or down in the speed range. Each gear clash in shifting means shorter transmission life. Frequently the shift into neutral, followed by a slight pause before proceeding into the gear chosen, will effect the silent shift by reason of the slower deceleration of truck type clutches. (See par. 67*e*.)

35. Lubrication.—*a. General.*—Positive lubrication is provided by the splashing and carrying action of the gears, provided the required oil level is maintained. The transmission case should be checked every 1,000 miles and kept filled to the level of the filler plug opening to the right on the rear side of the case. A high grade straight mineral gear oil equivalent to SAE 140 should be used for summer in temperatures above 75° F., and for winter in temperatures down to 32° F. Below 32° F., an oil of a grade equivalent to SAE 90 should be used. The transmission case capacity is 5 quarts. If an extreme pressure (EP) lubricant is used originally, only an identical EP lubricant or a straight mineral oil of similar base stock is to be used for make-up purposes to avoid difficulty.

b. Draining and flushing.—The object in draining the transmission oil periodically is to eliminate possible bearing surface abrasion and attendant wear. Minute metallic particles are deposited in and circulate with the transmission oil, and the oil itself changes chemically as a result of repeated heating and cooling, and churning in the presence of air. After the first 1,000 miles, and every 6,000 miles or seasonally thereafter, the used oil should be drained after the transmission case has become warm; care must be exercised to clean around the filler plug before opening for inspection. The case should be flushed by filling to the proper level with a light flushing oil, and a front wheel and a rear wheel should be jacked up. The wheels on the ground should be securely blocked to prevent motion of the vehicle, the transmission shifted into reverse gear and the engine operated at moderate speed for about 10 minutes. The flushing oil should be drained completely and the case should be inspected for foreign material before refilling with new fresh oil. Overfilling of the case must be avoided as the excess quantity will serve no useful purpose and may cause overheating or work into the clutch housing.

Section IX

TRANSFER CASE

	Paragraph
General	36
Construction	37
Auxiliary gear ratios and shifts	38
Lubrication	39

36. General.—*a.* The transfer cases or auxiliary transmissions (figs. 24 and 25) represent basic types as manufactured by the Wisconsin Axle Company and designated as follows:

(1) Model T-32-9 for the scout car, M3, group.

(2) Model T-32-15 for scout car, M3A1.

b. Each transfer case is mounted in rubber to the rear of the transmission on a special cross member of the chassis, and is the unit through which the front and rear axles are driven.

c. Field experience indicates that the bolts holding the transfer case may become loose by reason of the rubber mounting insulator taking a permanent set; these bolts will be checked regularly (at least once a week) and adjusted tightly at all times in order to preclude any failures.

d. Such a gear box serves to provide an additional speed reduction for extended slow-speed maneuvering and offsets the front propeller or drive shaft to clear the engine crankcase to the right. Direct or low-speed drive is provided.

37. Construction.—*a.* The cast iron transfer case (A) (fig. 24) incorporates a number of bearing caps (B) and oil seals (C), which enclose the main shaft (D), idler shaft (E), driven countershaft (F), and the main drive gear (I) with integral shaft (K). Each shaft is supported by two spherical roller bearings, and with the exception of the idler shaft, splined on the external end to facilitate connection of its respective propeller shaft companion flange.

b. The main drive gear (I), idler shaft driven gear (L), and countershaft driven gear (O) are of the helical type. The idler shaft low speed fixed gear (N) is of the spur type. The main shaft sliding or clutch gear (H) is of the spur type and under control of the shifter fork (G), provides direct drive by meshing with the internal teeth of the main drive gear (I) or extra low speed by meshing with the idler shaft gear (N). The speedometer drive gear (M) is on the idler shaft and fully enclosed in a small housing.

38. Auxiliary gear ratios and shifts.—*a. General.*—The transfer case selection of gear ratios is entirely independent of the transmission and controlled by an auxiliary gear shift lever in the driver's compartment.

b. Shifting.—Shifting of transfer case gears should be executed as indicated in paragraph 67*e* and be followed by conventional transmission shifts from neutral to whatever speed the situation requires. Ordinarily, with the transmission in gear, the clutch will not be disengaged to effect direct shifting through the transfer case. Direct drive of 1:1, with the transfer case shift lever pushed forward from the operator, is normally used but a low ratio of 1.94:1 and 1.87:1 may be obtained for scout car, M3, and for the scout car, M3A1, group respectively, by pulling the shift lever back toward the operator. The lower ratio is used primarily when the vehicle is accompanying slow-moving foot troops or to develop maximum traction.

39. Lubrication.—*a. General.*—Positive lubrication is provided by the splashing and carrying action of the gears, provided the required oil level is maintained. The transfer case should be checked every 1,000 miles and kept filled to the level of the filler plug opening to the left on the rear side of the case. A straight mineral oil equivalent to SAE 250 should be used for summer in temperatures above 75° F., and a grade equivalent to SAE 140 in temperatures between 32° F. and 75° F. For winter temperatures below 32° F., an oil of grade SAE 90 should be used. The transfer case capacity is 3 quarts.

b. Draining and flushing.—After the first 1,000 miles, and every 6,000 miles or seasonally thereafter, the used oil should be drained after the transfer case has become warm. The case should be flushed with a solvent or light engine oil, thoroughly redrained, inspected for sludge and metal chips, and refilled with new fresh oil. If facilities are available to support the vehicle off its wheels, it is practical to run the engine and operate the transfer case and transmission in gear at the same time to provide a thorough opportunity for the flushing medium to accomplish its purpose. (See par. 35*b*.) Overfilling of the case must be avoided as the excess quantity will serve no useful purpose but will cause overheating and damage to the oil seals. The drain plug is in the bottom of the case. The breather plug (J) should be inspected and cleaned to prevent clogging of the air passage.

Section X

PROPELLER SHAFTS

	Paragraph
General	40
Universal joints	41
Lubrication	42
Hand brake	43

40. General.—Three propeller or drive shafts with needle-bearing universal joints are provided to transmit power from the transmission. The type shown in figures 26 and 27 is manufactured by the Spicer Manufacturing Corporation and designated as its 1400 series for the scout car, M3 group; the 1410 series for scout car, M3A1, is similar except for length and minor variations. The longest shaft is for use between the transfer case and front axle, the medium length shaft between the transfer case and rear axle, and the shortest shaft as a coupling between the transfer case and transmission.

a. Coupling shaft.—The short main propeller shaft coupling between the transmission and transfer case incorporates a ball yoke universal assembly and splined shaft, a sleeve yoke universal assembly, yoke flanges, and companion flanges for the transmission and transfer case respectively. Arrows must be in line to aline trunnions or yokes.

b. Propeller shafts.—The two longer propeller shafts to the axles incorporate a tube assembly with a universal sleeve joint assembly at the splined end and a universal joint assembly at the yoke end. Beyond the universal joints are the flanges for connection to the transfer case and the respective axles. Arrows must be in line to aline trunnions.

41. Universal joints.—The universal joints are of the needle-bearing type and consist of two steel forged, one-piece yokes assembled into a unit with a single forged trunnion cross and four needle-bearing assemblies. The needle bearings which fit into the yoke holes are self-contained, the needle rollers being assembled in hardened steel retaining cups. The end thrust from the trunnion cross is carried on the hardened and ground surface of the needle-bearing retaining cup.

42. Lubrication.—*a. Universal joints.*—Universal joints of the needle-bearing type should be lubricated with an oil equivalent to SAE 140. A high pressure fitting is provided on the trunnion cross or journal assembly for lubrication. There is a large oil reservoir in each end of the journal which is packed with lubricant when the joints are assembled and additional oil will not be required except at 2,000-mile intervals. A relief valve is assembled to the central chamber to prevent damage to the oil seals when extremely high pressure is used to force in lubricant; this valve also serves as an indicator to show when the joint is completely filled.

b. Spline shaft.—A lubricating fitting is also provided to lubricate each splined sleeve or propeller shaft slip joint every 1,000 miles, using the same SAE 140 lubricant.

Caution: It is important to note that ordinary grease or heavy oil must not be used in needle-bearing universal joints as such lubricants will tend to block the oil passages.

43. Hand brake.—*a. Description.*—The disk type hand brake (fig. 28) is an American Cable "Tru-Stop" model, incorporating two shoes which operate on a disk that is mounted on a companion flange of the propeller shaft to the rear of the transfer case. The brake shoes are lined with a heavy duty molded lining, mounted on a shaft in brackets attached to a special cross member, and operated by linkage connected to the hand brake lever in the driver's compartment.

b. Adjustments.—When the brake lining wears so that the brake does not hold when the hand brake lever is pulled back as far as possible, adjustment should be made as follows:

(1) Place the hand brake lever forward in the fully released position to provide maximum clearance between the shoes and disk. Tighten the adjusting nut so that the release spring exerts enough pressure to bring the operating lever to stop solidly against the lever arm.

(2) Insert a $\frac{1}{32}$-inch shim between the front shoe lining and disk and adjust the pull rod from the driver's control lever to maintain this clearance.

(3) Tighten adjusting nut so that rear lining has $\frac{1}{32}$-inch clearance with the disk.

(4) See that the tension or brake shoe spring is in place and adjust the adjusting set screws so that the linings are parallel with the disk.

(5) Remove the shims.

c. Lubrication.—At intervals of 1,000 miles, the brake shoe anchor pins should be lubricated at the grease fittings provided. In the case of the scout car, M3, group there are also two grease fittings on the cross shaft for the operating linkage to the pull rod pin. In the case of scout car, M3A1, the brake and clutch pedal bushings should be inspected regularly for indications of binding which may be alleviated with penetrating oil.

TM 9-705

SCOUT CARS AND MORTAR MOTOR CARRIAGE 44

Section XI

AXLE ASSEMBLIES AND STEERING GEAR

	Paragraph
Front axle	44
Rear axle	45
Wheels and tires	46
Hydraulic brakes	47
Hydraulic brake servicing	48
Vacuum power unit	49
Springs	50
Shock absorbers	51
Steering mechanism	52

44. Front axle.—*a. Description.*—The front axle is of the spiral, bevel gear, single reduction, full floating type, with a straddle mounted pinion gear. As manufactured by the Timken-Detroit Axle Company, the type shown in figure 29 applies to the scout car, M3, group and to scout car, M3A1, with minor variations; assemblies are interchangeable as complete units, the latter having greater capacity.

b. Construction.—(1) The front axle consists of heat-treated tubing, pressed and riveted into the gear housings at the inner ends, and butt welded to the forged sockets at the outer ends. In the top and bottom of the sockets, hardened and ground kingpins are press fitted and welded to carry heavy duty, taper roller, kingpin or pivot bearings. These pivot bearings support the split socket housing and are shim adjusted, top and bottom, by means of steering knuckle caps on the steering arm. The inner end of the socket housing encloses a steering knuckle felt which rides upon a spherical wall of the socket, carrying a steering stop to limit the steering angle to 30°, and likewise a steering arm for tie rod attachment. The outer end of the socket housing carries a wheel spindle or knuckle and fully encloses the constant velocity, universal joint, drive shaft assemblies. Mounted upon the knuckle by means of tapered roller bearings is a full floating hub so the entire wheel end assembly carries the load independent of the shaft.

(2) The hub is attached to the universal drive shaft by means of a long, spline engaged drive flange directly attached to the hub by studs. Removal of this drive flange permits adjusting the inner and outer wheel bearings by means of two adjusting nuts secured with a tongued lock washer. The hub flange, in addition to carrying the wheel disk, mounts an iron brake drum with studs to suit the type of wheel. Against the knuckle flange is bolted the brake backing plate which fully encloses the two-shoe, internal expanding, hydraulic

brake with its wheel cylinder secured at the top. The brake lining is of ¼-inch molded type, readily adjusted for wear by externally operated adjustment cams near the top. It is not necessary to remove the drum or wheel in making adjustments to the brake.

(3) The tubular tie rod is mounted behind the axle for protection and is attached to each wheel end by a threaded and bolt clamped tie rod yoke. The tie rod yoke pin is bushed on the socket housing and fixed against rotation in the yoke.

(4) The upper and lower spring seats are of forged steel and welded to the housing arms or tubes. The steering arm ball stud is of carburized steel, ground and taper fitted to the steering arm.

(5) A modification (FSMWO G67-W3) has been effected for the axle by the addition between the spring seats of a truss rod fitted with a turnbuckle which may be tightened to relieve the strain on the axle proper.

c. Steering knuckle bearing adjustment.—Jack up the axle and remove the four cap screws at the upper and lower steering knuckle bearing caps. The caps can then be removed and adjustment of the bearings accomplished by means of shims located under these caps. The bearings should be adjusted until there is no end play of the knuckle assembly, but it should oscillate freely. Then remove caps and reduce shim pile .005-inch under each cap. After replacing caps, there should be a small amount of drag in rotating the steering knuckle but it should not bind.

d. Wheel bearing adjustment and replacement.—(1) Each front wheel is supported by two adjustable tapered roller bearings. The adjustment is initiated by first jacking up the axle until one wheel is free and removing the drive plate. The latter operation is accomplished by removing the drive shaft stud nuts and the center screw in which a lubrication fitting is mounted, and loosening the plate by means of two puller screws. The portion of the bearing lock which has been bent over is then straightened and the lock nut and nut lock are removed.

(2) The wheel should be spun slowly and the bearing adjusting nut should be turned up until the bearings bind slightly, then the nut should be backed off ⅛ turn.

(3) Replace the nut lock with a new one, if possible, and install the lock nut, making sure to hold the adjusting nut to prevent its turning. When the lock nut is tightened, the edges of the lock should then be bent over both the adjusting nut and lock nut, and the wheel checked for free rotation.

SCOUT CARS AND MORTAR MOTOR CARRIAGE

(4) The drive plate should then be reinstalled, making sure that the lubrication fitting on the outer edge of the plate is in line with the small hole in the gasket and the flange of the hub.

e. Caster or trailer effect.—The steering pivots or king pins are usually not perpendicular to the ground but inclined slightly to the rear in a vertical plane (fig. 29 ②). The main reason for this practice is that such construction gives a trailer effect which tends to cause the front wheels to right themselves automatically when deflected from the straight-ahead course. This effect is accomplished by the proper relation of the spring seat on the axle and the vehicle front springs. The correct amount of caster is 5° and the only method in the field of correcting any deviation from this angle is by the use of a wedge-shaped plate between the axle spring seat and the lower vehicle spring leaf.

f. Wheel camber.—Axle ends and steering axles are so designed that when the knuckles are in the position corresponding to straight-ahead driving, the knuckle spindle axis or wheel axis is not parallel with the plane on which the vehicle stands but inclines downward; hence the wheels are closer together at the bottom than at the top. This inclination is known as the camber angle and its principal purpose is to cause a vehicle to steer more easily. As shown in figure 30, the correct wheel camber of $\frac{3}{4}°$ per wheel is originally set in the axle and cannot be altered through any adjustments. If the reading is found to be greater than 1° or less than 0°, it is an indication that some part has been bent in service, and repair or replacement should be effected; usually replacement is preferable.

g. Toe-in or gather.—(1) The front wheels are not parallel when in the position of straight-ahead running, but are closer together at the front than at the rear. Toe-in has the effect of causing the natural paths of the wheels to approach each other and is introduced for the purpose of counteracting the tendency of the wheels to separate as a result of camber. Wheel toe-in, as indicated in figure 30, is originally set at $\frac{1}{8}$ inch, plus or minus $\frac{1}{16}$ inch, and should be maintained at this figure.

(2) Adjustment of toe-in is accomplished by removing the left-hand steering cross tube end pin and slipping the cross tube end or tie rod yoke off the cross tube steering arm or tie rod (fig. 29 ②). The cross tube clamp bolts are loosened to permit rotating the threaded yoke on the tube to increase or decrease its effective length. Toe-in is controlled by the length of the connecting tube assembly. After correct adjustment has been obtained, bolts, yoke, and pin must be secured in position once more.

h. Lubrication.—(1) *Oil seals.*—All oil seals should be periodically inspected and replaced if undue wear is apparent. If seals are allowed to operate after they have become worn, they no longer perform their function of retaining the lubricant in its proper location and many times allow the entrance of dirt, grit and other foreign matter which becomes mixed with the lubricant, causing premature wear and other difficulties.

(2) *Steering knuckle upper bearings.*—At 1,000-mile intervals, lubricate the upper steering knuckle bearings with a chassis lubricant.

(3) *Steering knuckle lower bearings and universal drive assembly.*—At 1,000-mile intervals, for summer lubrication, lubricate with SAE 250 through the trunnion socket for the Rzeppa type joint employed in production until level is reached through plug (X) (fig. 29 ②). For cold weather operation, use SAE 140.

(4) *Front axle center.*—After the first 1,000 miles of operation, drain the oil from the axle housing, flush out and refill with 4½ quarts of a gear lubricant using a straight mineral oil with a Saybolt viscosity of at least 150 seconds for summer use (SAE 140) and 85 to 115 seconds at 210° F. for winter use (SAE 90). At 1,000-mile intervals, check and add lubricant if necessary. At each 6,000 miles after the initial refilling, drain the lubricant from the axle housing, flush, and refill as above.

(5) *Front wheel bearings.*—Wheel bearings should be removed, cleaned, checked, and repacked every 6,000 miles. Lubrication through fittings inserted in cap recesses of the axle driving flanges is not recommended. For atmospheric temperatures down to plus 10° F., use a hard wheel bearing fibrous grease; for lower temperatures, use a medium wheel bearing fibrous grease.

45. Rear axle.—*a. Description.*—The rear axle (fig. 31) is manufactured by the Timken-Detroit Axle Company, applies to the scout car, M3, group and also to scout car, M3A1, with minor variations, and is interchangeable as a complete unit. This rear axle is of the spiral bevel-gear, single reduction, full floating type.

b. Construction.—(1) The rear axle consists of a housing which serves as the load-carrying member and is a steel stamping with a forged outer end. The differential and bevel ring gear assembly, together with the pinion, are mounted as a unit in the axle housing tube and carrier assemblies.

(2) The ring gear is riveted to a flange on the differential case which is mounted in tapered roller bearings. A backing-up block for the ring gear is provided to prevent excessive deflection under extreme loads.

(3) The pinion gear is straddle mounted with two opposed roller bearings in front of the gear head and a straight solid roller bearing at the rear.

(4) The wheels are mounted on two tapered roller bearings on the end of the axle housing tubes and are driven by a drop forged axle shaft. The outer end of this shaft has an integral flange which bolts to the wheel and the inner end is splined to the differential side gear.

c. Rear wheel bearing adjustment.—This adjustment must be made with the axle jacked up and the axle shaft removed.

(1) Draw the inside adjusting nut up tightly against the outer cone assembly, meanwhile rotating the wheel first in one direction and then in the other until the bearings bind and the wheel turns hard. Rotating the wheel in both directions causes the rollers to become fully and evenly seated.

(2) Back off the adjusting nut until the wheel turns freely without perceptible end play in the bearing. It may be necessary to tap the end of the axle housing while loosening the adjustment in order to move the cone on the axle.

(3) End play may be tested by placing the end of a short bar between the tire and the floor and at the same time holding a finger on the cage of the outer bearing. Work the bar up and down to detect any excessive play or looseness. If but a barely perceptible shake can be felt and the wheel turns freely, the adjustment is correct and can be locked as set, after which the axle shaft may be replaced.

d. Lubrication.—(1) *Rear axle.*—After the first 1,000 miles of operation, drain the oil from the axle housing, flush out, and refill with 3 quarts of a gear lubricant using a straight mineral oil equivalent to SAE 90 for winter and SAE 140 for summer. At 1,000-mile intervals, check the level of the oil in the axle housing and add lubricant if necessary. At each 6,000 miles after the initial refilling, drain the lubricant from the axle housing, flush, and refill as above.

(2) *Rear wheel bearings.*—At 6,000-mile intervals, remove the rear wheels, clean out the old grease and repack the bearings by hand with a wheel bearing lubricant. It is necessary that these bearings be repacked by hand with the correct amount of lubricant to eliminate the possibility of forcing the lubricant past the grease retainers such as when pressure guns are used. When reinstalling the wheels, care must be exercised to prevent damage to the oil seal at the inner bearings. Be sure to readjust the wheel bearings when the wheels are assembled.

46. Wheels and tires.—The front and rear wheels are the Budd Company's demountable 20 by 7, steel disk, spoke type, with six mounting holes. All wheels and tires of the scout car, M3, group and scout car, M3A1, are interchangeable.

a. Tire casings.—As originally equipped, the casings are 8.25 by 20, mud and snow tread, balloon type with a TR 77 type valve. Tires or casings should be repaired in accordance with conventional methods. Punctures or tears causing exposure of the cord or fabric should be vulcanized.

b. Tubes.—Bullet resisting inner tubes, with a puncture sealing element, are supplied in accordance with Rock Island Arsenal Tentative Specification RIXS–114. Pressure required is 60 to 70 pounds. Procurement of sponge rubber fillers for pneumatic tired combat vehicles has been discontinued (OFSC 116). Holes in bullet resisting and puncture sealing inner tubes should be repaired by cold patching with the method employed for conventional tubes. Hot patching or vulcanizing should not be attempted. The heat and pressure requisite for hot patching will destroy the sealing matrix and cause the inner walls to become vulcanized together. Tires must not be operated when underinflated, nor "bled" to reduce air pressure which increases during operation.

c. Preservation (OFSC91).—The deleterious effect of oil and grease on rubber is generally known, but precautionary measures to prevent contact are frequently neglected. Tires and tracks come in contact with oil or grease for various reasons, among the more common of which are faulty assembly of seals, worn or damaged seals, or carelessness in handling oil and grease when lubricating. The consequent deterioration of the rubber is slow and therefore unnoticed, since the oil gradually works into the rubber and leaves the outer surface normal in appearance, but an amalgam forms with the rubber to soften and reduce the heat and wear resisting qualities. When a lubricant is required to facilitate the installation of tires, a solution of liquid soap and flake graphite should be used. The liquid soap should be added to the graphite until the resulting solution can be applied with a paint brush. This solution has no deleterious effect on rubber and will retard rim corrosion.

47. Hydraulic brakes.—*a. Description.*—The service or wheel brakes comprise a 4-wheel, vacuum power, hydraulic type system (fig. 32) and are manufactured by the Wagner Electric Company (Lockheed). The brake proper consists of two internal expanding shoes for each of the front and rear wheels in iron brake drums with high wear resisting qualities. Shoes in both the front and rear brakes are expanded by opposed pistons acting in a cylinder and operating directly on each shoe.

SCOUT CARS AND MORTAR MOTOR CARRIAGE

b. Operation.—(1) This braking system consists of a combination brake-fluid supply tank and master cylinder, and hydraulic lines of copper tubing leading from the master cylinder to the flexible connections between the frame and axles which connect to the wheel operating cylinders. Foot pressure applied to the brake pedal forces fluid through the copper tubing and flexible connections into the wheel cylinders in the four-wheel brakes. The brake fluid enters the wheel cylinders between opposed pistons causing them to expand the brake shoes to contact the brake drums.

(2) As the pedal is moved forward the vacuum power unit piston and rod move, and greater hydraulic pressure is built up within the wheel cylinders to press the shoes against the brake drums. When the foot pressure is removed from the brake pedal, the release springs between the brake shoes contract, return the wheel cylinder pistons to their "off" position, and force the brake fluid from the operating cylinders back to the master cylinder. Since the pressure must be equal in all parts of the system, no braking action can take place until all shoes are in contact with the drums; the brakes, therefore, are automatically equalized.

c. Master cylinder and supply tank.—The master cylinder (fig. 33) is integral with the supply tank casting and is bracket mounted to the frame side rail. The supply tank carries a reserve of fluid which is fed automatically to the system as required, the master cylinder being submerged in the fluid. The tank is equipped with a combination filler and breather cap (A), which permits atmospheric pressure on the reserve fluid at all times and prevents the entrance of dirt and water and the evaporation of the alcohol content of the fluid. A conventional pressure type stoplight switch (fig. 43), with a ⅛-inch fitting and two screw terminals, is assembled to the master cylinder.

(1) *Function.*—The function of the master cylinder is to set up pressure in the system and force a sufficient quantity of liquid between the pistons of the wheel cylinders to apply the brake. The combination master cylinder and supply tank automatically maintains a constant volume of fluid in the system, compensates for expansion or contraction of the fluid caused by temperature changes, and replenishes any loss of fluid from slight leaks or seepage.

(2) *Operation.*—(a) When the foot brake pedal is released or in the "off" position, the piston (B) (fig. 33) in the master cylinder is held to its outer or released position by the return spring (G) and sealed by the rubber piston cup (C). When the piston is in

this outer position, it uncovers a compensating port (H) in the cylinder wall which connects to the supply tank.

(b) Increase in temperature causes the fluid in the braking system to expand, the expansion being bypassed through port (H) to the tank. A drop in temperature causes the fluid to contract and replenishment is effected through the same port from the tank so that a constant volume of fluid is maintained in the system. It is important, therefore, to adjust the rod to the power lever so that the piston may return to the extreme position against the stop wire (J) and permit the piston cup (C) to uncover the compensating port.

(c) The valves of the master cylinder, held in place by the return spring (G), are double check valves (K) and (L), which allow the brake fluid to flow in both directions. When the brakes are applied, the fluid is forced through the inner check valve (L) which is held against the large valve (K) by a spring (P) of low pressure. When the brake foot pedal is released, the master piston return spring forces the piston back to its position against the stop (J). At the same time, brake fluid enters the master cylinder through the outer larger valve (K), forced from the operating cylinders through the pipe lines by the brake release springs. The return pressure of the fluid decreases until it balances that of the master piston return spring (G) which is 6 to 8 pounds and is sufficient to keep the piston seal cups seated and prevent gravity leaks or unseating due to road shocks.

(d) Should the fluid returned from the system be insufficient to equal the displacement caused by the return of the master piston to its release position, a vacuum will be set up in the master cylinder sufficient to draw fluid into the master cylinder from the supply tank through six small ports in the master cylinder piston head, one of which is shown at (M). Secondary cup (D) is a seal to prevent loss of reserve fluid into the boot (F).

(e) The combination valve functions differently when bleeding or filling the system with brake fluid. Because of the fact that there is no pressure in the system to operate the valve against the 6- to 8-pound spring pressure of the master cylinder, fluid is continually passed by the operation of the foot brake pedal, through the smaller check valve (L), until air is entirely expelled from the system.

d. Brake connections.—The brake connections for the hydraulic brake system are of special annealed copper tubing and a flexible rubber and fabric hose designed for this particular purpose. The tubing is securely anchored to the frame or axle by clips to prevent vibration and whenever needed, protected by loom. One tube leads from the master cylinder along the inside of the frame left side member, and by flexible connection to the rear axle housing where it divides, serving both rear brakes. Separate tubes lead from the master cylinder to each front brake and these front tubes are carried inside of the frame side members leading by flexible connection to both front wheels. The pipe connection for the right front wheel brake is carried across the rear axle housing. The flexible connections should be renewed at the end of 2 years' service.

e. Wheel cylinders.—The four-wheel or operating cylinders are mounted rigidly to the dust shield. Each cylinder is fitted with two aluminum pistons, sealed with rubber piston cups, connected to the brake shoes. The open ends of the cylinders are protected by rubber boots which prevent the entrance of dust and grit. From the highest point of the cylinder and between the opposed pistons is a bleeder valve. This connection is used to expel all air from the system when it is being filled with brake fluid, an operation known as "bleeding."

f. Brake shoes.—The brake shoes in each wheel are lined with high grade molded brake lining, supported at the lower end by two eccentric anchor pins. Side play is limited by guide pins and retaining washers which are contracted by the brake release spring and bear on the edge of the brake shoe. At the top, the shoes are expanded by the operating cylinder.

g. Hydraulic brake fluid.—The Lockheed No. 21 hydraulic brake fluid is a special mixture of neutralized castor oil, denatured alcohol, and suitable chemical reagents to prevent any action of the fluid on the rubber and metal parts. Do not use any unauthorized substitute.

48. Hydraulic brake servicing.—*a. Fluid level.*—The level of the fluid in the supply tank should be inspected at least once a month. The proper level of the liquid is ¾ inch below the top of the tank. There should be practically no loss of fluid in the operation of the brakes and any noticeable loss indicates a leak in the system which should be located and stopped. If the tank becomes more than half empty, air will be drawn into the system when the brake is released. In such a case, filling the tank to the proper level is not enough, since the system must be bled at each wheel cylinder to remove the air.

b. Bleeding the line.—(1) *General.*—Bleeding is necessary only when some part of the hydraulic system has been disconnected or the fluid in the supply has become too low. To displace air which may have accumulated in the system, fluid is forced through the lines until it flows from the bleeder valve of each wheel cylinder in a solid stream. When bleeding, depression of the foot pedal forces the liquid from the master cylinder through the outlet combination valve into the lines to the wheel cylinders. When the brake pedal is released with no pressure in the system, the master piston return spring will return the piston against its stop and hold the return valve closed to create a vacuum within the master cylinder. The cup will collapse and bypass brake fluid through the drilled piston, allowing fluid to bypass from the supply tank and refill the master cylinder. Working the foot pedal thus gives a pumping action which forces fluid through the system and out at the wheel cylinder bleeder valve, carrying with it any air that may be present.

(2) *Procedure.*—Remove the filler plug (A) (fig. 33) and fill the supply tank with brake fluid. Remove the cap screw from the bleeder valve (R) of a wheel cylinder, and connect the bleeder drain tube provided for the purpose. Slide the bleeder valve wrench over the rubber tube, engage the hex of the bleeder valve and open the valve three-quarters of a turn. Place the free end of the tube below the brake fluid level and drain into a clean glass container comparable to a pint jar. Depress the brake pedal slowly by hand, allowing the spring to return the pedal to its released position. Approximately ten strokes of the pedal will be required to bleed each wheel cylinder until fluid issues from the tube end in a solid stream without bubbles. When bleeding, be sure to keep the supply tank more than half full of fluid, otherwise air will be drawn into the system at this point and necessitate rebleeding. As each wheel cylinder is bled, the bleeder valve is shut off tightly with the wrench, the bleeder tube is removed and the cap screw with the lock washer is replaced. After a cylinder has been bled, do not again depress the brake pedal until the valve of the next cylinder is opened, for the reason that air may be forced over from a line yet to be bled to a line on which this operation has been completed. When the bleeding operation is completed, refill the supply tank and replace the valve plug. See that the filler plug is screwed down tight. Fluid drained out in this operation should not be used again.

c. Adjusting brakes.—(1) *Lining wear.*—Raise the vehicle until wheels are free. Rotate the cam (T) by the nut (U) projecting through the dust cover until the brake shoe touches the drum. Back off this adjustment slightly until the wheel rotates freely without drag. Adjust all eight brake shoes in this manner. The cams are automatically locked in position by a friction spring and their shape is such that a wrench applied to the adjusting nut, with the handle pointing up and pulled toward the outside of the wheel, will push the brake shoe into contact with the brake drum.

(2) *Removing brake shoes.*—The washers are removed from the anchor pins (P) and guide pins (Q). After the brake shoe return

spring (O) is removed, the brake shoe may be taken off. In assembling, these operations are reversed. In case brake shoes are relined, it is imperative that the same kind of lining be used for all drums or the braking will not be uniform.

(3) *After relining.*—The brake shoe anchor pins (P) are eccentric and capable of adjustment. However, this is a factory adjustment and once correctly made should not be disturbed unless new linings are installed. The proper clearance between the lining and the drum at the point nearest the anchor pins is .006 inch measured with a feeler gage 1 inch from the end of the brake shoe lining. With correct clearance established at the anchor pins, the clearance for the toe of the brake shoe can be checked. Measure with an .008-inch feeler gage 1 inch from the end of the lining.

d. Disassembling brakes.—(1) To remove a front wheel cylinder, disconnect copper tubing from hose fitting at the frame, remove the nut and rotate cam (T) to bring shoes clear of wheel cylinder connecting links. Removal of the two cap screws (S), which hold the cylinder to the brake dust shield, allows the cylinder and hose to be withdrawn from the shield.

(2) To remove a rear cylinder, follow above instructions except that the copper tubing must be disconnected at the cylinder inlet.

(3) To remove wheel cylinder cups, the rubber boots on either end are removed and the pistons are withdrawn by inserting a hook in the hole of the piston skirt. The spiral spring placed between the wheel cylinder cups serves to keep the cups in contact with the pistons at all times. It is imperative that the spring bears evenly in the bottom of the cylinder cup and in no way disturbs the lip.

(4) To remove the piston from the master cylinder, it is necessary to remove the complete combination unit from the bracket. After the boot and stop wire are removed, the piston, primary cup, return spring, and combination valve can be withdrawn.

(5) It should not be necessary to disassemble any cylinder unless it is found to be leaking fluid past the cup.

(6) Before reassembling a cylinder, the bore should be thoroughly cleaned and washed with alcohol. Do not use kerosene, gasoline, etc. The bore should be free from any score marks, rust corrosion, or pits. It is always advisable to use new cups when servicing a cylinder, and cup and piston should be dipped in brake fluid before inserting into the cylinder.

e. Precautions.—(1) Do not use an unauthorized substitute for Lockheed brake fluid, as damage is very likely to result to some part of the system. Free acid will attack iron cylinders, free alkali will attack the aluminum pistons, and mineral oil will spoil the rubber piston cups, boots, and flexible connections.

(2) Do not allow grease, paint, oil, or brake fluid to come in contact with the brake lining.

(3) Do not clean rubber parts or inside of cylinders with anything but alcohol.

(4) Do not fail to replace flexible pressure line connection every 2 years.

49. Vacuum power unit.—*a. Description.*—The vacuum power unit (fig. 35) described as a Bragg-Kliesrath type RP66, is of the reaction type and so connected to the master cylinder and brake pedal that it supplies a percentage of the power applied to the master cylinder, the remainder being supplied by manual effort on the brake pedal pad. In this unit, the intake manifold is utilized as a source of partial vacuum to present a vacuum on both sides of the cylinder piston when the brakes are off and the engine is running, the vacuum line being connected from the rear of the power unit cylinder to the manifold (fig. 32).

b. Operation.—(1) The valve operating the power unit is contained in the unit and is operated by a rod extending through the power unit piston rod to the valve operating lever (figs. 34 and 35). If adjustments are correct, a movement of approximately 1 inch of the brake pedal pulls the valve toward the rear of the piston, admitting air to the forward side of the piston. The air, or atmospheric pressure, moves the piston toward the rear, and through the power lever connection, applies pressure to the master cylinder piston.

(2) Air enters the cylinder from the remote air cleaner through a connection in the end plate dust cover, holes in the hollow piston rod, and finally the valve to the front side of the piston. It is essential that about $5/32$-inch travel specified for the valve rod be obtained so that the valve may open the ports admitting air to the piston; $1/4$-inch travel is required for full opening of the valve when the clearance on the power lever is all taken up at (A).

(3) The amount of air admitted to the rear of the cylinder depends upon the brake pedal movement. If the operator stops the forward movement of the brake pedal, the piston will move until the valve closes off the port which admits air to the rear of the piston, the valve remaining in the neutral position to cover the ports and hold the air in the cylinder on the rear side of the piston. To accomplish any further movement of the piston or brake application, the pedal must be depressed further.

SCOUT CARS AND MORTAR MOTOR CARRIAGE

(4) When the operator releases the brake, the valve is positively moved to the released position by the valve lever attached to the brake pedal; this action closes the air passage to the rear side of the piston and opens a passage across the piston to restore the vacuum balance on both sides of the piston.

c. Adjustments.—The valve operating lever is attached to the brake pedal by two cap screws and a clamp with an oversize hole at the lower cap screw to permit adjustment. It is absolutely necessary that in the brake-released position the clearance of about $\frac{1}{32}$ inch between the shaft hole in the power lever and the brake pedal shaft must be on the forward side of the shaft as shown at (A) (fig. 34). Also, the power cylinder piston rod clevis pin must be against the rearward wall of the valve link bushing as shown at (B) (fig. 34) and A (fig. 35). Any improper adjustments will affect the application and operation of the brakes. It is important that adjustments be made as indicated and in the order given below.

(1) Loosen valve lever anchorage screws (C) (fig. 34) and remove master cylinder and power cylinder piston rod clevis pins (D) and (E). Be sure that the leverage system is clean and in correct alinement with no binding. Block brake pedal in the release position and check that clearance between the power lever and pedal shaft is at the front side of the shaft.

(2) Adjust master cylinder clevis to permit $\frac{1}{32}$ to $\frac{1}{15}$ inch lost motion in master cylinder piston rod and insert clevis pin (D) and cotter.

(3) Push power cylinder piston rod inward until piston bottoms; aline piston rod clevis with power lever eye by adjusting cylinder position at the mounting end (F). *Never attempt to adjust piston rod clevis as this affects valve positioning* which is correctly set at the time of factory assembly.

(4) Check that piston rod clevis pin (E) is against rear side wall of valve link bushings as shown at (B) then tighten valve lever adjustment screws (C) being careful not to disturb valve position. Be sure valve lever is central and square on valve rod bushing to avoid binding.

(5) When the brake pedal is moved by hand, the valve rod should move $\frac{1}{4}$ inch outward before any movement of the power line occurs.

(6) Check to be sure cotter pins are in place, lock nuts tightened, and cap screws tight.

d. Lubrication.—Every 6,000 to 10,000 miles, remove the pipe plug in the front end of the power unit and lubricate the cylinder walls with 2 ounces of Bendix vacuum cylinder oil, after which the pipe plug should be replaced. At every chassis lubrication, spray the valve and power lever linkage with light oil.

e. Cleaning.—The remote air cleaner should be examined and cleaned at least twice a year. Remove the hair, wash same thoroughly in kerosene, dry and then saturate with a light machine oil. Replace the hair in the cleaner and reassemble.

f. Inspection and maintenance.—In case of necessity, the following instructions for inspection and adjustment are available for the operator:

(1) Remove pipe plug at front of cylinder and connect in a vacuum gage.

(2) Start the engine and note reading on the gage which should show a vacuum of 17 to 20 inches. Stop the engine and note if vacuum is retained for a reasonable length of time. If gage shows a rapidly falling-off (more than 10 inches in 10 seconds), it indicates a leak which may be in the cylinder, in the line, or in the check valve in the inlet manifold connection. Leakage in the power cylinder may often be corrected by a thorough lubrication of the unit.

(3) Disconnect vacuum line between manifold and power unit and hold a finger over the end of the line. If the engine idling speed is slower than with the line connected to the power unit, it is an indication of a leak in either the lines or the power unit itself.

(4) Never attempt to replace the valve without also installing new piston rod. Piston rods are furnished with undersize bore and must be reamed to fit after assembly in piston.

50. Springs.—*a. Description.*—Semi-elliptic springs are used for the front and rear axles, being anchored at the front end and shackled at the rear. The pins which pass through the spring eyes and the shackle or brackets are hardened and ground and are fitted to reamed bushings of hard bronze. The rear springs, which employ the Hotchkiss drive principle, provide for easy riding when light but have ample capacity when loaded. Springs, while differing in design, are interchangeable between scout cars in pairs in case of emergency.

(1) *Spring clips.*—The use of the Hotchkiss drive, wherein the drive is taken directly through the rear springs, provides a simplified construction which eliminates radius rods and all component parts. It is very essential that spring clips are tight as considerable spring breakage can be eliminated by preventing the springs from flexing at the center bolt hole.

(2) *Spring clip adjustment.*—Spring clips which fasten the springs to the axle should be examined regularly and kept tight. Loose spring

clips may allow the axle to shift and cause shearing of the center bolt and breaking of the leaves. The spring clip nuts should be tried with a wrench each week during the first few weeks of operation and thereafter each month.

(3) *"Twin-back" principle.*—In order to provide a tight wrap around the spring eye sufficient to prevent breakage at this critical point, it is necessary to wrap both the first and second leaves around the bushing at the eye. To take care of the lengthening and shortening of the first and second leaf and still provide a tight wrap, it is necessary to split the second leaf into three sections. At the center of the spring underneath the clip bolts is an **H**-shaped section slightly thicker than the two outer ends of this leaf, and into the recess formed by the **H**, the tang end of the outer section is allowed to slide. The joint formed between the center section and the two outer sections of the second leaf gives the impression of a broken spring leaf and may lead to complaints resulting from a misunderstanding of the basic principle concerned in connection with the front spring assembly (White part No. 344977) of scout car, M3A1.

b. Lubrication.—At 1,000-mile intervals, lubricate all spring and shackle bolts, through the pressure fittings provided, with an approved grade of chassis lubricant. Spring leaves are lubricated or coated with graphite at assembly but the lubricating action is neutralized in time by the pressure of dirt and water. Leaves may be removed for cleaning and oiling, or sprayed with graphite oil while flexing the springs to assist penetration of the oil. Muck and old grease should be scraped off the sides of the leaves and removed from the shackles.

51. Shock absorbers.—*a. Description.*—The Houdaille shock absorber operates entirely upon the principle of hydraulic resistance in conjunction with the ASC type instrument, lever, link, and clip plate, left and right front assemblies and the BAG type instrument, lever, and link, left and right rear assemblies.

b. Operation.—Movement of the shock absorber lever, which is attached to a rotating shaft and wing, forces fluid from one chamber to another. The working chamber is divided into two sections by a stationary partition, in each side of which is located a check valve. The valves permit fluid to flow freely in one direction but close completely the instant the flow of fluid is reversed. When this action occurs, the fluid is forced out of the compression chambers, through an adjustable valve, and into the noncompression chambers, where upon the return stroke of the shock absorber lever, it is again forced into the compression chambers through the check valves in the stationary partition.

c. Adjustment.—The valve in the adjustable type of shock absorber automatically takes care of any variation in load and road conditions. Changes in temperature affect the coil in which the valve is mounted, thereby providing thermostatic control of the valve opening at any manual setting. The factory adjustment should be satisfactory for normal conditions and average driving; however, for unusual conditions, provision has been made for additional adjustments as follows:

(1) Remove the valve cap and gasket to expose the end of the shaft and the adjustable end of the valve. The wing shaft is marked with the letters "O" and "S" (open and shut).

(2) The valve end has two cross slots; the one marked with an arrow is for adjustment; the other contains a wedge which is used to stake the valve to the shaft. Unless the factory adjustment has been changed, the arrow will be directly in line with a punch mark between the letters "O" and "S."

Caution: The full range of adjustment lies between the letters "O" and "S", and the valve should never be turned beyond these points.

(3) To increase resistance, turn the arrow counterclockwise toward "S", not more than $\frac{1}{32}$ inch at one time, using the mark on the shaft as a guide. Test and repeat operation until satisfactory control is obtained.

d. Fluid.—(1) An auxiliary reservoir which is an integral part of the shock absorber contains a supply of fluid which automatically enters the working chamber through a replenishing ball check. To prevent air from entering the working chambers, the fluid level should be kept up to the bottom of the filler plug opening located at the top of this reservoir. Extreme care should be exercised when removing the filler plug, that no dirt falls into the reservoir. Such particles will enter the working chamber, pass to the top of the instrument, and eventually plug the air vent provided for the escape of gases formed under hydraulic pressure.

(2) Every 2,000 miles, remove the filler plug and check the fluid level. Use Houdaille No. 1400 shock absorber fluid or an authorized substitute having a glycerin base diluted with alcohol, a Saybolt-Universal viscosity at 100° F. of 800 seconds, at 130° F. of 310 seconds, and a pour point of minus 30° F. Initial filling capacity of the front unit is 130 cubic centimeters and of the rear unit, 180 cubic centimeters.

e. Interchangeability.—The Houdaille type A-4089 and A-4080 ASC instrument, lever, link, and clip plate assemblies (right and left front respectively), and the type A-4072 and A-4073 BAG instrument, lever, and link assemblies (right and left rear respectively) are used for the scout car, M3, group. Improved type A-4301 and A-4302 BEDVS assemblies (right and left front), and type A-5973 and A-5974 BBG assemblies (right and left rear) are applicable for similar purposes on scout car M3A1.

f. Lubrication.—The internal working parts are automatically lubricated by the fluid. Every 500 miles, lubricate with chassis grease the two ball joints on the connecting link by means of the pressure fittings provided.

52. Steering mechanism.—*a. Description.*—The Ross Gear and Tool Company steering gear, types 660 and T-26, respectively (figs. 36 and 37), is of the cam and lever type in which sufficient reduction is provided with ample leverage in the steering wheel to insure easy steering under all conditions. The angle of the steering column has been designed for the most comfortable operating position for the driver. The steering gear case is bracket mounted to the frame with the steering post held in a rubber bushing in the dash bracket. The cams, levers, and shafts are mounted in a malleable iron, oil tight case with full provision for the adjustment of both cam and cam follower.

b. Operation.—As shown in figure 37, the twin lever arrangement for scout car, M3A1, provides two integral follower pins to afford greater angular travel than in the case of the roller bearing mounted single pin (fig. 36) for the scout car, M3, group; this design permits the use of a shorter steering arm and more advantageous use of the effective leverage in the range of pin travel. As the gear moves away from the normal driving range into the parking range, one pin moves out of engagement leaving the other pin in the working position at which the effective leverage increases rapidly. The cam turns with the steering wheel, while the pins of the steering gear lever shaft engage with the thread of the cam. The groove is purposely cut shallower in the straight ahead driving position of each pin to permit a close adjustment for normal straight driving without binding elsewhere. Since the larger portion of driving is done when traveling straight ahead, more wear occurs in the steering gear within about one quarter wheel turn either side of the center position.

Caution: Do not attempt to cure wander, shimmy, or road shock by tightening the steering gear to dampen out such difficulties. Adjust the steering gear only to remove play in it. When making adjustments, follow the instructions exactly and in the order given, each adjustment being independent of the others. Improper adjustments will damage more gears than any other cause.

c. Adjustments.—Free the steering gear of all load by disconnecting the drag link from the steering gear arm and loosening the instrument board bracket which holds the steering gear jacket tube in place. Always make adjustment (1) below first.

(1) *Cam end play.*—End play of cam shows up as end play in the steering wheel tube. Before adusting the thrust bearings, loosen the housing side cover adusting screw and lock nut to free the lever shaft.

(*a*) In the case of the single lever type (fig. 36), back off the lock screw and turn the adjusting plug until a slight drag is felt when turning the steering wheel, and then back off plug about one-sixth turn until the wheel turns freely without any up and down movement of the wheel tube. Tighten lock screw and nut.

(*b*) In the case of the twin lever type (fig. 37), adjust the adjusting screw to a barely perceptible drag so that the steering wheel can be turned freely, with the thumb and forefinger lightly gripping the rim. Remove the four upper cover screws and raise the upper cover as far as possible, which will be about $\frac{1}{4}$ inch, to permit the removal of shims. (Combination of .003-, .010-, and .030-inch shims are used between paper gaskets.) Clip and remove shims as required and replace the clamp screws tightly. Test adjustment and if necessary remove or replace shims until the adjustment is correct.

(2) *Pin backlash.*—Backlash of lever shaft pins in the cam groove shows up as end play of the lever shaft, backlash at the steering wheel, and at the ball on the steering arm. Adjustment must be made within the high range through the midposition of pin travel. Do not adjust in the end positions, as play at the turn positions is not objectionable. Tighten the side cover adjusting screw until a very slight drag is felt through the midposition high range when turning the steering wheel slowly from one extreme to the other. The gear must not bind anywhere. Only a slight drag should be felt. A closer adjustment will not correct any steering condition, but will damage and wear the parts and impair operation. When proper adjustment has been made, tighten the lock nut for the adjusting screw and give the gear a final test. Make sure that the steering gear ball arm is tight on the splined shaft and that its nut and lockwasher are tight also.

(3) *Column alinement.*—Tighten the instrument board bracket. Turn the steering wheel to see if stiffness or binding occurs. If so, the gear has been adjusted too tightly or the steering column is out of alinement. The column must not be sprung in any direction. If misalinement occurs, it may be necessary to shim the dash

bracket. See that the frame bracket is tight to the frame and rigidly holds the gear assembly so that it does not spring when the wheel is turned (with the drag link connected and the wheels on the ground). Test the gear to make sure that tightening the brackets has not caused the gear to bind.

(4) *Connection to front wheels.*—Turn the steering wheel as far to the right as possible, then rotate the wheel in the opposite direction as far as possible to note the total number of turns. Turn back the wheel just one half of this total movement to secure the midposition.

NOTE.—With reference to figure 30, service experience shows that the steering angles indicated must be reduced several degrees for the most satisfactory operating conditions.

Place the wheels in position for straight ahead driving, and it should then be possible to connect the drag link to the ball on the end of the steering gear arm without moving the gear to any appreciable extent. If this cannot be done, remove the arm from the steering gear and place it on the splined shaft in the proper position. Ordinarily the latter action will not be necessary if all other settings are correct.

(5) *Steering wheel.*—The steering wheel can be adjusted up or down by first loosening the front bracket cap screw and the steering column dash bracket. After the desired position has been obtained, the assembly should again be securely tightened.

d. Lubrication.—Through the pipe plug hole, fill the housing slowly with steering gear lubricant, until it begins to run out the vent hole. Use SAE 250 for summer and SAE 140 for winter. Do not use grease of any sort. Repeat every 2,000 miles.

SECTION XII

ELECTRICAL EQUIPMENT; INSTRUMENTS

	Paragraph
Electrical system	53
Storage battery	54
Starting motor	55
Generator	56
Voltage regulator	57
Lighting, control, and accessory devices	58
Wiring	59
Instruments and gages	60

53. Electrical system.—The 12-volt electrical system is of the single wire, ground return type and energized from a 6-cell, 25-plate, lead acid type, 168 ampere-hour storage battery whose negative terminal is grounded to the frame. Included in the system are a direct electrical starter, generator, and voltage regulator, ignition equipment (sec. V), miscellaneous lighting, protective and control equipment, and necessary wiring.

54. Storage battery.—The battery is the source of supply for the current required by the starting motor, ignition system, and other electrical equipment until the engine is operating at sufficient speed for the generator to take over the load. The number of cells determine the nominal battery voltage and the size and number of plate per cell determine the capacity. Radio connection terminals are located on the positive or 12-volt terminal, and also on the 8-volt and 2-volt terminals. The location of the battery in the various vehicles is indicated in section II.

a. Specific gravity.—(1) Since specific gravity of acid in the electrolyte (battery solution) varies with and is proportional to the degree of charge, it is possible to determine the state of battery charge by an approved hydrometer designed for the purpose. The adjustment and operation of the battery system should be such that the specific gravity of all cells will be maintained normally above 1.250. It is important to note that the guaranteed performance of electrical accessories connected in the battery system is usually based on the requirement of a battery constantly and satisfactorily charged.

(2) Both temperature and electrolyte level affect the specific gravity reading, and it is desirable to record the temperature and electrolyte level in the cells in which gravity readings are taken at regular intervals, depending on operating conditions, at least once a week. The specific gravity with cells fully charged, electrolyte surface level maintained at least ½ inch above the top of the separators, and electrolyte temperature 80° F., should be between 1.270 and 1.290. A gravity reading of 1.220 indicates a half charged condition and a reading of 1.150 or lower indicates complete discharge. A d. c. voltmeter will not indicate whether or not a battery is fully charged; the effective voltage, however, on closed circuit at a period of high current discharge can be a measure of a battery's condition and capacity by indicating the drop in voltage from the nominal, open circuit value of 12 volts.

(3) Tests made immediately after water has been added will not register correctly since the solution must be given time to mix thoroughly. A test should be made before water is added or after the battery has been on charge or in use for a few hours. No gravity adjustment (addition of acid) should be required during the life

of a battery unless electrolyte is spilled, since only the water evaporates. Acid added in an effort to increase gravity will not charge the battery and will make hydrometer readings meaningless. Any electrolyte replacement should be effected by authorized maintenance personnel only.

b. Temperature effects.—(1) Check the battery for heating in warm weather. If the top connectors feel more than blood warm to the touch (approximately 100° F.), check the temperature with a dairy thermometer; if the temperature reaches 120° F., the battery may be ruined. If the battery feels more than blood warm, check for short circuits and excessive charging. If the battery continues to heat on long runs and authorized personnel are not available to test the system or adjust the voltage regulator to decrease the charging rate, disconnect the field circuit lead between the generator and regulator field terminals as an emergency expedient to cut out the generator.

(2) In tropical regions, great care must be taken to check the temperatures of batteries on charge as the danger of overheating is much greater than in cooler climates. An electrolyte of lower maximum specific gravity should be used so that the battery when fully charged will have a gravity of 1.225 if the temperature never drops to freezing.

(3) Except in cases where a specified temperature is stated in the rating itself, all capacity tests are conducted at 80° F. In addition to ordinary disadvantages of operating equipment at low temperatures, the ability of a battery to develop its capacity is materially reduced if it is not fully charged. Unless a full charge is maintained, the solution may freeze and in effect create sufficient damage to plates and containers to destroy the battery for all practicable purposes. A completely discharged battery may freeze at approximately 20° F.

(4) Batteries tend to "self-discharge" while standing idle, due to internal chemical action and, in case of dampness, electrical leakage between posts. Batteries kept in hot surroundings will discharge much faster than those stored in a cool place. A manufacturer's chart indicates, for example, that complete discharge may take place at 80° F. in about 4 months, whereas at 100° F. in about 50 days. The effect of allowing batteries to stand in a discharged or partially charged state is to cause the positive plates to buckle in service and shorten the battery life or preclude possibility of a thorough recharge.

c. Maintenance.—(1) The battery and battery compartment must be kept clean and dry and the vent plugs tightened although the breather holes in the latter must be kept open. If electrolyte is spilled or any parts are damp with acid, a solution of ordinary baking soda (1 pound of soda to 1 gallon of water) or weak ammonia should be applied and the surfaces should then be rinsed with fresh water and dried. No cleaning solution should be allowed to enter a cell. If the soda treatment is given several times a year and the battery is kept clean between times by means of weekly washings with water or blowing off with air, the life and service of the battery will be increased considerably. Whenever the tray or compartment is repainted, a soda treatment should first be given. Such a solution or ammonia will neutralize the effect of acid on clothing, cement, etc. Cleaning cloths contaminated with acid should be discarded and special care must be exercised to keep them away from matériel.

(2) Terminals should be scraped clean and coated with vaseline to protect the metallic surface from acid and corrosion. Cup grease should not be used since it gives less satisfactory results and may have a corrosive action on lead or brass.

(3) The level of the electrolyte must be maintained above the plates by adding pure (distilled) water whenever necessary to replace evaporation. In cold weather, water should be added just before or at the beginning of a charge so that gassing will insure thorough mixing and danger of freezing will be avoided.

(4) The battery compartment should be ventilated freely during charging, and an exposed flame should never be brought near the battery. Charging rates should be such as to prevent excessive gassing and keep the cell temperature below 110° F.

(5) If equipment is to be inoperative for some time (winter storage, etc.), batteries should be pooled together in a shop where they will be accessible for routine inspection and a freshening charge once a month to maintain the specific gravity at or above 1.250 at all times. The practice of removing electrolyte to store batteries is not recommended.

d. Cables.—Battery cables are frequently the source of trouble as a result of being undersized, of inferior quality, corroded, broken, or worn and frayed. Corrosion resulting from acid fumes or spray is unsightly, tends to "freeze" terminal nuts, and gradually consumes the terminal and cable ends to decrease capacity and eventually cause breakage. When corrosion is present, remove by brushing with a coarse wire brush and then wash with a strong solution of hot soapy

SCOUT CARS AND MORTAR MOTOR CARRIAGE

water before applying vaseline. Inspection of battery cables should always include the tightening of terminal nuts and bolts to insure proper contact with the posts.

e. Charging.—(1) When various cells of the same battery begin to show wide differences in gravity readings, or test below 1.200 on two successive testing dates, the battery should be removed for an equalizing charge in the shop or service station. Such action is recommended for a battery less than half-charged in a vehicle, likewise to expedite return of battery to a satisfactory operating state and not impose an unnecessary handicap on the electrical equipment operating in the same system.

(2) All batteries should have the terminals plainly marked. Positive terminals are marked (POS), (P), or (+), and the negative terminals are marked (NEG), (N), or (−). The positive terminal must always be connected to the positive or vehicle wire circuit and the negative terminal to the other cable or ground. If for any reason the polarity of the charging leads or battery is not known, it may be determined by a d. c. voltmeter or by inserting the bare ends of respective live wires in a glass of water to which a teaspoonful of common table salt or a few drops of battery acid have been added, and while bubbles will appear around both wires, there will be more bubbles at the negative lead.

(3) To charge a battery, a direct current is passed through it in the direction opposite to that in which current flows during discharge. It is the voltage of the direct current supply line which must be controlled to charge a battery properly and this open circuit voltage before application to the battery should not exceed 2.5 volts per cell, assuming that the battery is in normal condition and recommended charging current, based on state of charge, is not to be exceeded. Where alternating or direct current power supply is available in a maintenance shop, battery charging may be accomplished with three rectifiers, or resistors and/or lamp banks respectively. In such cases, the charging current remains practically constant, once adjusted, but attendants must check the system carefully until a practical schedule of time and rate is developed to prevent over (15 amperes) or under (1 ampere) charging. Provision is made on the vehicle for normal charging in service from a voltage regulated, battery charging, direct current generator, designed for, attached to, and driven from the engine as explained in subsequent paragraphs.

(4) The most desirable way to charge the vitally important battery is to begin with a comparatively high current and gradually

decrease the rate as charging progresses so that by the time the battery is completely charged the current has decreased to a low value. Voltage regulated equipment is designed to so control the generator field current that the generator armature voltage impressed on the circuit is nearly constant at operating speeds. The battery effective voltage, or potential on closed circuit to the load as contrasted to nominal rated open circuit voltage, varies with the state of charge. As the battery becomes charged, therefore, the effective voltage rises to gradually decrease the differential between it and the generator and the result is a decrease in the charging current supplied. These circumstances explain why ammeter readings may vary; if the ammeter pointer does not gradually indicate a decreasing charge, with all auxiliary electrical load disconnected and generator in operation for some time, a check-up will be in order by maintenance personnel. The voltage regulator coil may be adjusted for an incorrect open circuit voltage, leads may be shorting or grounding, or what is most probable, the battery may have developed a defective cell. The battery should be disconnected while leads are checked, adjustments made, etc.

(5) It is not economical to place a new battery, shipped dry, in service immediately after filling with electrolyte until an equalizing charge has been completed to obtain the correct specific gravity and voltage.

55. Starting motor.—*a. Description.*—The series starting motor (fig. 38) is the Auto-Lite model MAU 4006. It is a three-bearing, four-brush unit, having a clockwise rotation when viewed from the drive end and is secured to the flywheel housing on the right side of the engine by means of a standard, three-stud, No. 1 SAE flange mounting. Power is transmitted to the engine through a right-hand outboard Bendix drive. A cover band around the frame may be removed to permit inspection of the commutator and brush connections. The armature is carried on three plain bearings of a special absorbent type capable of absorbing oil up to about 20 percent of their volume.

b. Lubrication.—By reason of the special type of bearings used, no provision is made for the external oiling of either the intermediate or outer pinion housing bearings. An oil hole for the commutator end bearing is provided in the end of the bearing cap and is made accessible by swinging aside its cover. Two drops of medium oil should be added each 2,000 miles.

c. Maintenance.—Tension of the brush springs should be maintained at 42 to 53 ounces, and checked by attaching a small spring scale to the end of the spring bearing on each brush. Brushes must seat properly and not bind; they, along with the commutator, must be kept free from pits, dirt, and oil. If necessary to polish the commutator, use No. 00 sandpaper. Connections at the starting motor must be kept tight and clean. The Bendix drive should be cleaned and lubricated with a penetrating oil every 6,000 to 8,000 miles, as any accumulation of dirt at this point might restrict the free movement of the gear; for this operation, however, the starting motor must be dismounted. Check for loosened flange mounting bolts and oil seepage into the drive from the flywheel ring gear, indicating difficulties with the oil seals for the flywheel housing.

56. Generator.—Two types of d. c., voltage regulated, shunt wound, four-pole, four-brush, 12-volt, heavy duty generators are used on these vehicles, and they are belt driven clockwise from the engine crankshaft in connection with the radiator fan pulley.

a. Description.—In basic principles of construction, all generators are similar. The chief differences in the heavy duty types, as compared to standard units in modern passenger cars, are size, ruggedness of construction, and output capacity. The armatures are supported at each end by ball bearings supported and sealed in rigid end frames, and lubricated through oil wells. Forced ventilation is provided by a centrifugal fan mounted on the armature shaft. Generator output is controlled entirely by its associated current and voltage regulator unit, all adjustments being made on the regulator. The Delco-Remy unit (fig. 39) is designated as model 950 and rated at 50 amperes for use with the scout car, M3, group. The Auto-Lite unit (fig. 40) is designated as model GDJ-4802A and rated at 55 amperes for use with scout car, M3A1.

b. Brushes.—(1) All brushes should have a 75 percent seat or better to obtain correct generator output. The Delco-Remy unit has box type brush holders with the brushes under a spring tension of 22 to 28 ounces. The Auto-Lite unit employs reaction type brush holders with brushes under a spring tension of 64 to 68 ounces. Brush tension can be checked by hooking a scale at the end of the brush arm and taking the reading as the arm leaves the brush. Excessive tension will cause rapid brush and commutator wear, whereas low tension will cause arcing and reduce output.

(2) When installing new brushes, it may be necessary to seat the brushes by sanding to secure the correct fit. Wrap a strip of No. 00 or 000 sandpaper, cut to the commutator width, tightly around the commutator with the rough side facing the brush; turn the armature slowly in the direction of its driven rotation until the brush surface

is smoothed off to the proper profile. After surfacing, blow out dust, clean commutator segments of graphite deposits, and rotate awhile without load to obtain finished fit.

c. Commutator.—The commutator, accessible under the cover band, should be kept clean and free of grease and dirt. Clean surface with No. 00 sandpaper but do not attempt to remove the running polish a commutator secures in service. *Never use emery or carborundum cloth on commutator or brushes as particles of these abrasives embed themselves in the bars and brushes and continue a lapping action that greatly reduces brush and commutator life.* Roughened, pitted, or burned commutators will necessitate an overhaul.

d. Maintenance.—The generator should be removed every 6,000 miles for a thorough inspection, dismantling, and cleaning. Driving belts, pulley, and mounting details should be checked frequently. The belts should not be loose enough to allow slippage, nor so tight as to cause excessive side thrust on the driven end bearing. Belts and pulley must be kept free of oil and grease. Brush and external connections must be tight and clean.

e. Lubrication.—The armature bearings are packed at assembly. Add three drops of medium engine oil every 1,000 miles to the oilers provided. Do not oil or grease the commutator. Do not lubricate unit while it is in operation.

57. Voltage regulator.—The generator output to and connection with the electrical system is controlled automatically by a factory tested and sealed control device called the voltage regulator, which is mounted to the left on the engine side of the dash. The Delco-Remy type 5530 (fig. 41 ①) is designed for use with the Delco-Remy generator in the scout car, M3, group; the Auto-Lite type VRH-4102A (fig. 41 ②) is for use with the Auto-Lite generator in scout car, M3A1.

a. Description.—The regulator consists of three separate and distinct elements, described as the cut-out or reverse current relay, the vibrating voltage regulator relay, and the current regulator relay, all of which are mounted on the same base under a common cover and shielded.

(1) *Cut-out relay.*—The function of this relay or automatic magnetic switch is to close the circuit between the generator armature and the battery when the generator is operating at a speed sufficient to develop voltage (approximately 13.5 volts) in excess of the system to which it is connected and to open the circuit when the generator is at standstill or low speed and thus prevent discharge of the battery through the generator.

(2) *Voltage regulator relay.*—The function of the vibrating type regulator unit is to control the generator field strength by the insertion and removal of resistance in the field circuit and to prevent the generated voltage from exceeding a predetermined value (approximately 15.0 volts on open circuit). A constant potential is maintained and at the same time limited to protect the system equipment from excessive voltage surges. As the battery becomes charged, its resistance increases and the current input therefore decreases so the charging rate drops in direct proportion to the improvement in the battery's state of charge. The regulator cannot increase the generator output beyond the designed maximum.

(3) *Current regulator relay.*—This unit is similar in construction to the voltage regulator relay but its action depends on the line current rather than the generated voltage. It functions to protect the generator from an excessive current output by opening the circuit at a predetermined amperage value (50 to 55 amperes).

b. Contact point maintenance.—The contact points of the relays, like the distributor points, will not operate indefinitely without some attention. In normal operation, the gaps and point openings will not change and will not need to be reset if care is taken in clearing the points so that settings are not disturbed. Cleaning the points, tightening connections and, in an emergency, changing the spiral spring tension on the relay armatures will correct most troubles ordinarily encountered. Clean contact points with a thin, fine-cut contact file, free from grease or metallic particles. *Do not use the file excessively on the small contacts as the material is only a few thousandths of an inch thick. Never use sandpaper or emery cloth to clean contact points. Disconnect voltage regulator while servicing to prevent destructive arcs. Do not connect radio bypass condensers to the field terminal of the regulator or generator as such connection will have a detrimental effect on contacts.*

c. Failure in operation.—In the event of an emergency involving the voltage regulator, it would be practical for the vehicle operator to disconnect the field terminal lead at the generator to prevent the latter from developing any voltage while operating with the regulator out of action, or until the particular trouble can be identified and corrected. In case contacts of the regulator relays tend to seal, the generator has no protection electrically other than to have its field circuit opened, since it cannot be removed readily if the engine is to continue running and retain the belt drive for the fan.

58. Lighting, control, and accessory devices.—*a. Lighting equipment.*—Various lighting equipment, most of which is common to all vehicles, is listed in (1) to (5) below. The candlepower, voltage range, and description of the lamp bulbs are also noted for identification and replacement purposes. Great care should be exercised in dismantling and replacing lens and bulbs by reason of their fragility and the danger to personnel of broken glass. Prying or grasping with tools, unless protected by some soft buffer material, should be avoided. Lighting circuits should not be energized while such equipment is being replaced, to protect against short circuits and unnecessary blowing of fuzes. In cases where lamps must be operated without lens, cover the fixture body with a cloth and secure tightly to protect interior reflectors and sockets against the atmosphere.

(1) *Head lamps.*—Two Guide Lamp Corporation single bulb assemblies for each vehicle, incorporating models for the different groups, are employed as follows:

M3	*M3A1*
Model 828–M.	Model 364–E.
8¼-inch guide lens, Tiltray convex (#919730).	6¼-inch Cycleray lens (#918831).
21/21 candlepower, 12- to 16-volt, double-contact, candelabra-bayonet bulb (Mazda #1120).	32/21 candlepower, 12- to 16-volt double-contact, candelabra-bayonet bulb (Mazda #1122).

(2) *Tail lamps.*—Two Corcoran-Brown single bulb, tail and stop lamp assemblies, model CB–647135, with 4-inch reflex glass lens, model CB–2194. Bulb employed is a 21/6 candlepower, 12- to 16-volt, double-contact, candelabra-bayonet type (Mazda #1176).

(3) *Driving lamps (spotlights).*—Two Appleton assemblies, model 112, with 5¾-inch concentrated beam lens. Bulb employed is a 32 candlepower, 12- to 16-volt, single contact, candelabra-bayonet type (Mazda #1143). The lamp head turns through 360°. A fingertip control on-and-off switch is located in the operating handle.

NOTE.—The Appleton model 110, used on the scout car, M3, group is no longer manufactured; its parts are not interchangeable with the model 112 (stock No. 3017M).

(4) *Trouble lamp.*—The White Company, model B–16 trouble lamp assembly includes the 20-foot extension cord, lamp receptacle, and plug for insertion in the dash outlet. A 21-candlepower, 12- to 16-volt, double-contact, candelabra-bayonet type bulb is used (Mazda #1142).

(5) *Instrument panel lamps.*—Indirect light is provided for all instruments except the ammeter, and for the voltmeter. A Stewart-Warner model G–90865, and a Culver-Stearns' model G–723 are

SCOUT CARS AND MORTAR MOTOR CARRIAGE

provided respectively. Each unit includes a 3-candlepower, 12- to 16-volt, single-contact, candelabra-bayonet type bulb (Mazda #67).

b. Switches.—Switches for similar purposes are the same on all vehicles and interchangeable. The general location and appearance of these devices are shown in figures 43, 44, and 45.

(1) *Starter.*—Foot-operated, Auto-Lite model SW–4001.

(2) *Ignition.*—Key type, Douglas model 2980, with three keys.

(3) *Lighting.*—Pull type, off-dim-on, Douglas model 5400, with 20-ampere fuze; a dimmer coil is employed with middle position.

(4) *Head lamp beam.*—Foot operated, Douglas model 5530.

(5) *Stop light.*—Pressure type, F. A. Smith model 320.

(6) *Stop light cut-out.*—Toggle type, Arrow-Hart and Hegeman model 8961; a similar switch is used for the voltmeter.

(7) *Fuel gage.*—Toggle type, double throw switch, Cutler-Hammer model 8100.

(8) *Heater.*—Rheostat type, 12-volt, Tropic-Aire model A–33.

(9) *Miscellaneous.*—The instrument cluster panel light is controlled from the lighting switch. The switch for the voltmeter light fixture is incorporated therewith. The horn button (Ross Gear and Tool model 465312) is included in the steering wheel assembly. The switch for a spot light is incorporated in the control handle.

c. Protective devices.—The customary automotive type, glass tube inclosed fuzes are mounted in brass femules on a fuze and junction block which is secured behind the instrument panel within the instrument shielding box. Access to the fuzes is obtained by loosening the wing nuts below the box and removing the cover plate. A set of spare fuzes should always be available. For the capacity and electrical location, refer to the wiring diagram in figure 42.

d. Other Accessories.—(1) *Horn.*—A single horn, Auto-Lite part EO–3918, is employed with the scout car, M3, group while a dual horn, Delco-Remy type K–335–206–1 and 2, is employed with scout car, M3A1.

(2) *Heater.*—A hot water heater, Tropic-Aire Universal model 20300X (12-volt), is employed for all vehicles. Water circulation may be shut off from the engine by a plug where the inlet hose connects to the engine, but there is no valve or shut-off cock at the outlet. (See figs. 11 and 13.) Repair or replacement of the heater or its hose usually will require drainage of cooling system.

(3) *Junction box.*—A radio terminal box, with several terminals for extending the battery connections to a convenient point for the radio hook-up, is mounted on the bulkhead, facing the crew compartment.

(4) *Windshield wipers.*—Two Trico model 618A automatic windshield wipers are employed for each vehicle. They are mounted at the base of the windshield with the operating mechanism inside and tube-connected to the intake manifold. With the armor shield lowered, it is necessary on scout car, M3A1, to fit the projecting spring retainers into slots provided in the armor plate.

59. Wiring.—The wiring diagram or schematic for the system is shown in figure 42. It is imperative that all electrical connections are complete, tight, and clean, and that wires and cable are secured properly to prevent fouling with or chafing from associated mechanisms, with resulting grounds and trouble. Avoid the practice of testing unidentified leads by the indiscriminate grounding of same to discover if circuit is "alive", since dangerous and destructive arcs may be drawn as long as the battery itself is grounded in the system.

60. Instruments and gages.—*a. Electrical.*—(1) *Ammeter.*—This unit of the Stewart-Warner instrument cluster (fig. 43) is that company's part G–96647, and is used in conjunction with a shunt, part G–96672. The ammeter is graduated to read 100–0–100 amperes and indicates total current discharge ($-$) under any load, with the generator inoperative, and the net charge ($+$) to the battery when the generator is functioning, regardless of auxiliary loads. The ammeter, as normally connected, does not indicate total generator output, although it can be utilized for test purposes to do so by shifting the generator lead to the battery terminal of the ammeter shunt.

(2) *Voltmeter.*—This separately mounted unit is an Arrow, Hart, and Hageman model 8961, graduated for 0 to 20 volts, direct current. It may be connected to or disconnected from the system at will by means of a suitable switch. The voltmeter is not a substitute for a hydrometer in determining the state of a battery's charge. Relative effectiveness, however, may be checked by the proper use of the voltmeter. With the generator inoperative and the same load applied each time, the variance in the system voltage at different intervals will provide a clue as to the performance that can be expected of the battery. The relative drop in effective voltage, with starter engaged, is another means of determining a battery's condition to produce. If lights dim exceedingly or go out when engine is cranked, there is no need to check with a voltmeter as the battery definitely is down. Once the generator is operating, checks of system voltage reflect the results of the average potential impressed by the generator rather than the battery, and that voltage will change very little depending on the pre-set open circuit voltage. The open

circuit generator voltage may be checked readily by disconnecting the generator lead in the instrument box, running a jumper between it and the ungrounded voltmeter terminal, with the voltmeter switch open, and operating the engine at moderate speed.

(3) *Fuel gage.*—This electrical unit of the Stewart-Warner instrument cluster consists of the indicating instrument, part G–95622, and the actuating unit in the tank, part G–95457 which are wired together. The gage is graduated to indicate "Empty–¼–½–¾–Full" readings, has the inherent characteristic of being unaffected by variations in voltage, and is energized only when the ignition switch is turned on; at other times the pointer will register empty. The transfer switch permits readings for either tank from one gage. The tank fitting consists of a rheostat or variable resistance which is altered by a float mechanism to affect the current through the gage coil. Since this fitting is grounded by the screws attaching it to the fuel tank, *care must be exercised in removing to have ignition switch off to prevent danger of sparks.*

b. Mechanical.—(1) *Oil pressure.*—This unit of the Stewart-Warner instrument cluster is that company's part G–95614, a direct reading, segmental model graduated for 0–40–80 pounds and tube-connected to the engine.

(2) *Heat indicator.*—The remaining unit of the Stewart-Warner instrument cluster is that company's part G–95620, a vapor bulb model of the remote capillary type, graduated for 100°–180°–220° F., and tube-connected to the engine.

(3) *Speedometer.*—The Stewart-Warner, full dial magnetic type, model SW–585AM, speedometer includes the speed unit which is graduated to indicate 0–80 miles, and the odometer element which indicates total mileage (up to 99999 miles) and trip mileage (0–100 miles). The speedometer flexible drive shaft is connected into the transfer case and lubricated with a mixture of flake graphite and oil.

Section XIII

OPERATING INSTRUCTIONS

	Paragraph
Requirements for efficient operation	61
Preliminary instructions	62
Vehicle controls	63
Placing vehicle in service	64
Inspection by driver	65
Starting and warming up engine	66
Operating the vehicle	67
Driving handicaps	68
Signals for the driver	69

	Paragraph
Road rules	70
Marching	71
Operating inspections	72
Maintenance by driver	73
Reports by driver	74
Examination and operator's permit	75
Troubles and remedies	76

61. Requirements for efficient operation.—*a. Factors affecting operation.*—Factors which materially affect the service rendered by automotive vehicles should be impressed on all personnel who are concerned with the supervision, operation, maintenance, and inspection of motor transport equipment. These factors include—

(1) Understanding of the capabilities and limitations of the vehicles in operation.

(2) Serviceable condition of vehicles.

(3) Organized maintenance with adequate repair facilities and the performance of routine maintenance and inspection functions.

(4) Careful reconnaissance of routes to be traveled.

b. Selection of drivers.—An individual selected for training as an assigned driver should be physically fit, dependable, alert, sober, steady, and ambitious and should have good judgment and mechanical sense.

c. Assignment of drivers.—A driver and an assistant driver should be assigned to each vehicle. Except for instruction and inspection purposes, prolonged marches, or casualties, the vehicle should not be operated by various individuals. All crew members, however, should be capable of performing the duties of a driver at the direction of the car commander.

d. Training of drivers.—The manner in which individual drivers perform their duties determines the mobility and dependability of the entire command as well as that of the single vehicle. Training schedules should include a maximum of practical instruction and a minimum of classroom work. Complete details for the various arms are not within the scope of this manual but basic technical items concerning the vehicle and its operating problems are covered.

e. Elimination of vehicle abuse.—Vehicle abuse is the chief cause of mechanical failures, excessive operating and maintenance costs, and general unsatisfactory performance of the vehicle and its component parts. The following forms of vehicle abuse are prohibited:

(1) Improper use of controls, particularly gear shifts, clutch, brakes, and choke.

(2) Racing engine, especially when cold, and before stopping.

(3) Overspeeding, particularly over rough roads and across country.

(4) Improper lubrication.

(5) Deferred maintenance.

(6) Lack of systematic inspection and follow-up.

(7) Overloading.

f. Speed limits.—The caution plate mounted on the vehicle indicates the maximum safe speed for which the vehicle is designed and it should not be exceeded.

62. Preliminary instructions.—The driver's responsibility, which should be shared by the crew, includes the operation, maintenance, and inspection of his vehicle in accordance with instruction; care and condition of vehicle tools and equipment; accomplishment of vehicle reports and records. Disregard of the same may entail the loss of a vehicle and casualties.

a. Fire precautions and fire fighting.—(1) Pools of fuel and oil must not be permitted to collect under vehicles. Leaky lines must be repaired or promptly replaced.

(2) The friction of gasoline flowing through fuel pump hose creates static electricity. To prevent a gap discharge between the nozzle and fuel tank, the former must be in contact with the tank at all times during the filling to ground the charge. Ignition will be off for such operations.

(3) To put out a gasoline fire, use chemical (pyrene or carbon dioxide type) fire extinguishers, sand, or dry dust. Water must not be used because the lighter gasoline will float, spread, and continue to burn. All motor vehicles should be equipped for fire fighting with suitable fire extinguishers, properly charged, and a shovel.

b. Accident prevention.—The formulation and observance of definite rules will eliminate the majority of accidents incident to the operation and maintenance of vehicles.

(1) Place the transmission gear shift lever in neutral and set the hand brake before hand cranking an engine or starting with the motor.

(2) Make sure the way is clear before a vehicle is moved. If the driver cannot see the road, he should be directed by a dismounted individual, particularly if a vehicle is backed or moved through bivouac areas and across country at night without lights.

(3) Stop the engine before anyone gets under a vehicle. If it is necessary for a mechanic to work under the vehicle while the engine is running, precaution must be taken that the vehicle cannot move accidentally.

(4) Block up a vehicle safely before the wheels are removed. Do not place reliance on jacks for prolonged support.

(5) Remove battery when vehicle is taken to the shop for major repairs.

(6) Provide ample ventilation for garages, shops, vehicle cabs, and vehicles carrying personnel.

(7) Insure adequate ventilation when it is necessary to operate a gasoline engine within an enclosure of any kind, or provide for the removal of exhaust gases through a safe outlet fixture.

(8) In case of carbon monoxide poisoning, remove the patient to open air, keep him quiet, apply artificial respiration and warmth, and obtain medical assistance as soon as possible. Administer no liquid stimulants unless it is certain the patient can swallow, and then only a light stimulant such as coffee or tea. Beware of an unreasonable feeling of drowsiness combined with a headache, when driving or riding in a closed vehicle, as these may be symptoms of gas poisoning.

c. Vehicle nomenclature.—Preliminary instruction should cover the nomenclature and purposes of major assemblies only, in order that the operator may become familiar with his vehicle without being confused by details. Detailed instruction in nomenclature, function, operation, use, lubrication, maintenance, and limitations of motor vehicles, and the nomenclature, care, and use of vehicular tools and equipment should be given in subsequent periods.

63. Vehicle controls.—The nominal condition and the ultimate service of a vehicle, as well as safety to life and property, depend upon the condition and proper use of the controls. The various controls shown in figures 44 and 45 for the scout car, M3, group and scout car M3A1, respectively, are employed according to current automotive practice. Before attempting to operate a vehicle, the driver must become thoroughly familiar with the location and use of control levers and pedals.

a. Mechanical.—(1) *Clutch and brake pedals.*—These pedals are conventional in usage and location relative to the steering column and the driver's customary foot position. The pedals and column for scout car, M3A1, are outside the frame, however, by reason of the driver's wider compartment.

(2) *Choke and spark.*—Cable connected control buttons are mounted on the instrument panel as indicated; for normal running, these buttons are pushed all the way in against the panel.

(3) *Throttle.*—The throttle is cable controlled by the foot accelerator pedal and by a manual control button; the latter is used mainly to facilitate starting and not to control the engine speed while driving and is not affected by actuation of the accelerator

pedal. The latter is actuated, however, by movement of the hand throttle.

(4) *Gear shift levers and hand brake.*—The main and auxiliary gear shift levers and the propeller shaft brake lever are located and used in the customary manner; smooth, firm control is required without the application of excessive force. The ratios in the auxiliary transmission should not be changed when the vehicle is in motion.

(5) *Radiator shutter.*—The lever for closing or opening the radiator shutters is to the right in the driver's compartment.

(6) *Ventilator.*—The right and left ventilators below the dash in the driver's compartment of scout cars, M3A1, are controlled by cable connected buttons mounted on the instrument panel.

(7) *Windshield wipers.*—These devices are controlled by buttons at the base of the mechanism when the engine is running.

b. *Instruments, gages, and switches.*—The various other aids for operation of the vehicle are described in paragraphs 58 and 60.

64. Placing vehicle in service.—These instructions and information are for use by the personnel charged with the operation, maintenance, and repair of vehicles when new or after a period of inactivity or storage. It is presumed that relatively skilled automotive personnel will be charged with the inspection and care of such vehicles and only a brief résumé, therefore, is given of the general procedure which is required.

a. *Initial inspection.*—(1) *Shipment overland.*—When a vehicle arrives at a new station under its own power, the operator will give a full report of observations en route and advise as to the vehicle's peculiarities, precautions to be taken, and matters requiring immediate or current attention.

(2) *Shipment by carrier.*—Vehicles shipped by freight, boat, or other carriers will be inspected before the chocking is removed. Trace all oil or grease seepage for determination of its origin and cause. Check tires for pressure, cuts, or chafed spots due to chocking or previous service. Check general appearance of vehicles for evidence of damage or mishandling while in transit, such as indications of excessive shock, broken seats or locks, burned or torn canvas, damage due to hoisting slings, or rigging. Locks and keys must be available.

(3) *Equipment and spare parts.*—Unpack the boxed equipment and check all tools, accessories, and spare parts against the lists furnished. Make entries in the log book as called for therein. Install interior and exterior equipment and the armament, if required immediately. Check the fire extinguisher for liquid.

b. Electrical system.—(1) *Battery.*—Inspect all cells of the battery for quantity and specific gravity of the electrolyte. Check for perfect battery terminal connections and remove all traces of sulphation. With the clutch released but no ignition, engage the starter and note if the starter whirls the engine satisfactorily. In extremely cold weather it may be necessary to ship the battery separately, in which case it should be examined closely for evidence of mishandling resulting in acid leaks or broken cells. Batteries shipped "dry" must be serviced.

(2) *Ignition.*—Test the ignition circuit by closing the switch and noting the ammeter response. Ignition tests should be made before water is placed in the cooling system so that the engine will not freeze during cold weather while possible malfunctions are traced.

(3) *Lighting.*—Test all lamps and electrical equipment. As additional load is connected, the ammeter should indicate an increasing "discharge."

c. Lubrication.—Check at this stage of preparation.

d. Fuel.—Fuel tanks will be shipped dry but should be checked and drained of all condensation before refilling; make note of fuel gage corrections in the log book. Crank engine several revolutions to check operation of fuel pump and filling of carburetor.

e. Cooling system.—Check and fill with water and/or antifreeze.

65. Inspection by driver.—As far as the driver is concerned, a vehicle is not ready for operation until certain items have been checked. Before moving his vehicle for its daily schedule, the driver will make his inspection and report the results to his section chief or other designated individual. The inspection should be divided into two phases as follows:

a. Before engine is started.—(1) Check fuel supply, oil in crankcase, water and antifreeze in radiator, and electrolyte in battery.

(2) Examine surface under vehicle for evidence of leaks.

(3) Inspect engine for loose parts or electrical connections, and fuel and oil lines for leaks.

(4) Inspect all tires for inflation and casing injuries.

(5) Inspect front axle and steering linkage.

(6) Check all lights and the horn for proper functioning.

(7) Check tools and equipment belonging to the vehicle or to be carried extra on the trip.

(8) Examine connection and condition of towed load, if any.

(9) Check for supply of necessary instructions and report forms.

b. After engine is started.—(1) Observe operation of instruments, gages, and windshield wiper.

(2) Check operation of cooling system.

(3) Check engine for loose parts and unusual noises.

(4) Test action of brakes.

(5) Test action of clutch.

(6) Test action of gear shifts.

66. Starting and warming up engine.—*a. General instructions.*—Special attention should be devoted to the starting and warm-up period in order that unnecessary engine wear may be prevented. The procedure outlined below is satisfactory under average operating conditions:

(1) Set hand brake securely and place transmission gear shift lever in neutral position.

(2) Check selection and opening of fuel transfer valve.

(3) Pull out choke and spark control buttons to close the choke valve and retard the spark; pull out hand throttle button about ¼ inch. (One or more of these operations may be eliminated eventually, based on engine peculiarities, climatic conditions, and the operator's familiarity with the respective engine's starting performance.)

(4) Disengage clutch.

(5) Switch on ignition and engage starter.

(6) Release starter the moment engine begins to run.

(7) After the engine has started, release the clutch, push in spark control, and adjust hand throttle to a position that prevents the engine from racing. As soon as the engine runs smoothly or warms up (approximately 140° F.), push in choke control.

b. Starting hints.—With the battery, fuel system, and ignition in satisfactory condition, difficulties other than mechanical failures may develop in connection with the starter itself.

(1) The starter should not be engaged for periods longer than 10 to 15 seconds. If the starter engages the engine flywheel but the engine fails to start after several attempts, report the trouble to the proper authority. Continued cranking consumes too much electrical energy.

(2) If the starter device engages the engine flywheel and locks, release starter switch, turn off ignition, place transmission in high gear, release brake, and rock vehicle backward. If the gear still sticks, loosen starting motor bolts and shake the motor until its gear releases. Retighten bolts and test again.

(3) If the starter does not turn but the lights dim when the starting switch is engaged, the starter bearings may be "frozen"; gummed bearings can usually be freed with penetrating oil.

(4) If there is some doubt as to the ability of the electrical equipment to crank the engine, especially in cold weather, break the engine free by a few quick strokes of the hand crank or bar the engine over, and then use the starter. Pull up on a crank with a short, quick movement; never push down.

(5) The easiest way to overcome difficulty in starting is to have the vehicle pushed either by another vehicle or by hand. With high gear engaged, throttle slightly open, ignition on, and choke control fully out, engage clutch gradually when the vehicle has attained a speed of from 5 to 10 miles per hour. Even though the battery is weak, the engine usually can be started in this manner.

67. Operating the vehicle.—*a. Starting on level ground.*—The engine having been thoroughly warmed up and checked for satisfactory operation, the vehicle is placed in movement as follows:

(1) Release hand brake.

(2) Disengage clutch fully.

(3) Move transmission gear shift lever to selected position.

(4) Release clutch pedal gradually, and at the same time gradually depress accelerator pedal to increase the speed of the engine, care being taken not to race the engine.

b. Starting on a grade.—If the vehicle is on a grade, one method of starting is as follows:

(1) Release hand brake and hold vehicle with foot brake.

(2) Disengage clutch fully.

(3) Move gear shift lever to first speed position.

(4) Gradually engage clutch, and at the same time gradually release foot brake and accelerate engine with hand throttle.

c. Preliminary driving.—In the case of a new driver or vehicle, initial driving should be conducted on a large open field where steering is of secondary importance. The operator should familiarize himself with the control peculiarities of his vehicle and perfect his correlation of gear shifting, braking, clutch usage, and engine response.

d. Position of driver.—The proper position of the driver is to have the body erect but in a relaxed position, with his hands on the steering wheel and approximately opposite each other. The right foot should be on the accelerator (or brake) and the left foot should be on the floor in a position to reach and move fully the clutch pedal. The eyes observe straight to the front along the road, although the driver must often glance to either flank, at the rear view mirror, and at the instrument board.

SCOUT CARS AND MORTAR MOTOR CARRIAGE

e. Shifting gears.—Practice will enable a driver to judge at what rates of speed the vehicle should be moving before he shifts from a lower to a higher speed. An engine should never be permitted to labor unduly when a change in gear ratios would improve operation.

(1) *Transmission.*—In shifting synchro-mesh gears from any speed to a lower speed ratio, disengage the clutch, make the shift to the next lower position, engage the clutch and at the same time depress the accelerator to maintain engine speed.

(2) *Transfer case.*—In shifting the auxiliary transmission from high (direct) to low (underdrive) for heavy going, stop the vehicle, disengage clutch, shift main transmission into low gear, lightly engage and disengage clutch while shifting transfer case gears, and then fully engage clutch to operate vehicle. Shift main transmission from low to high thereafter, as the situation permits, all regular speed ratios being reduced. When the vehicle is being operated with the underdrive and it is desired to shift back to the direct range, the shift can be made with the vehicle moving at any general speed, due attention being given to the use of the clutch and the speed ratio of the main transmission to prevent shock to the propelling mechanisms.

Caution: In shifting from one speed ratio to another, do not skip positions. *Do not ride the clutch. The driver's foot should rest on the clutch only when he is operating it.* When the clutch is to be disengaged, it should be disengaged fully to avoid gear damage and shifting difficulties. A sudden engagement is injurious to the mechanism and may stall the engine.

f. Braking.—The brakes should be in such condition that a hard application will cause all wheels to be locked, but the driver must realize that the maximum retarding effect occurs just before the wheels lock. Intermittent application will reduce the wear of brake linings and drums. Application should be gradual with just enough force to accomplish the desired result.

(1) *Usage.*—Judicious use of the breaking effect of the engine will increase the serviceable life of the brake linings and drums. When the driver anticipates a stop, he should make full use of the engine braking effect, disengaging the clutch in time to avoid stalling the engine. When descending hills, a driver should use the engine as a brake by selecting and engaging the proper gear ratio, and use the intermittent application of the brakes to prevent overspeeding the engine. The ignition should not be turned off. The engine speed when descending a hill should be no greater than the speed necessary to ascend the hill when using the same transmission gear ratio. On steep hills, the gear train necessary to give the desired results should

be engaged before the vehicle is committed to the hill. Attempting to shift gears after the vehicle has started down a steep slope may result in a run-away vehicle.

(2) *Moisture effect.*—At all times, a driver should know the performance and the general condition of his vehicle brakes. When operating conditions require vehicles to move through water, the brakes become very inefficient because of moisture on the brake linings and in the brake drums. If the distance to be traversed is short, considerable water may be kept out of the brake assemblies by a slight application of the brakes while the vehicle is in the water. After passing through water, the brakes should be set slightly and the vehicle operated until sufficient heat has been generated to dry the brakes.

(3) *Stopping distance.*—Vehicle stopping distances are dependent upon the nature and condition of the road surface, condition of the brakes, weight of the load, and kind and condition of tire treads. When operating at a speed of 20 miles per hour on a dry, smooth, level road free from loose material, every motor vehicle or combination of motor vehicles having brakes on all wheels should be capable, at all times and under all conditions of loading, of stopping within 30 feet when the foot brake is applied.

Caution: Drivers should be cautioned concerning the use of brakes when a vehicle is skidding or operating on ice covered roads.

g. Maneuvering.—After the driver has acquired facility in starting, simple driving, and stopping, he should practice maneuvering in difficult places. The ability to turn a vehicle in a confined space, back it accurately, and park it properly under various conditions are essential requirements.

(1) *Turning.*—Turns should be made at speeds commensurate with the road, load, and traffic conditions: A vehicle driver should always give the appropriate arm, electrical, or mechanical signal in sufficient time to afford ample warning that a change in direction is to be made. Turns should start and end in appropriate traffic lanes and should be made with as little confusion to other traffic as possible. At least one hand should be kept on the steering wheel when the vehicle is in motion.

(2) *Backing.*—A driver should never back a vehicle until he is certain that the way is clear. When the driver's view is obstructed, he should act as directed by an assistant on the ground. When backing unassisted, the driver should always give warning of the movement by sounding his horn. Considerable practice is necessary

to back a vehicle safely and accurately. This is particularly true when the driver is required to back a towed load.

(3) *Parking.*—Parking includes turning and forward or backward moving of the vehicle in more or less restricted space. Factors which should be given consideration when parking are space for maneuvering the vehicle, solid standing, interference with other traffic, and cover if applicable.

68. Driving handicaps.—*a. Skidding.*—When a vehicle skids, the front wheels should be turned in the direction of the skid and the throttle closed gradually until it is only partly open. Closing the throttle quickly or braking will accentuate the skidding.

b. Obstacles.—After the driver has acquired skill in driving and maneuvering, he should become proficient in handling his vehicle in the face of such difficulties as mud, sand, ditches, ruts, holes, narrow defiles, woods, steep slopes, sharp curves, etc. Training should include the use of chains and traction devices and field expedients. (See sec. XIV.)

c. Night driving.—In forward areas, movements must be made without lights if casualties are to be minimized and secrecy preserved. Night movements are particularly difficult because of the limited control that can be exercised and the obstacles that must be overcome.

d. Curves.—Close the throttle before coming to a turn. If necessary apply the brakes to reduce speed of the vehicle below that at which it is safe to make the turn. On the turn, open the throttle to keep the wheels rolling under power and reduce the chance of skidding. On entering a curve inadvertently at high speed, jiggle the steering wheel rapidly and repeatedly to the right and left, just enough to move the front wheels slightly until the curve is passed. Make a long swing in returning to the right lane after making turns or passing obstacles.

69. Signals for the driver.—*a. Arm signals.*—(1) *Turn right.*—Extend left arm outward at an angle of 45° above the horizontal.

(2) *Turn left.*—Extend left arm outward horizontally.

(3) *Slow or stop.*—Extend left arm outward to an angle of 45° below the horizontal.

b. Command signals.—Refer to manuals for the arms and services.

70. Road rules.—*a. General.*—The following general rules are presented for automotive vehicle operation:

(1) Vehicles will keep to the right of the road.

(2) The appropriate warning signal will be given before changing direction, slowing down, or stopping.

(3) The right-of-way will be given promptly to faster moving vehicles.

(4) Speed will be reduced on dry, dusty roads, especially in combat zones.

(5) Lights will be dimmed when meeting another vehicle or for driving in populated areas.

(6) A disabled vehicle will not delay unnecessarily a column's march.

(7) A driver who has been assigned a place in a column will not pass another vehicle unless he receives a signal to pass.

(8) A driver when meeting and passing an oncoming vehicle will pass on the right giving at least half the road, slow down if operating conditions are hazardous, and permit the vehicle having a clear road ahead to have the right-of-way.

(9) Vehicles will not be permitted to coast down hills with the clutch disengaged or the transmission in neutral.

(10) Vehicles will clear the roadway before being halted, and will not be halted on bridges, in defiles, at points where the vision of other drivers is restricted, or in such a manner as to block cross traffic or entering side traffic.

(11) Vehicles will be slowed down to a safe stopping speed at all road intersections not covered by traffic control personnel or devices.

(12) Personnel will not mount or dismount from moving vehicles.

b. Doubling.—Passing other vehicles moving in the same direction is strictly forbidden under the following conditions:

(1) When going around a corner or blind curve.

(2) When ascending or descending hills unless safe passage is assured.

(3) At street intersections, crossroads, and railroad crossings.

(4) When road is too narrow to allow at least 2 feet between vehicles.

c. Railroad crossings.—Vehicles will be halted at railroad crossings not guarded by military personnel or civilian watchmen.

d. During a halt.—When halted, the following rules will be observed:

(1) The engine will be stopped if the vehicle is to stand longer than a few minutes.

(2) All personnel will keep to the right of the vehicles.

(3) Wheels will be blocked if on a grade for a prolonged stay.

(4) Prescribed inspection will be performed.

71. Marching.—*a. Close column.*—During training in close column marching, special attention should be paid to safe intervals between vehicles. The following rule, properly modified to meet special

SCOUT CARS AND MORTAR MOTOR CARRIAGE

conditions, indicates that for safe marching *the distance in yards between vehicles should be not less than twice the speedometer reading.*

b. Rolling terrain.—When marching over rolling terrain, a higher rate of march and smoother marching may be attained if drivers are permitted, within maximum prescribed speed, to increase the speed of their vehicles before commencing to climb. Vehicles should be slowed down while going down grades to compensate for the distance gained when running a hill. This practice will prevent excessive jamming and will allow drivers to take advantage of power and momentum to negotiate hills without excessive shifting of gears. Running hills is particularly advantageous when march columns are made up of mixed vehicles.

c. Map routes.—Drivers of military vehicles should receive sufficient instruction and training in map reading to enable them to follow routes on marked maps, to choose routes, and to recognize terrain features represented on topographic maps. Training should include the use of commercial highway maps, military topographic maps, airplane photographs, and mosaics.

72. Operating inspections.—During operation, the driver should be alert to detect unusual engine sounds or vehicle noises and follow the proper procedure when they occur; he should glance frequently at the instruments and gages to check the charging, fuel supply, oil pressure, and water temperature and be forewarned by abnormal readings in time to obtain assistance and prevent serious trouble.

a. During halts.—At every scheduled halt on the march or at intervals during the day's run, the driver should make a careful inspection of his vehicle to determine its general mechanical condition and make a pertinent report accordingly to his section chief. A suitable routine is as follows:

(1) Allow engine to run a short time and listen for unusual noises. If unusual sounds or knocks are heard with the engine running but with the vehicle stopped and the clutch disengaged, practically everything but the engine assembly is eliminated.

(2) Observe around the vehicle for fuel, oil, and water leaks; check fuel, oil (after engine is stopped a few minutes), and water supply and replenish if possible.

(3) Inspect all tires for inflation, cuts, imbedded objects, and misalinement. On track-laying vehicles, examine tracks for adjustment and for worn, loose, broken, or missing parts. Note condition of traction devices, if used.

(4) Feel brake bands, wheel hubs, and gear cases for evidence of overheating.

(5) Examine front axle, steering assemblies, and brake lines.

(6) Tighten equipment fastenings, secure curtains and top, and check towed load, if any.

(7) Remove debris which may have accumulated on the vehicle.

b. After operation.—At the conclusion of the day's run, the driver should make an inspection similar to that made at halts, but more thorough and detailed, and report his findings and the day's developments for action by the section chief.

(1) Check all items included in the inspection at the halt, testing lights in all cases.

(2) Raise the hood and look for loose, missing, or broken parts, and indications of improper operation.

(3) Examine grease seals for evidence of failure or over lubrication.

(4) Check axles, springs, and shackles for condition and attachment.

(5) Examine propeller shafts and brake linkage.

(6) Check body bolts; tighten or replace as required.

(7) Check tools and equipment; secure replacements if necessary.

73. Maintenance by driver.—Efficient enforcement of preventive maintenance is the responsibility of commanding officers of all units operating automotive vehicles. In connection therewith definite maintenance duties will be assigned the driver (or crew) and he will be prohibited, except in an emergency, from performing any maintenance function not specifically listed below. (See par. 84.)

a. Inspections.—The driver is charged with routine inspections outlined in paragraphs 65 and 72.

b. Servicing.—Servicing involves the check and necessary replenishment of fuel, oil in the crankcase, water or antifreeze in the cooling system, and air and valves in the tires.

(1) Precautions concerning the handling of gasoline must be enforced rigidly.

(2) Take every precaution to prevent dust and other foreign matter from entering the crankcase with the oil. Wipe out oil measure, spigot on oil drum, funnel, and oil filter pipe with a clean cloth before refill oil touches any of the surfaces. Do not spill or overfill. Post record of replacement. A simple test to check the suitability of an oil for operation at the prevailing atmospheric temperatures is to leave a small quantity outdoors in an open bottle overnight. Obviously, if the oil is not in a liquid state by morning, it is not a suitable oil for vehicles parked in the open.

SCOUT CARS AND MORTAR MOTOR CARRIAGE

(3) The water in the radiator should be maintained at the proper height below the overflow pipe and the latter must not be clogged. A hot engine should be allowed to cool before any considerable quantity of water is added to the radiator, or the engine should be running while the water is added slowly.

(4) Tires should be inflated to recommended pressures and checked daily with a reliable gage. Wheels, including any spares, should be changed periodically to secure uniform tire wear and to maintain resiliency in the spare tires. All wheel drive vehicles should have tires with the same inflation and outside diameter. Do not bleed air to lower tire pressures during a trip, provided original pressures were correct.

c. Lubrication.—(1) Parts that should be lubricated by the driver, in the case of decentralized lubrication, include spring and spring shackle bolts, spring pivot seats, steering knuckle pivots, steering knuckle tie rod pins, drag link ends, clutch and brake pedal and brake lever pivots and linkage, throttle linkage, door hinges, locks, and other slow-motion friction surfaces.

(2) Equipment furnished the driver includes a high pressure lubricator and an oilcan for whose care and condition he is responsible. The two types of lubricant used include oil and chassis lubricant; the use thereof should be in accordance with a lubrication schedule, and reported for record purposes. (See pars. 91 and 92.) Grease fittings and oilholes should be cleaned before any lubricant is applied.

d. Tightening.—The distinction between tightening and adjusting must be understood, otherwise drivers will undertake operations which they have not the knowledge, experience, or equipment to perform. In general, adjustment involves placing moving parts or assemblies in the proper relative position and securing them in that position. Adjustments, except specified emergency adjustments, are prohibited to the driver.

(1) When a driver discovers a loose or lost nut, bolt, screw, stud, or cotter key, he should tighten or replace it unless the adjustment of a part or assembly is affected. If adjustment is involved, a report should be made to the section chief.

(2) A driver should be taught the correct use of the tools furnished and the proper degree of tightness of the various nuts, bolts, and screws.

e. Cleaning.—(1) A vehicle should be cleaned after operation to prevent hardening of dirt accumulations and to keep dust and other foreign particles from working into bearing surfaces. The body and exterior parts of the chassis should be washed, using a hose if available. Keep water off the engine; dirt should be wiped from the engine and its accessories. Gasoline should not be used to clean an engine; use a cleaning solvent instead. Fuel and oil lines should not be polished. The use of paint on radiator covers is prohibited.

(2) A vehicle should be inspected *before* it is washed because of the greater ease in detecting loose parts and assemblies, broken dust films being the best evidence of looseness. Scheduled lubrication should be performed *after* washing so that any water or dirt which has entered bearing surfaces may be forced out by the pressure of the new lubricant.

f. Tools and equipment.—The driver is responsible that tools, spare parts, chains, paulins, and equipment furnished with his vehicle are in their proper places, clean, and in condition at all times for immediate use. Any equipment which becomes unserviceable should be repaired or replaced promptly. Shortages or unserviceable equipment should be reported to the section chief.

g. Tires.—(1) The chief responsibility of the driver in caring for tires is that of proper inflation and checking valves and caps, but he must be alert constantly to detect evidences of excessive or unusual tire wear, the most common causes of which are as follows:

(*a*) Improper inflation, including under and over inflation and bleeding.

(*b*) Poor driving, including fast starting and stopping; improper breaking; striking sharp objects; rubbing curbstones, ruts, and car tracks.

(*c*) Wheel misalinement.

(*d*) Tight chains.

(*e*) Overloading.

(2) In general, tires should be removed from their wheels at least yearly to permit conditioning of wheel rim surfaces.

h. Storage battery.—The driver should have a general knowledge of the functions and care of the battery since it is the vehicle's most important accessory. (See par. 54.) Unusual performance or changes in the battery condition must be reported immediately. Keep the battery terminal connections clean and tight and check the electrolyte at least once a week.

i. Duties during scheduled maintenance and technical inspections.—Before his vehicle is submitted for scheduled maintenance or technical inspection, the driver should correct such mechanical defects as are within the limits of his ability and faculties. He should report known mechanical defects which he is not authorized to correct, and accompany his vehicle to the shop to further his knowledge of the vehicle and receive pertinent instructions for future procedure.

j. Emergency roadside repairs.—In performing emergency repairs, the driver should not force any part nor attempt the repair unless he is reasonably sure that he has diagnosed the trouble correctly. Tampering with mechanisms is prohibited. At the first opportunity after an emergency repair has been effected, the driver should report the fact to his section chief in order that proper action may be taken. The following are examples of emergency roadside repairs which a driver should be permitted to perform after he has received the proper training:

(1) Remove, clean, and install spark plugs.

(2) Adjust fan belt.

(3) Remove, blow out, and install fuel lines only.

(4) Tighten nuts and/or cap screws around leaky gaskets.

(5) Tape leaks in gas or oil lines and tighten connections.

(6) Tape electrical lines; replace fuzes; replace light bulbs.

(7) Plug leaks in the cooling system and tighten water pump connections.

(8) Loosen tight brakes.

74. Reports by driver.—There are two driver's reports generally applicable to all arms and services operating and maintaining automotive vehicles.

a. Driver's Report, Accident, Motor Transportation (Standard Form No. 26).—In case of injury to person or property, the driver of a motor vehicle will stop the vehicle and render such assistance as may be needed, complying with State and local regulations relative to reporting pertinent accidents outside combat areas. He will fill out immediately at the scene of the accident Standard Form No. 26 and deliver it to his commanding officer immediately upon return to his station. This action must be executed in every case regardless of how trivial the accident may appear to be or whether Government property or personnel only is injured (AR 850-15). Proper use of accident report form protects the careful driver in that it presents data secured immediately after the occurrence of the accident and permits completion of an investigation before facts become distorted.

b. Driver's Trip Ticket and Performance Record (W.D., Q.M.C. Form No. 237).—A properly completed driver's trip ticket furnishes valuable data for organization maintenance records as well as a written report of performance defects and emergency repairs affected. The report of defects protects the driver and puts the responsibility for repair on the shop maintenance personnel. When driver's trip tickets are not used, an oral report should be made by the driver.

75. Examination and operator's permit.—*a. Examination.*—Motor vehicle operator's permits will be issued only to individuals who have satisfactorily passed an examination conducted by a qualified commissioned officer covering the subjects listed.

(1) *Mechanical.*—Nomenclature and functions of major units of the vehicle.

(2) *Operation.*—Actual driving of the vehicle, involving use of controls; reversing and parking under usual conditions of traffic and terrain; traffic regulations; road procedure; safety precautions; speed limits and vehicle abuse.

(3) *Maintenance.*—First echelon (vehicle operator's) maintenance.

b. Operator's permit.—The U. S. Army Motor Vehicle Operator's Permit (W. D., Q. M. C. Form No. 228) will be issued by commanding officers to all enlisted and civilian operators of Regular Army motor vehicles (AR 850–15). Possession of a motor vehicle operator's permit should be a guarantee that the individual is a safe driver. The permit will be revoked immediately when an accident or other cause so warrants.

76. Troubles and remedies.—*a. Gasoline boiling in carburetor.*—Some engines, when stopped after reaching an operating temperature, radiate enough heat to cause boiling of the gasoline in the carburetor float chamber. This condition, especially prevalent during hot weather operation, causes a rich mixture in the intake manifold. To start the engine, open the hand throttle fully and leave choke in the normal operating position. The throttle should be adjusted to the desired engine speed only after the engine begins to run smoothly. Intermittent depression (pumping) of the accelerator when the engine is not running will also produce a rich mixture.

b. Vapor lock.—Excessive heat causes vaporization of the fuel before it leaves the carburetor jets, resulting in too lean a mixture to sustain engine operation. For such a condition, the fuel must cool and return to liquid form, and matters may be expedited by opening the hood to release the entrapped hot air around the engine. Improved insulation may be required.

c. Overheating of engine.—Overheating is caused by faults in the cooling system (par. 27 *b*), the air-fuel system (par. 16), the ignition system (par. 23), and also by mechanical defects (par. 11). In connection with the latter three items, difficulties are usually indicated by other symptoms but all are treated in greater detail in appropriate sections. Stop engine.

SCOUT CARS AND MORTAR MOTOR CARRIAGE

d. Stiffening of engine.—As a contributing factor to overheating, an engine may tighten up due to lack of lubrication. Check oil supply in crankcase. If there is doubt as to the operation of the oil pump, disconnect the oil line to the filter, slowly run engine, and observe flow of oil; the suction pipe in the oil pan may be clogged. High pressure readings on the gage do not necessarily mean that the lubrication system is functioning properly.

e. Clogging of exhaust or muffler.—An accumulation of carbon or dirt in the tail pipe or muffler will reduce engine efficiency. Try the vehicle on a pull with the muffler removed to check difference in power. Material may be loosened and blown out after tapping pipe with a hammer.

f. Knocks.—An unnatural sound or noise in an engine is a warning that some part of the engine is not functioning as it should. An engine in perfect mechanical condition and operating under ideal conditions gives out a continuous rhythmic sound with no sharp or metallic clicks. Correct adjustment, together with adequate lubrication, prevents or muffles the sound of metal moving over metal or striking against other metal. Knocks are caused either by an operating condition over which the driver of a vehicle can exercise some control, or by a mechanical condition, such as an incorrect adjustment of parts or an excessive wear of parts.

(1) *Operating knocks.*—Operating knocks, or detonations, are caused by engine overload; carbon in the combustion chamber; advanced spark; poor fuel; auto-ignition.

(*a*) Excessive carbon in the cylinders is indicated by a sharp knock which is most noticeable when the engine is accelerated or put under load and occurs only when the engine is hot.

(*b*) The spark too far advanced will cause a knock that may be mistaken for a carbon knock or the engine may also kick back when starting.

(*c*) Spark plugs of incorrect thermal fit will contribute to pre-ignition.

(2) *Mechanical knocks.*—These knocks result from wear or improper adjustment and are not always easy to locate or identify. They include crankshaft and bearing knocks; piston and connecting rod knocks; camshaft knocks; valve and valve sifter knocks; water pump knocks; miscellaneous knocks and noises; timing gear noises; fan noises. Analysis by and attention of maintenance personnel are usually required.

Section XIV

FIELD EXPEDIENTS

	Paragraph
General	77
Difficult operations	78
Traction aids	79
Pioneer work	80
Repair expedients	81
Camp expedients	82

77. General.—Field expedients covering the more common conditions which arise for the operator are described herewith.

a. Points to be observed.—(1) On approaching doubtful crossings or steep hills, a quick reconnaissance to determine the best route should be made on foot.

(2) A decision must be made promptly in the case of a stalled vehicle as to whether or not it can be moved by a companion vehicle or by men at hand, or requires a pioneer crew and trouble truck.

b. Factors.—The ability of a vehicle to negotiate difficult terrain depends upon its power, momentum, traction, and flotation. A proper appreciation of these related factors will assist military personnel in the choice of a practical expedient to meet most road difficulties.

78. Difficult operations.—*a. Ascending steep slopes.*—Where the grade is slippery or the slope particularly steep, the leading driver on approaching the hill should select a sufficiently low gear and continue on to gain the maximum momentum which his load and the road conditions permit. The driver of the next vehicle should slacken speed and halt before he arrives at the approach, and wait long enough to see that the vehicle ahead has cleared the crest.

(1) *Stalling.*—On a steep ascent, stalling usually occurs because of either power or traction failure. Several solutions include making another run in lower gear, applying traction devices, or utilizing towing power.

(2) *Precaution.*—As a precaution, when a vehicle stalls on a hill, the driver should not shift gears until he has tested the brakes by disengaging the clutch gradually. After the brakes have been tested and found to hold, the driver should shift to reverse and back the vehicle down the hill or to the side of the road in gear.

b. Descending steep slopes.—Very steep slopes should be descended straight down so that in case sliding occurs, the vehicle will not get out of control. All personnel except the driver should be dismounted. As a rule, the same gear is required in going down a hill as would be used in coming up the same hill; a sufficiently low gear should be selected so that the brakes need not be used. During intermittent brake applications, care should be exercised not to lock the wheels. Outside assistance should be given to vehicles, if the situation permits, through block and tackle, other vehicles, etc.

c. Muddy roads.—The usual muddy road that will be encountered is soft and slippery on the surface, while underneath it is generally hard or will pack sufficiently to support a vehicle. Soft spots will allow spinning wheels to dig in quickly. The following principles are applicable:

(1) *Traction aids.*—Chains usually give the best aid to traction and prevent skidding.

(2) *Gear.*—In general, the highest gear that will give sufficient power is selected. As the loss of momentum and the sudden application of increased power at a critical point starts the wheels to spin, the need for a gear reduction must be anticipated.

(3) *Momentum.*—Momentum should be maintained across slippery places and up grades.

(4) *Choice of tracks.*—Old ruts are the hardest packed and should generally be chosen. When road centers are high, ruts should be straddled or a new track should be made.

(5) *Stalling.*—Once a vehicle has come to a complete stall in mud, the clutch is disengaged at once. No new trial is attempted until an outside check-up is made. Proper procedure for extricating a stalled vehicle is dependent on judgment and experience but the following possibilities are suggested:

(a) If personnel are carried, they should dismount and try to push the vehicle, with power gradually applied.

(b) Usually a vehicle can be moved backward for a new trial easier than it can be moved forward.

(c) Combine assistance of a tow from another vehicle and help by manpower.

(d) Where a vehicle is hopelessly stalled, a winch, tractor, or tackle must be employed.

(e) Because of the danger of slipping under the vehicle, personnel should be cautioned against pushing on the side of a moving vehicle that has slipped into the ditch from a high crown road or on a vehicle that has slipped into old wheel ruts.

(f) A vehicle operating alone must have one or more wheels jacked or raised to permit insertion of brush, rock, or similar material thereunder and facilitate traction and flotation.

(6) *Digging out.*—Ditches dug in the direction that the wheels are expected to move will assist operations. For deep ruts, cross

ditches are dug at an angle to the ruts with dirt thrown back into the old ruts to guide the wheels to a straddle position.

d. Swamps.—Lacking supporting matériel, boggy or swampy soil should be avoided by keeping on relatively high ground. The main requirement is to move over such areas as rapidly as possible, with least amount of wheel spinning and loading. Personnel should dismount and assist with prolonges. Each vehicle should follow a separate track by reason of the weak crust of such soil, and have a guide, if possible, testing the route in advance. No attempt should be made to remove a vehicle stalled in a swamp without outside power.

e. Gumbo or sticky soil.—Such soils present a problem similar to swampy ground, but in addition provide little traction and stick to the wheels. It may be necessary to fasten devices under the fenders to scrape off the muck as the wheels revolve.

f. Sand.—Flotation in sand increases more or less below the surface and support is usually available for rapidly moving vehicles. Traction is limited due to continual slipping, and as soon as a driving wheel starts to spin it digs in rapidly. As long as the vehicle continues to move, however, the wheels may be kept turning to allow the vehicle to dig itself out. Vehicles should follow the tracks of the vehicle ahead. Hog or chicken wire fencing staked on the surface of the sand will usually make a satisfactory surface for movement of automotive vehicles.

g. Snow and ice.—On soft snow, flotation is at a minimum, while on ice, traction is at a minimum. In addition to the principles already listed, the following are applicable for winter driving:

(1) *Chains.*—Chains on all wheels are usually the best safeguard, although on ice they add little or no traction and are likely to give a false feeling of security because they increase skidding.

(2) *Fresh snow.*—Manpower should be available to push or tow the first vehicle to break trail. Other vehicles will follow exactly in track.

Caution: The engine should be used as a brake and rapid acceleration should be avoided. Where necessary, men with prolonges may hold vehicles on dangerous icy roads.

h. Ditches.—Ditches in width up to nearly the diameter of the tire and wider shallow ditches should always be traversed at an angle so that the drive wheel on one side will take hold of the far edge of the ditch at the same time that the opposite wheel is going into it. As this angle of crossing is a severe strain on the frame, springs, and driving mechanism, personnel should be dismounted to assist by pushing at the critical point. Ditches must be crossed slowly. When a ditch is wider than the diameter of the tire and deeper than the running board or undercarriage clearance, no attempt should be made to pass it until the banks are thrown in and the bottom filled up. Such ditches should be crossed at right angles. If they are wet, they should be approached slowly and the vehicle speeded up without wheel slipping just as the front wheels cross the lowest point.

i. Shelled areas.—Shelled areas vary from those that have been sparsely shelled to those in which the craters interlock or the terrain has been completely upheaved. Occasional craters in roads, trails, or other positions can usually be detoured; if not, they must be filled or bridged to permit passage. A thorough reconnaissance is necessary before badly torn areas can be crossed and the best route must be marked and all pioneer work completed in advance. Where the soil has been badly torn, it may be necessary to corduroy short stretches with any suitable material at hand. Care should be exercised to prevent stalling or damaging vehicles against hidden stumps or rocks, or in deep craters filled with water.

j. Shallow streams.—Fordings should be attempted only after a careful reconnaissance for bogs, holes, and depth. The height of the lowest electrical equipment and fuel accessories is a limiting factor. Other points to be observed are as follows:

(1) *Reduce speed.*—As a rule, nothing is to be gained by attempting to use momentum in crossing streams; they should be crossed slowly in low gear.

(2) *Disconnect fan.*—If there is any danger of the water surging or splashing to the fan, the fan belts should be slipped off before the crossing to prevent water from being thrown under the hood.

(3) *Dry brakes.*—After crossing a stream, brakes should be applied intermittently until dry enough to hold.

(4) *Check lubrication.*—At the first opportunity, wheels, crankcase, universal joints, differentials, transmission, and transfer case should be checked.

k. Bridges.—Narrow bridges should be approached with caution and at reduced speed. The risk of an accident on bridges having no side rails should not be taken, as a wheel over the side represents real trouble. A timber or rail should be screwed in place. Signs indicating maximum capacity must be given due consideration.

l. Overturned vehicle.—In order to get a maximum leverage on an overturned vehicle, a cradle of two ropes should be passed over the body of the vehicle, one in front of the windshield and the other in rear of the center of the vehicle. Preferably, both should be tied to the body frame or spring shackle. Brakes should be applied before the vehicle is righted. Any of the usual towing means may be used on the ropes, holding lines being employed to prevent damage to the vehicle from settling too rapidly. Before the vehicle is moved under its own power, necessary fuel and oil and battery and radiator water should be replaced, and a careful inspection made of the damage to determine servicing necessary or possible for the particular situation.

79. Traction aids.—*a. General.*—Chains and traction devices should always accompany the vehicle to which they pertain. They should be kept in serviceable condition and in proper adjustment to permit installation with a minimum of delay. Prompt removal should be effected, when the necessity for their use no longer exists, to prevent unnecessary damage to tires and roads.

b. Chains.—Chains are generally necessary in mud, sand, snow, or slush ice. The following general rules apply:

(1) The chains are applied before the vehicle becomes mired, and in such a manner that rotation of the wheel tends to close the chain fastenings. If improperly installed, rotation of the wheels opens the fastening and the chain will be lost.

(2) Fairly loose adjustment gives better traction and less tire wear than tight adjustment.

(3) Chains must be installed on all wheels of all wheel drive vehicles to prevent unnecessary strain.

80. Pioneer work.—*a. Mission.*—The mission of a pioneer party is to perform such road work as is required to make the route passable.

b. Allowances.—Each vehicle carries some pioneer tools and equipment to assist in crossing difficult terrain, varying according to Tables of Basic Allowances. In general, allowances include pick, shovel, tow chain, prolonge, axe, crosscut saw, bucket, and set of skid chains per vehicle. Other vehicles in a march unit carry additional equipment for the pioneer party, or a regular trouble truck is made available.

c. Precautions.—(1) *Barbed wire.*—Entanglements are cut out and towed away by means of a smooth wire or chain passed around them. In an emergency, a vehicle may go through entanglements under 4 feet in height with a fairly good chance of success but with some damage (particularly steering, axles, drums, and drive shafts).

(2) *Chemical agents.*—Sections of roads and bridges which have been sprayed with persistent chemical agents are decontaminated.

SCOUT CARS AND MORTAR MOTOR CARRIAGE

Where decontamination is not immediately practicable, detours are selected.

81. Repair expedients.—The usual limitations for repair of a vehicle by the driver are stated in paragraph 73 *j*. However, the following temporary expedients may be practiced in an emergency:

a. Blown fuzes.—*Locate and correct short circuit first.* Tinfoil may be employed then if fuze supply is exhausted.

b. Fan belt.—Replace with rope or fasten old belt together with wire and wrap with friction tape.

c. Springs.—The broken ends of a spring leaf may be held together by a splint secured by wire. If necessary, a block of wood is secured between the frame and axle to prevent spring action. A heavy wire or chain run from the front spring hanger, and another from the axle, to the rear spring shackle will hold the axle in alinement so that the vehicle can be driven slowly.

d. Broken fuel lines.—These can be repaired temporarily by slipping a section of tight fitting hose over the break; small leaks may be stopped by soap over the openings.

e. Wet ignition.—Wipe water away from plugs; dry distributor cap.

f. Cracked water jacket.—Temporary repair may be possible by draining cooling system, cleaning crack on either side with a file or steel brush, and cementing a patch over the crack with ordinary tire patching material.

g. Leaky hose.—A hose leak can be repaired with electrical or adhesive tape.

h. Leaky radiators.—Chewing gum, sealing wax, or plastic gasket material pushed into a leak will often reduce or stop the loss of water.

82. Camp expedients.—*a. Weather effects.*—(1) During cold weather, rubber tires adhere to wet soil and freeze. Before moving vehicles, the tires should be broken free from the ground.

(2) In parking overnight, ground should be selected that will remain firm regardless of storms. Provision must be made for satisfactory driving-wheel traction for one vehicle at least so that the other vehicles may be towed to solid ground with the least delay.

(3) When snow freezes to fenders and other painted parts of the vehicle, it should not be removed by force as the paint may come off with it. The best method is to melt the ice.

b. Supply problems.—(1) When the available water is too dirty for use in the cooling system, it should be strained; if time and means permit, water can be boiled and the floating sediment skimmed off or allowed to settle out. Rainwater, etc., may be used for batteries.

(2) It is not to be expected that the many various types of fuels and lubricants required for various vehicles will always be obtainable. It is more than probable that the supply services will be able to send forward only the fuels and lubricants of greatest general utility; any grade of gasoline, oil, and grease, provided it is of good quality, will meet immediate emergency needs for considerable periods and operators should be guided accordingly in keeping their vehicles in action.

Section XV

MAINTENANCE

	Paragraph
General	83
First echelon (driver, assistant, and crew)	84
Second echelon (troop or battery)	85
Third and fourth echelons	86
Maintenance operations	87
Maintenance on the march	88

83. General.—Military vehicles operate under difficult conditions and unusually good care is essential. Losses due to mechanical failure must be kept at a minimum and minor repairs accomplished quickly in order to keep motor transportation at the highest possible level of efficiency.

a. Functions.—The Army system of automotive maintenance is based on certain maintenance functions as follows:

(1) Scheduled preventive maintenance operations, unit replacements, repairs, and inspections with the primary objective of economical, uninterrupted vehicle service.

(2) Systematic detection and correction of incipient causes of vehicle casualties before they occur and the action necessary to maintain satisfactory day to day operating condition of automotive vehicles.

b. Unit replacement.—The principle of unit replacement rather than major repair of a unit while installed in the vehicle is practiced in all cases where such assembly is available. Where minor repair only is required and can be made without dismantling the unit or removing the unit from the vehicle, the unit replacement principle is not followed.

c. Essential elements.—Within the automotive maintenance system of operating organizations will be included only the tools, equipment, and personnel which are necessary to insure combat efficiency.

d. Field maintenance.—Care must be exercised by all personnel to retain the distinction between the proper functions and scope of the automotive maintenance of operating organizations and those of the supporting services under field conditions.

e. Maintenance echelons.—There are, in general, four divisions of Army maintenance called the first, second, third, and fourth echelons. The first and second echelons of maintenance are the responsibility of the using arms and services, while the third and fourth echelons are the responsibility of the supply service (quartermaster or ordnance) personnel. The work performed in the various echelons is limited by the restrictions of one or more of the four elements essential to maintenance functions, comprising personnel, equipment, supplies, and time.

84. First echelon (driver, assistant, and crew).—The first echelon maintenance is driver's maintenance which covers the simple operations that can be trusted to the skill of the average driver using tools and supplies available on the vehicle. These operations include driver's inspections (pars. 65 and 72); servicing (replenishment of fuel, oil, water, antifreeze, and air); lubrication (except items requiring special lubricants, equipment, or technical knowledge); tightening or replacement of nuts, bolts, screws, and studs; cleaning; care of tools and equipment, tires, and storage battery; preparation of the vehicle for maintenance operations and for command and technical inspections; emergency repairs (limited by tool kit and spare parts carried on the vehicle). For further details see paragraph 73.

85. Second echelon (troop or battery).—*a. Unit commander.*—The unit commander is directly responsible for the first echelon maintenance and for part or all of the second. The success of preventive maintenance will depend upon the judgment, energy, common sense, and ability not only of the unit commander but also his subordinates including a motor officer, motor sergeant, and motor mechanics. (See chart below.)

b. Regimental.—In most arms and services there is provided by Tables of Organization a regimental second echelon maintenance organization. The personnel are a part of the headquarters company, battery, or like unit of the regiment and are administered by the commanding officer of that unit.

86. Third and fourth echelons.—As between the two services in wartime or emergency, either the Ordnance Department or the Quartermaster Corps will perform such third and fourth echelon maintenance as may be requested and facilities permit.

a. Third echelon maintenance is that normally performed in the field by quartermaster and ordnance personnel, embracing principally the replacement of unserviceable unit assemblies by similar unit assemblies held in third echelon stock. In addition to unit replacement, the third echelon supports and extends maintenance facilities to the using arms and services by making repairs involving the use of medium mobile shop equipment and by the services of general mechanics and a limited number of trade specialists; by the supply of unit assemblies and parts to the second echelon; and by the evacuation

MAINTENANCE ORGANIZATION CHART (SECOND ECHELON)

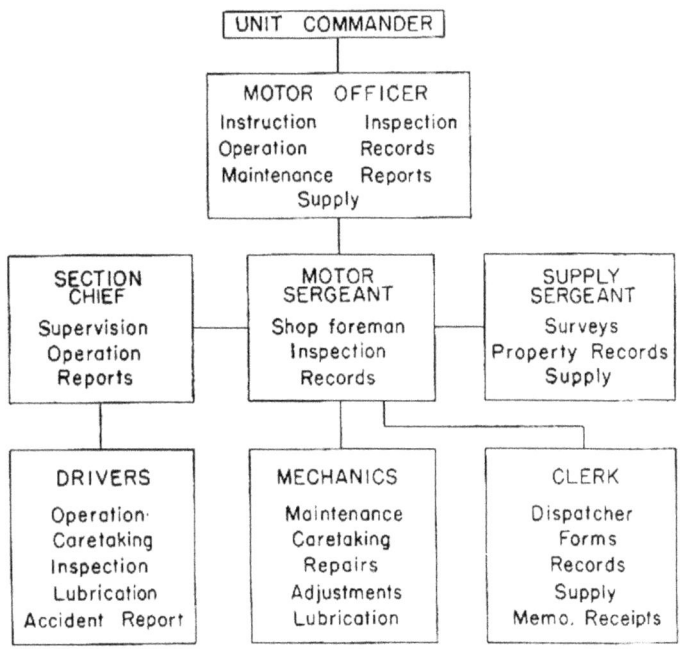

RA FSD 746

to the third and fourth echelon shops of vehicles which require repairs beyond the scope of second and third echelon facilities.

b. Fourth echelon maintenance is that normally performed in the rear areas by the quartermaster or ordnance personnel embracing the disassembly and repair of any or all unit assemblies which are used in the automotive vehicles of the command to which the fourth

SCOUT CARS AND MORTAR MOTOR CARRIAGE

echelon shop is assigned. Salvage and reclamation service is also included.

87. Maintenance operations.—*a. General.*—In order to maintain the vehicles in as near perfect condition as possible, scheduled maintenance operations followed by maintenance inspections are necessary, all being performed in accordance with a definite schedule based on time, mileage, or a combination of both.

(1) *Repair.*—Repair consists of adjusting, tightening, replacing, or reconditioning any part, subassembly, or assembly of a vehicle.

(2) *Adjustment.*—Adjustment consists of placing parts, subassemblies, or assemblies in correct working relation to each other and securing them in that position. Examples are fan belt tension, breaker point clearance, brake and clutch pedal clearance.

(3) *Tightening.*—Tightening consists of drawing up nuts and screws where adjustment is not involved. Examples are body bolts, body screws, bumper bolts, fender and running board brackets, floor board bolts or screws. A clear distinction should be made between tightening (driver's responsibility) and adjusting (mechanic's responsibility).

(4) *Replacing.*—Replacing consists of exchanging any part, subassembly, or assembly and placing them in proper adjustment. Examples are fuel and oil lines, distributor head, radiator hose, muffler, oil filter, carburetor, generator, battery, brake parts.

(5) *Reconditioning.*—Reconditioning consists of restoring any part, subassembly, or assembly to a state of serviceability. Examples are refacing valves, welding broken parts, patching tubes, turning down an armature.

b. Daily.—Daily maintenance consists of cleaning, servicing, tightening, and emergency repairs. In general, daily repairs will be of an emergency nature based on defects reported by the driver and supervisory personnel. After an examination of these reports, the work will be allotted to the various mechanics according to their ability, or it will be sent to the shop. Except in an emergency, a vehicle will not be sent out before defects are corrected.

c. Weekly.—Weekly maintenance is a continuation and check of the driver's daily maintenance, performed at least once each week by the driver under the direct supervision of the section chief and under the technical supervision of the motor maintenance personnel. Operations to be performed should include the maintenance in conjunction with the inspection after operation (pars. 72 and 73) and a report to the motor officer of any defects observed but not corrected.

d. Lubrication.—Lubrication operations should be performed by designated personnel in accordance with manufacturer's recommendations as amended by military authority. (See sec. XVI.)

e. Monthly (1,000 miles).—This maintenance operation is performed normally by the troop, battery, or similar unit mechanics under the supervision of the motor sergeant. A record is made to show the defects that could not be corrected, the time of accomplishment, the mechanic who performed the operation, and the officer who made the maintenance inspection. This record should be retained until the semiannual (6,000-mile) maintenance operations and technical inspection, at which time it may be disposed of as the unit commander sees fit. The guide as shown below for this maintenance may be modified as necessary for the different vehicles; items marked with an asterisk may require tools and parts not available or authorized, in which case the defect should be corrected by the next higher echelon.

MAINTENANCE OPERATION GUIDE (MONTHLY)

Vehicle road test

1. Bring engine to operating temperature and examine for smoke or fumes.
2. Examine condition of oil on measuring stick; observe any evidences of blow-by or leaks.
3. Test horns, lights, and windshield wipers.
4. Test for proper steering.
5. Check engine for power delivery, acceleration, and unusual noises.
6. Test clutch action; stop and investigate unusual noises.
7. Test gear sets and final drives for ease of shifting and unusual noises.
8. Test brakes for equalization, stopping distance, pedal travel, and "feel."
9. Observe action of panel instruments.
10. Observe final drives and propeller shafts while another person drives or while the vehicle is blocked up with the wheels off the ground. Note any overheating of units.

General maintenance

1. Clean and tighten storage battery, terminals, and carrier bolts; test battery and refill to proper level.
2. Tighten body bolts, fenders, running boards, bumpers, brush guards, headlamp brackets, mirrors, tow hooks, pintle, body parts, radiator shell, hardware, and windshield equipment.
*3. Repair body injuries.
4. Replace unserviceable instruments, safety devices, and gages.
5. Adjust lights; controls.

Driving axles; wheels

1. Tighten loose driving flange nuts and cap screws.
2. Tighten and properly secure all assemblies, pinion carriers, cover plates, spring seats, bolts and nuts.
*3. Correct any leakage of lubricant.
*4. Remove any excessive play or backlash.
5. Remove looseness or bind from wheel bearings.
6. Tighten wheel stud nuts.

Engine

1. Service air cleaner; replace oil filter if required.
2. Tighten engine mountings, flywheel housing, oil pan, timing gear cover, manifold, accessory attachments, and other bolts and nuts.
*3. Correct all breakage, cracks, or leaks.
*4. Repair unserviceable breaker points.
5. Replace all damaged wiring and shielding.
*6. Correct malfunctioning generator or starter.
*7. Correct generator output.
8. Adjust noisy valves.
*9. If missing occurs on road test, ignition system should be checked and spark plugs removed, examined, cleaned, reset, and replaced if necessary.
*10. Remove causes of other knocks, noises, and unsatisfactory engine performance. (Vacuum gage is valuable for diagnosis of trouble.)

Fuel system; cooling system

1. Clean dirty sediment bowls.
*2. Correct fuel pump leakage.
3. Tighten connections; repair or replace tubing; check valves.
*4. Correct malfunctions of fuel pump.
5. Tighten radiator supports, braces, and attachment of shell to core.
*6. Correct all evidences of water leakage.
7. Adjust incorrect fan belt tension; replace unserviceable belts.
8. Replace unserviceable hose and hose clamps; check heater.

Brakes; springs

*1. Replace worn brake lining.
2. Correct any leaks in system.
3. Fill master cylinder to level.
4. Centralize and adjust hydraulic brakes.

Brakes; springs—Continued

5. Correct malfunctioning of system.
6. Adjust propeller shaft hand brake.
7. Replace unserviceable shock absorbers and linkage; replenish fluid.
8. Repair broken or loose spring hold-down bolts, clips, and center bolts.
9. Tighten loose shackle bolts.

Steering mechanism

1. Adjust or repair excessive play in—

*Steering knuckle bearings.
Tie rod and drag link ends.
*Bushings.
Sector shaft and steering gear.

2. Tighten attachment of steering mechanism to frame, and of steering column to body.
3. Replace any excessively worn or bent parts.
4. Tighten, replace, or secure properly all lock washers, cotter keys, nuts, and similar items.
*5. Adjust wheel stops when turning radius is incorrect; note any wear on drag link.
6. Lubricate entire mechanism while front wheels are off the floor. Turn wheels from side to side to insure distribution of lubricant and to ascertain whether or not the entire mechanism works freely.

Clutch; transmissions; shafts

1. Adjust incorrect clutch free travel and floor clearance.
*2. Repair defective shifter mechanisms.
3. Tighten all loose bolts and nuts, supports, carriers, and cover plates.
*4. Correct any leakage of lubricant.
5. Correct misalinement of universal joints.
*6. Repair all fractures.
*7. Replace excessively worn spline and universal joints.
8. Open vents.
9. Repair or replace muffler or tail pipe.

Final record	Final record—Continued
1. Check road test.	Signature of mechanic.
2. Record of defects remaining:	Signature of sergeant.
Unit.	4. Maintenance inspection certificate by motor officer (required by AR 850-15).
Correction necessary.	
3. Mechanic's certificate:	
Date.	RA FSD 747

f. Semiannual (6,000 miles).—Maintenance operations are normally performed by the regimental second echelon of maintenance. Under extremely severe operating conditions, certain items may have to be checked every 2 or 3 months. An instructional guide similar to that used for the monthly maintenance operations should be drawn up. All accessory units are disassembled, cleaned, inspected, and lubricated, and they are repaired or exchanged if necessary. Maintenance operations which should be included normally at this period are as follows:

(1) *Records.*—Included should be inspection of vehicle, repair, and operating records for the period followed by a road test.

(2) *Engine tune-up.*—Included should be a check of the oil filter and air cleaner; a vacuum and compression test; cleaning of engine interior and oil pan; adjustment of valves; servicing of ignition system, generator, and starter; a check on the tightness and serviceability of all parts and accessories.

(3) *Fuel system.*—Included should be examination and servicing of the fuel pump, carburetor, fuel lines, and tanks.

(4) *Cooling system.*—Included should be examination and servicing of the radiator, fan belts, and water pump.

(5) *Instruments.*—Included should be a check, servicing, and replacement if necessary of horns, lights, wiring, windshield wipers, and panel instruments, gages, and controls.

(6) *Clutch, transmission, and transfer case.*—Included should be a check of clutch travel and floor clearance, shifter mechanisms, transmission and transfer case supports, grease seals, tightness, and lubrication.

(7) *Propeller shafts and universal joints.*—Included should be an examination for slackness, free movement of splined joints, grease seals, and lubrication.

(8) *Driving axles.*—Included should be a check of backlash; inspection, lubrication, and adjustment of wheel bearings, spring clips, and holddown bolts, shackles, and driving flanges; a check for leaks; examination of grease seals; lubrication.

(9) *Steering mechanism.*—Included should be a check of the attachment of the steering mechanism and column, steering linkage, excessive play, steering stops and turning angle, and lubrication.

(10) *Front end.*—Included should be a check of spring hold-down bolts, rebound clips, shackles, shock absorbers, lubrication and adjustment of wheel bearings, tie rods, and tires for wear and alinement.

(11) *General.*—Included should be an examination of the battery, body and attachments, curtains, top, windshields, muffler, and tail pipe.

(12) *Engine.*—Check engine by bringing engine up to operating temperature and checking results of tune-up for quietness; idling speed; acceleration; leaks in carburetor, fuel pump and lines, cooling system, oil lines and seals.

(13) *Road test and record of operation.*

g. Troop, battery, and regimental second echelon repairs.—The examples below do not indicate all the operations performed but show some of the common ones. Circular 1–10, OQMG, covers the operations in detail for the entire second echelon.

(1) *Troop or battery.*—(*a*) *Adjustments.*—Wheel bearings; pedal clearances; steering gear and linkage; fan belts; water pump; spring shackles; lights.

(*b*) *Replacements.*—Carburetor; generator; distributor cap and rotor; fuel pump; batteries and cables; manifold; instruments and switches; oil lines and filter; brake shoes.

(2) *Regiment.*—(*a*) *Adjustments.*—Steering geometry; voltage regulator; carburetor; generator; valve tappets; timing.

(*b*) *Replacements.*—Tie rods; distributor points; valve springs; carburetor; fuel pump diaphragms.

88. Maintenance on the march.—*a. Maintenance personnel.*—Where marches of tactical units are involved, each organization will have the maintenance personnel allowed by Tables of Organization, and possibly some attached third echelon personnel. Maintenance personnel of batteries, troops, or similar units normally ride at the tail of their respective units.

b. Equipment, spare parts, and spare units.—The repair equipment available consists of the tools and equipment allotted by Table of Basic Allowances for each organization. The parts and units carried should be sufficient to cover all malfunctions and failures that experience has shown will probably occur. Where small organizations such as batteries, troops, or similar organizations operate by themselves, sufficient spare units should be furnished from the regimental second echelon or from the third echelon.

c. Repair procedure.—During marches, roadside repairs to disabled vehicles are frequently temporary in character. Upon reaching its destination, the vehicle should be repaired properly. The driver always remains with the vehicle unless ordered by competent authority to abandon it.

d. Towing disabled vehicles.—Arrangements in any column for towing disabled vehicles will depend upon the type of vehicle, road conditions, type of march, and other considerations. Towing vehicles should be provided with tow bars, tow ropes, or tow chains. When repair personnel are working by the side of the road, warning guards, signs, or flags must be put out unless the vehicle is completely off the road. At night, red lanterns should be utilized.

e. Abandoning vehicles.—When vehicles on the march become disabled and for some reason are not towed or are not capable of being towed with vehicles within the organization, they may be abandoned either temporarily or permanently.

(1) When the abandonment is temporary, the driver and possibly a mechanic are left with the vehicle. In the combat zone, consideration must be given to the possibility of not recovering the personnel and facilities thus detached. Every effort should be made to remove to other vehicles all essential combat equipment prior to abandonment of the vehicle. A driver left with a vehicle awaiting maintenance or salvage personnel should be given explicit orders concerning the removal of the load.

(2) If the abandonment is permanent, the proper steps should be taken to comply with orders covering such action. Vehicles should be tagged to show the reason of their unserviceability. When opering units abandon vehicles, the supply service concerned must be furnished accurate reports as soon as practicable of the location and general condition of such vehicles.

Section XVI
LUBRICATION

	Paragraph
General	89
Methods	90
Schedules	91
Lubricants	92
Application	93

89. General.—Lubrication is an essential part of preventive maintenance; it determines to a great extent the serviceability of parts and assemblies; it influences materially repair and operation costs; it is one of the most important factors affecting dependable mobility and useful vehicle life.

SCOUT CARS AND MORTAR MOTOR CARRIAGE

90. Methods.—Lubrication operations may be decentralized or centralized. In either case, the unit commander assigns definite responsibility for these functions. The motor officer, assisted by the motor sergeant, prepares lubrication schedules, supervises lubrication, and makes frequent inspections to assure himself that all vehicles are properly lubricated. Good team work must be developed if the desired results are to be accomplished.

a. Decentralized lubrication.—This method is particularly applicable to field service operations, and will give excellent results when personnel are properly trained and supervised and lubrication schedules are carefully followed. Responsibility is divided as follows:

(1) *Driver.*—The driver performs the prescribed driver's lubrication functions (par. 73c).

(2) *Mechanics.*—The mechanics perform special lubrication to include gear cases, steering gear housing, wheel bearings, universal joints, starting motor, generator, distributor, clutch release bearing, water pump, fan, air cleaner, and changes of crankcase oil.

(3) *Supervisors.*—Chiefs of sections or truck masters are charged with direct supervision of lubrication by the driver. They should make frequent inspections to insure correct lubrication in accordance with the lubrication schedule.

b. Centralized lubrication.—When this method is employed, all lubricating functions are carried on at a central point and drivers are relieved of all responsibility for lubrication except the replenishment of crankcase oil. Vehicles should be sent to the central station when lubrication is required, accompanied by the driver whose services should be utilized to expedite the work. Centralized lubrication is not recommended for field service operations.

c. Detached service.—When automotive vehicles are detached from their organizations for such periods of time that they will miss their scheduled lubrication service, provision should be made for the performance of the lubrication functions. Arrangements should be made to send qualified personnel and the necessary supplies and equipment with the vehicles, have lubrication performed by other units, or provide the necessary supplies and equipment for the driver to perform the operations.

91. Schedules.—Lubrication schedules are required for each make of vehicle. The schedule or chart furnished by a manufacturer forms the basis for organizational lubrication procedure. In cases where recommended periods are too infrequent to provide the desired lubrication for military purposes, necessary modifications must be effected. In general, the chassis and slow-motion parts should be lubricated every 7 days or 50 hours of vehicle operation, while the crankcase oil should be checked frequently and changed after not more than 1,000 miles of operation, or more often during prolonged periods of cross-country driving, hard pulls, or idling. Gear lubricants should be checked weekly and changed seasonally unless operating mileage requires more frequent changes. Severe operating conditions may require immediate attention, especially in cases where vehicle components have been submerged in water, chemicals, snow, or mud.

a. Records.—A complete record of lubrication will be kept for every vehicle. Responsible personnel will accomplish a check sheet at regular intervals to indicate the actual mileage and date at which each component receives such attention as prescribed.

b. Instructions.—Lubrication instructions for the various components of these vehicle groups, as discussed in detail in preceding sections, are consolidated and charted for review in the lubrication schedule and chart below.

c. Supplies.—Lubricants and application equipment should conform to the recommendations of responsible manufacturers or the supply services concerned. When these recommendations are inconsistent, authorized bulletins and circulars published by the supply services and local regulations should govern. During field service, it may not be possible to supply a complete assortment of lubricants called for by the schedule to meet the recommendations and it will then be necessary to make best use of those available, subject to inspection by the regimental motor officer in consultation with responsible ordnance personnel.

92. Lubricants.—Correct lubrication requires the use of several types of lubricants and the application of each type in accordance with the lubrication schedule below.

a. Symbols.—The SAE identification numbers are used to indicate the viscosity (body) of an oil but do not in any sense reflect quality or specific characteristics. Government symbol (Navy contract) numbers and the SAE viscosity equivalents for engine, transmission, and differential oils are tabulated in the lubricating oil viscosity chart below. Federal or U. S. Army specifications for greases and fluid lubricants are incomplete and Navy contracts do not apply.

(1) *Selection.*—Some confusion in the selection and use of straight mineral oils available under the Navy contract have resulted from the fact that certain oils may be used for either the transmission or the engine. For example, Navy symbol No. 3100 is classified as SAE 90 when required for a transmission, and SAE 50 when required for the engine. Actually there is no difference in these oils.

SCOUT CARS AND MORTAR MOTOR CARRIAGE TM 9–705

LUBRICATION CHART

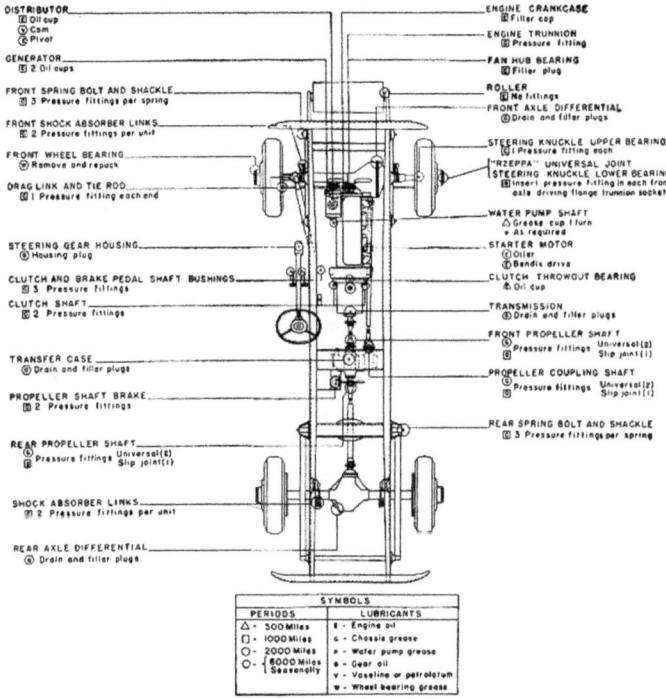

RA FSD 713

LUBRICATION SCHEDULE

Part and application	Amount	Lubricant	Below 32° F	32° F 75° F	Above 75° F	Remarks
500 MILES						
Clutch throwout bearing oil cup.	7 drops	Engine oil	SAE 20	SAE 30	SAE 40	Oil line extends through clutch housing.
Shock absorber arm pressure fittings (8).	As required	Chassis lubricant	Soft	Medium		Apply until fresh clean grease extrudes from bushing.
Water pump grease cup (one turn).	As required	Water pump grease				Never use chassis or fiber type grease.
1,000 MILES						
Clutch shaft pressure fittings (2).	As required	Chassis lubricant	Soft	Medium		Apply until fresh clean grease extrudes from bushing.
Differential housing plugs (2)	As required	Gear oil	SAE 90	SAE 140		Check and maintain proper level. Drain, flush, refill after first 1,000 miles.
Distributor shaft oil cup	3 drops	Engine oil	SAE 20	SAE 30		Do not over lubricate.
Drag link and tie rod pressure fittings (4).	As required	Chassis lubricant	Soft	Medium		Apply until fresh clean grease extrudes from bushing.
Engine crankcase	6 quarts	Engine oil	SAE 20	SAE 30	SAE 40	Check gage daily. Maintain proper level. Drain thoroughly while hot. Add flushing oil, idle engine 5 minutes, redrain. Do not use kerosene or solvent.
Engine crankcase flushing oil	4 quarts	Engine oil	SAE 10	SAE 20		
Engine front trunnion pressure fitting.	As required	Chassis lubricant	Soft	Medium		Apply until fresh clean grease extrudes from bushing.

Fan hub bearing plug	Fill	Engine oil	SAE 20	SAE 30	Remove slotted head screw. Do not over lubricate.
Generator oil cups (2)	3 drops	Engine oil			
Linkage; bumper roller; pintle	As required	Engine oil			Avoid waste.
Pedal shaft pressure fittings (3)	As required	Chassis lubricant	Soft	Medium	Apply until fresh clean grease extrudes from bushing.
Propeller shaft brake anchor pin pressure fittings (2).	As required	Chassis lubricant	Soft	Medium	Apply until fresh clean grease extrudes from bushing.
Propeller shaft slip joint pressure fittings (3).	As required	Gear oil	SAE 140	SAE 140	Avoid excessive lubrication.
Spring shackle and bolt pressure fittings (12).	As required	Chassis lubricant	Soft	Medium	Apply until fresh clean grease trudes from bushing.
Steering knuckle lower bearing and Rzeppa universal joint trunnion socket channels (2).	As required	Gear oil	SAE 140	SAE 250	Remove relief plug before filling and to check level. Insert fitting in axle driving flange. Do not use chassis lubricant.
Steering knuckle upper bearing pressure fittings (2).	As required	Chassis lubricant	Soft	Medium	
Transfer case housing plug	As required	Gear oil	SAE 140	SAE 250	Check and maintain proper level. Drain, flush, refill after first 1,000 miles.
Transmission housing plug	As required	Gear oil	SAE 90	SAE 140	Check and maintain proper level. Drain, flush, refill after first 1,000 miles.

LUBRICATION SCHEDULE—Continued

Part and application	Amount	Lubricant	Below 32° F	32° F 75° F	Above 75° F	Remarks
2,000 MILES						
Air cleaner reservoir	As required	Engine oil	SAE 20	SAE 30	SAE 40	Drain, clean, and refill. Check daily and maintain proper level.
Brake fluid reservoir plug	As required	Lockheed #21 Hydraulic brake fluid with level ¾-inch below top of tank.				
Engine crankcase oil filter	As required	Replace				Replace filter cartridge as required to maintain clean oil.
Propeller shaft universal joint pressure fittings (6).	As required	Gear oil	SAE 140	SAE 140		Do not use chassis lubricant. Apply until overflow at relief valve.
Shock absorber reservoir plug (4).	As required	Houdaille #1400 fluid				Maintain reservoir level. Keep out foreign matter.
Spring leaves (spray)	As required	Penetrating oil				Optional; not recommended by manufacturer.
Starting motor oiler	2 drops	Engine oil	SAE 20	SAE 30		Do not overlubricate. Keep oil off commutator.
Steering gear housing plug	As required	Gear oil	SAE 140	SAE 140/250		Use steering gear lubricant if available. Fill housing.
6,000 MILES OR SEASONALLY						
Cooling system	19 quarts					Clean water or antifreeze solution. Drain, flush, and refill. Check daily.

TM 9-705

Distributor breaker arm felt wick oiler	1 drop	Engine oil	SAE 20	Do not overlubricate.
Distributor cam	Wipe	Vaseline or petrolatum		Do not overlubricate.
Front axle differential housing filler plug.	9 pints	Gear oil	SAE 90 / SAE 140	Drain, flush, and refill. Seasonal changes to be made regardless of mileage.
Rear axle differential housing filler plug.	3 quarts	Gear oil	SAE 90 / SAE 140	Drain, flush, and refill. Seasonal changes to be made regardless of mileage.
Speedometer cable and gear housing.	As required	Graphite		To be done only by ordnance repair shop.
Starter Bendix drive	As required	Engine oil	SAE 10 / SAE 20	Remove, clean, and dip in oil.
Transfer case housing filler plug	3 quarts	Gear oil	SAE 140 / SAE 250	Drain, flush, and refill. Seasonal changes to be made regardless of mileage.
Transmission housing filler plug	5 quarts	Gear oil	SAE 90 / SAE 140	Drain, flush, and refill. Seasonal changes to be made regardless of mileage.
Vacuum power unit cylinder cap plug.	2 ounces	Bendix vacuum cylinder oil		Be sure to replace cap after lubricating every 6,000 to 10,000 miles.
Wheel bearings	As required	Grease	Medium / Hard	Disassemble, clean, and repack 6,000 to 10,000 miles. Do not lubricate through wheel cap fitting. Use wheel bearing grease. Do not overlubricate.

NOTE.—Clean around filler plugs and wipe off fittings before applying lubricant. Lubricate chassis parts after washing vehicle or after prolonged maneuvering through water and/or snow.

Requirement	Contract or designation	Substitute specification	Emergency conditions
Engine oil:	Annual Navy contract:		Specify for emergency requirements branded, "premium" or "regular" first quality automotive engine oils produced by reputable and experienced companies.
SAE 10 (10 W)	Symbol 2110 [4]		
SAE 20 (20 W)	Symbol 3030	VV–O–496, SAE 20	
SAE 30	Symbol 1065 [5]	VV–O–496, SAE 30	
	Symbol 3065		
SAE 40	Symbol 1080 [5]	VV–O–496, SAE 40	
	Symbol 3080		
Gear oil: SAE 90	Annual Navy contract: Symbol 1100 (medium) Symbol 3100	SAE 90/140/250 specifications for transmission, differential, transfer case, steering gear housings, and universal joints.	Specify in addition to SAE designations, branded, highest quality, noncompounded automotive gear lubricants produced by reputable and experienced companies.
Gear oil, extreme pressure:			
SAE 90 (EP)			
SAE 140 (EP)	T. P. S. class 14: [1] Supplied by contractors.	VV–L–761, Class B [2]	
SAE 250 (EP)		VV–L–761, Class C [2]	
Chassis lubricant:			
Winter grade (soft)	T. P. S. class 14: [1] Supplied by contractors.	Chassis grease (grade 1 or soft)	
Summer grade (medium)		Chassis grease (grade 2 or medium).	
Water pump grease	T. P. S. class 14 [1]	Water pump grease (calcium)	
Wheel bearing grease:			
Winter grade (medium)	T. P. S. class 14 [1]	Wheel bearing grease (grade 2 or medium).	
Summer grade (hard)		Wheel bearing grease (grade 3 or hard).	

Petrolatum or vaseline	Fed. Stock Catalog 14–P–95	U. S. Army No. 2–67
Penetrating oil	Fed. Stock Catalog 14–O–3217	Oil, penetrating, noncorrosive
Hydraulic brake fluid	QMC ES 377	"Lockheed" No. 21 hydraulic brake fluid
Shock absorber fluid		"Houdaille" No. 1400 fluid
Solvent	T. P. S. class 14, 51 [3]	P–S–661A
Vacuum cylinder oil		Bendix vacuum cylinder oil

[1] Treasury Department, Procurement Division, General Schedule of Supplies, Class 14, quarterly grease contract.
[2] Will be used by Treasury Department, for contracts beginning Oct. 1, 1940.
[3] For delivery in the District of Columbia, nearby Virginia and Maryland, only.
[4] For temperatures from +10° F. to −15° F.; below −15° F. add 55 percent transformer oil (Navy symbol 9045) to engine oil SAE 10 W (Navy symbol 2110).
[5] These oils recommended by reason of higher viscosity indices.

ORDNANCE DEPARTMENT

LUBRICATING OIL VISCOSITY CHART

Item	Navy symbol	Saybolt universal viscosity (seconds)		SAE No.	
		At 130° F.	At 210° F.	Engine	Gear oils [3]
1	2075 Refrigeration oil	70–90			
[1] 2	2110 Forced feed oils	90–120		10W	
3	2135 Automotive and general oils.	120–145		20	
4	2190 Automotive and general oils.	185–205		30	
5	2250 Automotive and general oils.	245–280		40	
*6	3050 Automotive and general oils.		45–55	20W	
7	3065 Automotive and general oils.		60–70	30	80.
8	3080 Automotive and general oils.		75–90	40	90 (low).
9	3100 Automotive and general oils.		90–105	50	90 (high).
10	3120 Automotive and general oils.		115–125	60	110 (low).
[2] 10½	1065 Class A oils		62–68	30	80 (medium).
[2] 11	1080 Class A oils		76–84	40	80 (high).
12	1100 Aviation oils		93–103	50	90 (medium).
13	1120 Aviation oils		115–125	60	140 (low).
14	1150 Aviation oils		140–160	70	140 (medium)
15	4065 Compounded oil		65–75	[4]	
16	5065 Mineral marine engine and cylinder oils.		65–75	[4]	
17	5150 Mineral marine engine and cylinder oils.		135–165	[4]	
18	5190 Mineral marine engine and cylinder oils.		180–220	[4]	
19	6135 Compounded steam cylinder oils.		120–150	[4]	
20	7105 Compounded steam cylinder oils.		95–110	[4]	
21	8190 Compounded air cylinder oils.	180–200		[4]	
22	9045 Transformer oil	50–65			

[1] For temperatures between minus 10° F. and plus 10° F.
[2] These oils recommended by reason of higher viscosity indices.
[3] Except when extreme pressure (EP) or hypoid lubricants are recommended.
[4] Not used.

RA FSD 715A

SCOUT CARS AND MORTAR MOTOR CARRIAGE

(2) *Classification.*—The SAE numbers used to classify transmission oils are derived from viscosity measurements in Saybolt furol seconds taken at 100° F., whereas the SAE numbers used to classify engine oils are derived from viscosity measurements in Saybolt universal seconds taken at 130° F. and 210° F. For approximate conversion, Saybolt furol viscosity values when multiplied by ten give the Saybolt universal equivalents.

b. Types.—(1) *Lubricating oils.*—Lubricating oils are selected from the mineral oils specified in the Navy Department contract. They are characterized by physical properties such as viscosity, flash point, and pour point and should be used in accordance with recommendations as approved or amended by military authority. In these vehicles, lubricating or engine oils of the proper viscosity are employed to lubricate engine bearings, the electric starter, generator, distributor, fan bearings, and slow-moving surfaces such as brake pedal pivots, linkages, hinges, etc.

(2) *Chassis lubricant.*—A grease of light consistency which has a tendency to spread rapidly over bearing surfaces, cling to them for a long period, and resist the action of and seal against water and dirt, is required in high-pressure greasing equipment to lubricate slow-moving elements of the chassis equipped with pressure fittings. Several basic types of greases are commercially available for chassis lubrication of components such as spring shackles, kingpin upper bearings, pedal shafts, the tie rod and drag link, etc., but excluding wheel bearings, the water pump, and universal joints except under certain conditions. These types incorporate a calcium, aluminum, or soda soap base and generally range in consistency from a semifluid to a medium grade or an unworked penetration (A. S. T. M.) of about 300.

(*a*) *Calcium soap grease.*—This grease has been in use for the longest period. It is yellow in color, smooth in texture, and contains a low viscosity mineral oil. It is insoluble in water but has a very low melting point and will leak out readily at moderate temperatures.

(*b*) *Aluminum soap grease.*—This grease is light amber in color and quite adhesive. While it is not soluble in water, the latter has the effect of destroying the lubricant's adhesive properties.

(*c*) *Soda soap grease.*—This grease has the highest melting point of the several types mentioned and will not separate at temperatures in excess of 250° F. It has been found that a soda soap grease having a low soda soap content under 8 percent in combination with a very high viscosity cylinder oil stock is usually water resistant to road wash or submersion. The lubricating and load-carrying properties of such greases are governed by the quality and viscosity of the mineral oil used as a base stock and not by the grease consistency which is proportional to the soap content. Specifications for grades are indicated by numbers to facilitate selection based on the desired ease and manner of application, in consideration of the temperatures and equipment involved.

NOTE.—For general summer conditions, use a grade No. 2 (medium) such as Marfak 2 or equivalent. For general winter conditions where the lubrication is performed in an enclosed or heated building and where the prevailing outdoor temperatures are below 32° F., use a grade No. 1 (soft) such as Marfak 1 or equivalent. For very low atmospheric temperatures where lubrication is performed outside at temperatures generally below 32° F., use a grade No. 0 (semifluid) such as Marfak 0 or equivalent. (Refer to current contract schedules.)

(3) *Water pump grease.*—This grease is developed specifically for water pumps which employ gland packing. Such a grease should be high in calcium soap content to obtain the required consistency and melting point for adherence of the lubricant to the shaft when in contact with hot water.

(4) *Wheel bearing grease.*—This grease, fibrous in nature, has a high melting point and a very strong tendency to cling to bearing surfaces which makes it particularly suitable for the lubrication of parts and assemblies where centrifugal force tends to throw out the lubricant, but it is usually soluble in water. In all atmospheric temperatures down to approximately plus 10° F., use a grade No. 3 (hard) such as Marfak 3 or equivalent for roller bearings and in lower temperatures, use a grade No. 2.

(5) *Gear oils.*—These lubricants are heavy bodied pure mineral oils that are used for the lubrication of axle differentials, the steering gear, transmission and transfer case, and universal joints. Current SAE practice discontinues the use of references to SAE 110 and 160 gear oils in favor of SAE 140. Generally, the SAE 140 and SAE 90 grades of quality lubricants will serve for most equipment under ordinary summer and winter operations respectively. The SAE 140 is given a viscosity range in Saybolt universal seconds of 120 to 200 at 210° F. and must have such a consistency so as not to channel in service at plus 35° F. Extremes in temperature or service conditions may necessitate the use of SAE 80 (below minus 20° F.) or SAE 250 (high limit). Straight mineral oils rather than hypoid lubricants are recommended by reason of their stability and wide source of supply. Characteristics to be considered include such factors as sufficient viscosity to prevent wear, resistance to channeling at low temperatures, physical stability, facilitation of gear shifting during cold weather, and freedom from

gear clashing during warm weather. Another factor, while not related to lubrication proper, frequently causes modifications of specifications as concerns leakage and its elimination.

(6) *Fluid gear lubricant.*—Under certain conditions, a substitute for gear oil may be preferred in the form of a fluid gear lubricant of the Marfak grease type for use in the drive shaft and front axle universal joints to counteract the effects of water and limit loss of lubricant due to leakage through worn seals or loosened housings.

(7) *Miscellaneous fluids.*—(*a*) *Penetrating oil.*—This oil is used principally to get into places that have become very dry or rusty, such as brake linkage, nuts or bolts that cannot be loosened or tightened with a reasonable amount of effort, and to free or clean other mechanisms. It will not corrode any metal in machine construction.

(*b*) *Petrolatum.*—This compound is used for the distributor cam and to coat battery terminals and connections to reduce corrosion.

(*c*) *Cleaning solvent.*—This solvent is a compounded fluid used for washing engines, parts, and assemblies. It is not highly inflammable but should be employed with caution when used around hot engines.

(*d*) *Alcohol.*—Hydraulic brake parts should be cleaned with denatured alcohol. Gasoline, kerosene, cleaning solvents, and oils must not be used.

c. Weather factor.—In general, a lighter or lower viscosity lubricant is used in cold weather. Viscosity may be described incidentally as that quality of oil which increases or decreases under heat or the lack of it respectively. Like butter in the summer heat, it thins out whereas the same substance in the cold thickens and becomes hard, and the handling in lubrication equipment is affected accordingly.

93. Application.—Lubricants are applied to vehicles by employing the equipment provided by Tables of Basic Allowances.

a. Lubricating oils.—Oil should be poured into the engine crankcase through the filler pipe. Extreme care should be taken to prevent dirt and other foreign materials from entering the crankcase. Oil measures and funnels should be scrupulously clean. Oil is applied to other required surfaces by using an oil or squirt can.

b. Gear lubricants.—Gear lubricants should be introduced into gear cases through filler pipes. If a gear lubricant bucket with pump is available, it should be used to expedite the work. Care should be taken to prevent overfilling and the level should be checked after the mechanism has been warmed in operation.

c. Chassis lubricants.—Chassis lubricants should be applied by using a high pressure hand gun or a power operated grease gun. Lubrication fittings should be cleaned before the grease is applied.

Grease should be forced through the bearing until clean grease is visible on both ends of the bearing.

d. Water pump grease.—Water pump grease, when required, should be applied by using the grease cup.

e. Fiber greases.—To lubricate wheel bearings, the wheels should be dismounted, old grease removed, and bearings cleaned, dried, and inspected. The bearings should then be dipped or coated with engine lubricating oil (in order to cause the grease to adhere to the balls or rollers) and repacked with the grease. Care should be taken that the correct amount of lubricant is used and that the wheel bearings are properly adjusted. Close adherence to approved recommendations is essential.

f. Miscellaneous lubricants and fluids.—(1) *Spring lubricant.*—If the spring is provided with a spring cover, the lubricant should be forced into the cover. If no cover is provided, the spring should, when necessary, be removed, disassembled, cleaned, and thoroughly lubricated. Partial lubrication may be achieved by jacking up the vehicle, separating the spring leaves, and applying lubricant between the leaves with a putty knife, or by spraying.

(2) *Penetrating oil.*—If supplied in small quantities, the penetrating oil will usually be furnished in a can, similar to a squirt can, ready for use. If furnished in quart or larger containers, the oil should be removed from its container as required and applied with a squirt can.

(3) *Petrolatum or vaseline.*—Petrolatum or vaseline should be applied with a brush or in small quantities by hand.

(4) *Cleaning solvent.*—Cleaning solvent should be used with a stiff bristle brush or applied by an air operated cleaning gun. Metal brushes should never be used when cleaning an engine and the solvent should not be introduced into the interiors of the accessories, conduit, or oil lines.

g. Common mistakes.—Inexperienced men often make the following mistakes when lubricating vehicles:

(1) Ignoring lubricating charts and instructions.

(2) Substituting inferior or improper lubricants.

(3) Neglecting fittings or special lubrication requirements by reason of lacking proper lubricant for same instead of reporting circumstances promptly and securing necessary supplies.

(4) Changing the engine oil when the oil is cold. The oil should be changed immediately after a run of not less than 10 miles so that the solid contaminates (dirt, carbon, and metal particles) will be in suspension and drain out with the old oil.

(5) Maintaining the level of the engine oil too high, resulting in excessive oil pumping, plug fouling, and valve sticking.

(6) Diluting lubricating oil with kerosene except in an emergency when recommended oils are not available. When low prevailing temperatures warrant, lubricating oil dilution should be effected with electric transformer oil, Symbol 9045, which has a viscosity of 50 to 65 seconds at 130° F. Since the viscosity of kerosene is about one half as much, approximately double the quantity of kerosene ordinarily suggested will be required when the transformer oil is used but since the latter actually is a lubricant in effect, and kerosene has a mild abrasive action, the reason for the substitution is obvious. For instance, where the prevailing temperature is lower than 15° below zero, a mixture of 55 percent of the oil recommended by the manufacturer and 45 percent of Symbol 9045 will facilitate starting without affecting adversely the viscosity, lubricating film, or quality of the oil.

(7) Applying too much pressure on the water pump lubricant fitting, which forces away the packing and permits the escape of the lubricant into the cooling system.

(8) Maintaining the lubricant level too high in the transmission, transfer case, and differentials, which causes too much heat to be generated and permits the lubricant to escape to parts where it is undesirable. Grease retaining washers in the transmission and differential should be replaced as soon as they become unserviceable.

(9) Applying too much pressure to universal joints, which destroys the effectiveness of the grease retainers.

(10) Over lubricating rear wheel bearings, which forces grease past the retainer into the brake drum.

(11) Applying grease to a bearing whose parts are wet with kerosene or any other solvent. Such practice invites trouble. Bearing must be bone dry before grease is applied.

(12) Mixing extreme pressure greases made by one manufacturer with those made by another.

Section XVII

INSPECTIONS

	Paragraph
General	94
Command	95
Maintenance	96
Technical	97

94. General.—*a. Purpose.*—Inspection has as its purpose the detection of deficiencies of mechanical condition, quality of maintenance

TM 9–705

ORDNANCE DEPARTMENT

INSPECTION

WAR DEPARTMENT
QMC Form No. 260 **TECHNICAL INSPECTION REPORT OF MOTOR VEHICLES**
Tentative

This form indicates the scope of complete technical inspection of all motor vehicles for all echelons. It does not prescribe a required routine or procedure. Items will be checked to the extent of ability of personnel and adequacy of equipment available.

Date _____
Vehicle Nomenclature _____
U. S. A. Registration No _____ Mileage _____
Organization _____ Station _____
Supply Arm or Service Maintaining Vehicle _____
Check ✓, is satisfactory, X adjustment made, X X repair or replacement needed.

EXTERNAL INSPECTION

1. Bumpers _____
2. Boards, running ____
3. Body _____
4. Bows _____
5. Camber** _____
6. Carrier, tire _____
7. Caster** _____
8. Curtains _____
9. Doors _____
10. Fenders _____
11. Gate, tail _____
12. Glass _____
13. Guards, headlight __
14. Guard, radiator ___
15. Hood _____
16. Hooks, tow _____
17. Lights _____
18. Paint _____
19. Pintles _____
20. Radiator _____
21. Tires _____
22. Top _____
23. Toe-in _____
24. _____
25. _____

HOOD UP (ENGINE STOPPED)

26. Anti-freeze _____
27. Assembly, breaker pt _____
28. Baffles, intercyl.* _____
29. Battery _____
30. Belt, fan _____
31. Cleaner, air ____
32. Compressor, air __
33. Engine, oil _____
34. Fan, cooling ____
35. Filter, fuel _____
36. Filter, oil (external) _____
37. Filter, oil (in eng.)* _____

38. Fluid brake _____
39. Governor, seal __
40. Housing, steer. gear _____
41. Pump, water ___
42. Shroud, engine* _
43. Spark plugs ____
44. Strainer, fuel pump _____
45. Strainer, scavenge oil* _____
46. System, fire exting _____
47. _____
48. _____

HOIST VEHICLE (IF PRACTICABLE)

(Except full track & rear end of half-track vehicles)

49. Axle, front _____
50. Axle, frt. drive, lubr'n _____
51. Axle, rear _____
52. Axle, rear, lubr'n _
53. Body, bolts ____
54. Engine, side pans _
55. Frame, distortion _
56. Frame, rivets ___
57. Joints, universal _
58. Lines, brake (hydr.-air) _____
59. Linkage, brake (mech) _____
60. Linkage, steering _____
61. Shafts, propeller _
62. Spring, front assembly _____
63. Spring, rear assembly _____
64. Shock absorbers, fill _____

65. Tank, air _____
66. Trf. case - sub - trans _____
67. Trf. case-sub-tr., lubr'n _____
68. Transmission ___
69. Transmission, lubr'n _____
70. Wheels, front, adjustment and trueness ____
71. Wheels, front, lubr'n _____
72. Wheels, rear ___
73. _____
74. _____
75. _____

INTERNAL INSP. (START ENGINE)

76. Ammeter _____
77. Accelerator ____
78. Choke _____
79. Cut-out _____
80. Extinguisher, fire _
81. Filter, trans. oil* _
82. Gauge, air _____
83. Gauge, fuel ____
84. Gauge, oil _____
85. Generator _____
86. Horn _____
87. Indicator, heat __
88. Insulation, hull* _
89. Lights _____
90. Pad, protecting* _
91. Protector, peep hole* _____
92. Pump, priming* _
93. Seats, troop ____
94. Starting motor __
95. Switch, battery* _
96. Switch, ignition _
97. Switch, mesh. starter* _____

* Ordnance vehicles.   ** Normally 3d and 4th echelons.

TM 9-705

SCOUT CARS AND MORTAR MOTOR CARRIAGE   94

SCHEDULE

98. Switch, sol. starter*_____
99. Switch, starter_____
100. Tachometer*_____
101. Tools_____
102. Throttle_____
103. Upholstery_____
104. Wiper, windshield_____
105. Viscometer_____
106. Voltmeter*_____
107. _____
108. _____

HOOD UP (ENGINE RUNNING)

109. Engine noise_____
110. Engine, smoothness_____
111. Engine mounting_____
112. Gaskets (all)___
113. Leaks, fuel_____
114. Leaks, oil_____
115. Leaks, water___
116. Valves, noise___
117. Wiring, ignition___
118. Wiring, other___
119. _____
120. _____
121. _____

ROAD TEST VEHICLE

122. Body, noise_____
123. Brakes, hand____
124. Brakes, service_
125. Brakes, steering*_____

126. Clutch_____
127. Drive units, noise_____
128. Engine, noise___
129. Engine, smoothness_____
130. Engine, power__
131. Gear shift_____
132. Governor_____
133. Shock absorbers
134. Speedometer___
135. Steering mech__
136. _____
137. _____
138. _____
139. _____
140. _____

COMBAT VEHICLES*

SUSPENSION (FOR FULL TRACK AND REAR END OF HALF-TRACK VEHICLES)

141. Arm, bogie_____
142. Bearing, bogie arm_____
143. Final drive, lubr'n_____
144. Leaks, final drive_____
145. Leaks, wheel bearing_____
146. Springs, suspension_____
147. Sprocket_____
148. Tires, bogie____
149. Track, adjustment_____
150. Track, metal compon'ts___

151. Track, rubber compon'ts___
152. Tube, axle_____
153. Wear, bogie link
154. Wear, bogie link pin_____
155. Wear, gudgeon
156. Wear, gudgeon guides_____
157. Wear, sprocket_
158. Wheel, bogie___
159. Wheel, idler____

TURRET

160. Insulation_____
161. Locks, top door_
162. Lock, turret____
163. Mech. traversing_____
164. Protective, peep hole_____
165. Rollers, turret supporting___

AMMUNITION RACKS

166. Condition_____
167. Packing, leather_____

GUN MOUNTS (TO BE LISTED)

168. _____
169. _____
170. _____
171. _____
172. _____
173. _____
174. _____
175. _____

REPAIRS REQUIRED (EXPLANATION)

_____
_____
_____
_____
_____

REMARKS AND RECOMMENDATIONS: _____

_____
_____
_____

----------------------------   ----------------------------
         Inspector.   Supervising Officer.

RA FSD 547

operation, appearance, servicing, vehicle operation, and the recommendation of corrective measures to prevent recurrence of such deficiencies.

b. Scope.—While the appearance of the vehicle as a whole is of some concern, the important inspection is that which covers the normal adjustments and mechanical condition of operating units and investigates the lubrication requirements of the vehicle with a view to maintaining the standards of reliability and performance originally built into the vehicle. Such inspections are classified as command, maintenance, and technical.

(1) *Negligence.*—Visual detection of negligence is possible resulting in accumulation of grease, oil, and dirt in the vehicle, rusty unpainted surfaces, and loose equipment representing elementary faults which may lead to trouble.

(2) *Faulty practices.*—Such practices, common to both operation and maintenance, include speeding, riding the clutch, habitually clashing gears, refilling grease guns indiscriminately with any lubricant at hand, and overlooking vital points during inspection routines. It is also improper to alter or modify any vehicle or part thereof without authority. Special devices may not be added to a vehicle except in cases where experimentation is authorized, and no component or equipment may be removed or omitted unless specifically ordered.

(3) *Corrective measures.*—Suggestions toward changes in design prompted by chronic failure or malfunctions, equipment changes, inspection and maintenance methods, safety, efficiency, economy, and comfort should be forwarded to the ordnance officer.

95. Command.—It is the duty of all commanders to make regular and frequent inspections of their motor vehicles and of the operation and maintenace activities of their commands.

96. Maintenance.—These inspections are a preventive maintenance function, the responsibility of operating organization commanders, and a part of scheduled maintenance operations.

a. Daily and weekly.—Such inspections are made normally by the chief of section under supervision of unit officers and consist in checking and supervising the maintenance work of the vehicle operator. The serviceability and completeness of tools and other equipment should be checked thoroughly. A guide for his weekly inspection should be drawn up and issued to fit the particular vehicles assigned. (See inspection schedule below.)

b. Monthly (1,000-mile).—The monthly maintenance inspection is a check on the maintenance of the unit's vehicles. Normally it is made by the motor officer of the unit concerned but may be made by

TM 9-705

SCOUT CARS AND MORTAR MOTOR CARRIAGE 96-98

the regimental, battalion, or similar unit motor officer. The motor officer spot checks such items as he believes necessary, including those that are inaccessible or frequently neglected. He should make a short road test of the vehicle.

97. Technical.—*a. Purpose.*—Technical inspections are a follow-up and check on maintenance functions and determine whether the vehicle should be continued in service or withdrawn from operation for overhaul.

b. Period.—Except as otherwise specified in service manuals or handbooks pertaining to special purpose and combat vehicles, all vehicles will be given this inspection by personnel of third or fourth echelon maintenance units once every 6 months, or after 6,000 miles of operation whenever a vehicle is run more than 6,000 miles in a single 6 months' period. Commissioned officers supervising technical inspections of motor vehicles will enter under "Remarks" on W. D., Q. M. C. Form No. 260, all repairs found due to vehicle abuses and will report such abuses to the regimental commander. If repairs are considered not due to vehicle abuse, this fact will be stated.

Section XVIII

GENERAL CARE; PRESERVATION; RECORDS

	Paragraph
Cleaning	98
Painting	99
Storage	100
Ordnance Motor Book	101
Transfer of vehicles	102

98. Cleaning.—*a. General.*—Grit, dirt, and mud are the sources of greatest wear to a vehicle. If deposits of dirt and grit are allowed to accumulate, particles will soon find their way into bearing surfaces, causing unnecessary wear and eventually serious difficulty. Before removing engine parts or any other units, making repairs and replacements, or inspecting where working joints or bearing surfaces are to be exposed, carefully remove all dirt and grit that might find their way to the exposed surfaces. Use clean tools and exercise care to eliminate the possibilities of brushing dirt or grit accidentally into the openings. To cut oil-soaked dirt and grit, hardened grit, or road oil, use dry-cleaning solvent applied with waste, rags, or a brush.

b. Water.—The vehicle is so designed that the possibility of interfering with its proper operation by the careless application of cleaning water is very small. However, care should be taken to keep water from the engine as it might interfere with proper ignition and carburetion. Water should not be permitted to stand on exposed metal parts as it will cause rust. Such exposed parts shall be painted as soon as conditions permit. Rust may be softened by using dry-cleaning solvent or penetrating oil and scraping with a piece of wood. Oilholes which have become clogged should be opened with a piece of wire; wood should never be used for this purpose, as splinters are likely to break off and permanently clog the passages.

c. Reference.—For further instructions in cleaning and description and use of cleaning and preserving materials, see * TM 9–850.

d. Chemicals.—Particular care should be taken to clean thoroughly all vehicles that have been involved with chemicals. Vehicles that have laid smoke screens or gas barrages will have deposited a substance that is extremely irritable to the skin, even after long periods of storage, and should be thoroughly washed with a cleaning solution as soon as possible after the maneuver is completed. An engine that has had chemicals introduced through its carburetor may have to be exchanged for a new one, as such engines must be disassembled by the service personnel for cleaning.

99. Painting.—*a. Issue.*—The paints issued for painting scout cars are olive-drab, black, red, and white, put up in cans ready for use, and applicable to both wood and metal parts. The olive-drab paint is used for the outside of the vehicle. Black paint is used on the floors and to coat the various implement fastenings. Red paint is used to make oil and grease fittings stand out prominently.

b. Preparation.—If paint is too thick, turpentine should be used as a thinner, but not to exceed 2 percent by volume. All parts to be painted should be free from dirt or grease. They may be washed in a liquid made by dissolving ½-pound of sal soda in 8 quarts of warm water. Rinse in clean water and wipe thoroughly dry. Where the vehicle surfaces are in fair condition and marred only in spots, the marred places should be primed with olive-drab paint, second coat, and permitted to dry. The whole surface should then be dulled with flint paper, receive another coat of paint, and be allowed to dry thoroughly before use. After repeated painting, the paint may become so thick as to scale off in places or give an unsightly appearance. It may be removed for repainting by using paint and varnish remover. Use the solution freshly mixed and apply to the parts where paint

---

*See Appendix.

is to be removed with a brush or with waste tied to the end of a stick. When the solution begins to dry on the surface, use a scraper to remove the old paint and complete the cleaning of the surface with rags and water. Before painting, wash the surface with a sal soda solution, rinse with clean water and wipe thoroughly as described above.

c. Equipment.—Vehicle equipment will be painted the same as when issued. The shovel, ax, hatchet, and mattock should be painted to conform to the exterior. After camouflage, which includes exterior accessories, the items should always be in conformity to the vehicle pattern from which removed to avoid interruption of the color scheme.

100. Storage.—All vehicles to be stored for an indefinite period (dead storage) are, if possible, placed in good mechanical condition before storing; otherwise each vehicle is tagged to show what repairs are required before it is returned to service.

a. Removing parts.—All removable parts such as spark plugs, lamps, carburetors, distributors, starting motors, generators, etc., and small tools are removed, wrapped in oiled paper to exclude moisture, and packed in a separate box for each vehicle. Each box is marked to identify it with the proper vehicle and may be stored separately in warehouses, if practicable. All tires and batteries are removed and stored as indicated in *f* and *h* below.

b. Draining.—Fuel tanks are drained and the openings plugged. The cooling system is drained also, and all drain cocks are opened and cleaned with a wire to insure removal of sediment that may impede the flow of water. A light oil should be placed in the water pump.

c. Blocking.—All vehicles in storage, whether in the open, in sheds, or in closed warehouses, are jacked up and blocked to keep the wheels off the ground.

d. Engine.—The crankcase is drained and flushed with a light oil other than kerosene which causes corrosion. About half a pint of heavy mineral oil is poured into each cylinder and distributed by cranking the engine. Oil, grease or graphite is placed in the threads of the spark plug holes. All openings are plugged with tapered, fitted wooden plugs. All exposed metal parts are given a coating of suitable slushing oil. A tag is placed on the engine on which inspectors enter initials and inspection dates.

e. Chassis.—Vehicles are completely serviced before storing and all exposed metal parts are slushed.

f. Tires.—Pneumatic tires and tubes should be kept in a cool, dark, dry place (50° to 60° F.). Used casings should be repaired, cleaned, and wrapped in burlap, paper, or cloth, and stored vertically side by side. Tubes should be deflated, removed from the casing, cleaned, repaired, folded loosely, and stored in pasteboard cartons. Care should be taken that there are no sharp folds and that a small amount of air should be left in the tube to keep creases from forming.

g. Bodies.—All exposed metal parts of the body should be slushed thoroughly. Collapsible tops should be raised. Vehicles stored in the open should be covered with paulins.

h. Storage batteries.—Batteries removed from vehicles will be pooled with the general stock of issue batteries and kept charged and in service whenever possible. For details of care and maintenance see paragraph 54.

i. Equipment.—Leather equipment will be preserved in accordance with instructions contained in AR 30–3040. Web equipment, felt washers, and other textiles will be sprinkled with flake napthalene as a moth preventive. The recommended concentration is obtained with about 1 pound of naphthalene per 100 cubic feet of material. Thick paper gaskets and paper gasket material will be kept impregnated with light oil to prevent shrinkage and drying. Carbon tetrachloride types of fire extinguishers must be kept filled with liquid to avoid decomposition and deformation of the cork seats and washers therein. Water is permissible in stored extinguishers in lieu of regular extinguisher liquid in emergencies only. Flashlights must be stored without battery cells to avoid sulphation which otherwise will occur with a resultant ruination of the flashlight housing and terminals. All other tools and accessories will be repainted or regreased if necessary.

j. Inspection of vehicles in storage.—Inspection of vehicles in storage will be made not less than once each month, under the direct supervision of a commissioned officer, to see that instructions contained in AR 850–15 are being complied with.

k. Slushing oil.—Oil drained from crankcases, gear oil thinned with crankcase oil, or oil purchased for the purpose may serve as a slushing oil.

101. Ordnance Motor Book.—An accurate record must be kept of each automotive vehicle issued by the Ordnance Department. For this purpose the Ordnance Motor Book, generally called "Log Book", is issued with each vehicle and should accompany it in service at all times. The book will habitually be kept in a canvas cover to protect it from damage. Instructions for making the entries are printed within the binder.

102. Transfer of vehicles.—Records involved in a transfer of vehicles include the following:

a. Memorandum receipt of the responsible officer.

b. Mechanical inspection report.

c. Vehicle "Log Book."

Section XIX

SPARE PARTS AND ACCESSORIES

	Paragraph
Spare parts	103
Accessories	104

103. Spare parts.—*a. General.*—Parts become unserviceable through breakage or through wear resulting from continuous usage. For this reason, certain parts are provided for replacement purposes. These parts are divided into two groups, spare parts and basic spare parts. The using arm has no concern with basic spare parts except possibly to draw a part from the ordnance maintenance company. They should be kept clean and lightly oiled to prevent rust.

b. Spare parts.—These are extra parts provided with the combat vehicle for replacement of those most likely to fail and are for use by the using arms in making minor repairs. Sets of spare parts should be complete at all times as far as possible. The allowances of spare parts are prescribed in pertinent Standard Nomenclature Lists.

104. Accessories.—Accessories include tools and equipment required for disassembling and assembling, cleaning and preservation of the equipment, and tools which may be termed "trouble tools" such as axes, shovels, etc. They also include covers, tool rolls, chests, etc., necessary for storage and protection when the equipment is not in use or when traveling. Accessories should not be used for purposes other than as prescribed and when not in use should be stored in the places or receptacles provided. There are a number of accessories, the names or general characteristics of which indicate their uses or application, therefore detailed descriptions or methods of use are not outlined herein. However, accessories embodying special features or having special uses are described below.

a. Accessories carried on the vehicle.—Accessories issued with scout cars, M3 and M3A1, and mortar motor carriage, M2, are listed in Standard Nomenclature List No. G–67. Those carried on the vehicle are located as shown in figures 1, 2, and 44 for scout car, M3; figures 5 and 6 for mortar motor carriage, M2; and figures 7, 8, and 45 for scout car, M3A1.

b. Special accessories.—(1) *Book, Ordnance Motor.*—The motor book is used for the purpose of keeping an accurate record of each vehicle. It must always remain with the vehicle regardless of where it may be sent. This book should be in possession of the organization at all times, and is solely the responsibility of the company commander as to the completeness of the records and as to its whereabouts. It must also contain date of issuance of the vehicle, to and by whom issued, and place where issued.

NOTE.—Data pertaining to the records of assignment must be removed and destroyed prior to entering combat.

(2) *Extinguisher, fire, Pyrene.*—A 1-quart Pyrene type fire extinguisher is mounted in the driver's compartment. The extinguisher should be frequently checked for leakage and if found to be leaking or after having been partially or fully discharged, should be replaced as soon as possible.

(3) *Helmet.*—The helmets issued are of padded leather construction. They provide protection to the wearer against possible head injuries.

(4) *Wrench, combination, oil adjusting, crowfoot.*—The purpose of this wrench is stated in paragraph 7*k* (2) and its method of use shown in figure 12.

c. Armament accessories.—Information pertaining to the spare parts and accessories issued with each gun and mount listed in paragraph 4*b*, their maintenance, or their care and preservation, may be found in pertinent Standard Nomenclature Lists or appropriate Field Manuals.

SECTION XX

ARMAMENT AND MOUNTS

	Paragraph
General	105
Tripod mount, M2	106
Tripod mount, M3	107
Elevating mechanism	108
Tripod mount, M1917A1	109
Pedestal mount, T34	110
Elevating and traversing mechanism	111
4.2 chemical mortar mount	112
Carriage mount, M22	113
Carriage mount, M21	114
Carriage mount, D36961	115

105. General.—*a. Armament.*—The type and number of weapons provided for the vehicles are tabulated in paragraph 4*b*. References in connection with pertinent Standard Nomenclature Lists and Technical Manuals are given in the Appendix.

SCOUT CARS AND MORTAR MOTOR CARRIAGE

b. Ammunition.—The ammunition is carried in ammunition chests which are stored in the various racks and space available.

c. Mounts.—The type and number of gun mounts provided for the vehicles are also tabulated in paragraph 4*b* and described in succeeding paragraphs.

106. Tripod mount, M2.—The tripod mount shown in figures 46 and 47, is a fixed height, folding tripod with tubular legs. Rigidity in firing position is obtained by fixed stops and by the use of the traversing bar which converts the rear legs into an **A** truss. The traversing bar also forms the rear gun support through the elevating mechanism and serves as the elevating and traversing base. The tripod head houses the pintle bushing which assembles the tapered pintle of the machine gun.

a. Purpose.—This mount supersedes the emergency tripod, Mk. IA1, and is suitable for use with all caliber .30, heavy barrel, Browning machine guns. It is used by the Cavalry in pack transport, and as a ground mount for caliber .30 machine guns in the scout car, M3, group.

b. Description.—Referring to figure 46, the tripod consists of the tripod head (1) which connects the right (2) and left (3) rear legs and the front leg (5); a traversing bar (4) mounts between the rear legs.

(1) *Tripod head.*—The tripod head is machined to seat the bronze pintle bushing (6), graduated traversing dial (7), pintle lock (8), and dial locking screw (9). The traversing dial is adjustable, rotates in the pintle bushing, and is held in place by a flange on the inside diameter of the dial which slides in the under cut bearing on the shoulder of the pintle bushing. The dial is clamped in any desired position by means of the dial locking knob (10). Turning the knob clockwise will fasten the dial, and vice versa. The dial locking knob stop (11) is provided to prevent loss of the knob.

(2) *Pintle lock.*—The pintle lock is assembled in the pintle lock housing (12) and attached by screws to the under side of the tripod head. The pintle lock is constructed to engage a groove in the pintle, thereby securing the gun pintle in 360° traverse. The upper side of the pintle lock is beveled to allow assembly of the pintle in the pintle bushing without withdrawing the pintle lock. The assembly consists of the flat pintle lock (13) actuated by two helical pintle lock springs (14) by means of the pintle lock knob (15). To disengage the pintle lock, the knob is pulled back and turned until the projection of the knob rests on the housing.

(3) *Tripod legs.*—The tripod legs are made from seamless steel tubing, assembled with welded spades. Steel leg hinges are in-

TM 9-705
106   ORDNANCE DEPARTMENT

serted in the other end of the tubing and welded for connection with the tripod head by bolts (16) and (17).

(4) *Traversing bar.*—The traversing bar is graduated to form the seat for the traversing slide of the elevating mechanism. Connection of the traversing bar (4) and the rear legs is through bolts (16) in the sliding sleeves, right (18) and left (19). The sleeves slide on the legs between the stops provided and the sleeve latch (20), assembled at the right leg, locks the sliding sleeve and retains the traversing bar in firing position. When folding the rear legs, the sleeve latch is released by pressing down the handle; the sleeve on the right leg is pushed toward the bottom and the sleeve on the left leg is pushed toward the top.

(5) *Pintle.*—The pintle (21) is attached to the bracket on the under side of the machine gun by the pintle bolt (22) which forms the connection between the tripod and machine gun. The pintle consists of a tapered stem made integral with a yoke that straddles the gun connection. The stem is hollow but closed at the top by an expansion plug. This pintle is made interchangeable with tripod mount, M3, by the two angular grooves in the stem which engage the pintle lock on the tripod. The upper groove is for the caliber .30 mount and the lower, for the caliber .50 mount.

c. Mounting.—(1) Remove gun with elevating mechanism and tripod from vehicle. It is recommended that the sliding sleeves on tripod legs, traversing bar, traversing slide, pintle, and pintle bushing be cleaned and lubricated prior to mounting.

(2) Spread rear legs of tripod until traversing bar slides into place against stops and sleeve latch is engaged.

(3) Swing tripod forward to throw front leg into place against stops and place tripod in position.

(4) Assemble gun on tripod by inserting pintle on gun into place in pintle bushing on tripod, secure elevating mechanism, and place traversing slide on traversing bar.

d. Dismounting.—(1) Disengage pintle lock from groove in pintle by pulling back knob and turning it until projection knob rests on the housing.

(2) Release traversing slide lock lever and swing out elevating mechanism.

(3) Lift gun, with pintle and elevating mechanism attached, from tripod.

(4) Push down sleeve latch thereby releasing the sliding sleeve on right leg and permitting it to slide toward the bottom while the sliding sleeve on the left leg goes toward the top.

(5) Assemble gun and tripod in carriage and hanger respectively.

107. Tripod mount, M3.—The tripod mount shown in figures 48 and 49 is a variable height, folding tripod with telescoping legs. Rigidity in firing position is obtained by fixed stops and the use of the traversing bar which converts the rear legs into an **A** truss. The traversing bar also forms the rear gun support and serves as a base for manipulating the gun in elevation and traverse. The tripod head houses the pintle housing which assembles the tapered pintle of the machine gun. The height of the mount, adjustments, and leveling may be varied by positioning the front leg in addition to adjusting the length of all three legs by the telescoping extensions. Normal mounting of the tripod is with the front leg set at an angle of 60° and all extensions home. In this position on level ground, the center of the gun trunnion is at a height of 10 inches and the mount is stable. If this height is increased, the recoil of the caliber .50 gun destroys stability and makes mandatory the extension of the rear legs if stability is to be retained.

a. Purpose.—This mount is complementary to the caliber .50, heavy barrel, Browning machine gun. It is issued to the Cavalry for use in pack transport and as a ground mount for caliber .50 machine guns in combat vehicles.

b. Description.—Referring to figure 48, the description of this tripod is similar to that in paragraph 106*b*.

(1) *Tripod head.*—See paragraph 106*b*. (1).

(2) *Pintle lock.*—See paragraph 106*b*. (2).

(3) *Tripod legs.*—The tripod legs are made from seamless steel tubing. The lower sections are made integral with the formed steel feet (15) and (16) and assembled with welded spades (17) and (18). The leg extensions are controlled by the spring actuated indexing lever (19) assembled in a bracket in each upper leg section, engaging holes drilled at regular intervals in the telescoping sections. Clamping the telescoping sections is accomplished by means of the threaded handle (20) welded to the lower split end of the upper section. The front leg upper section is equipped with a serrated yoke which engages serrated plates (21); the latter are fastened to the tripod head by clamp screw (22), nut (23), and handle (24). Pin (25) is assembled to the nut to prevent it from being lost. The rear leg upper sections are equipped with steel hinges (26) and are secured to the tripod head by bolts (27).

(4) *Traversing bar.*—The traversing bar is graduated and forms the seat for the traversing slide of the elevating mechanism. Connection of the traversing bar (4) and the rear legs is through bolts (31) in the sliding sleeve (28) and the permanent sleeve (30). The

sleeve on the right rear leg slides between stops provided and the sleeve latch (29) locks the sliding sleeve and retains the traversing bar in firing position. When folding the rear legs, the sleeve latch is released by pressing down the handle and the sliding sleeve pushed toward the bottom.

(5) *Pintle.*—The pintle (32) is atached to the bracket on the under side of the machine gun by the pintle bolt (33) which forms the connection between the tripod and machine gun. The pintle consists of a tapered stem made integral with a yoke that straddles the gun connection. The stem is hollow but closed at the top by an expansion plug. This pintle is made interchangeable with tripod mount, M2, by the two angular grooves in the stem which engage the pintle lock on the tripod. The lower groove is for this mount.

108. Elevating mechanism.—The elevating mechanisms shown in figure 50 are generally similar in function and also apply for use with the caliber .30 gun mounts for scout car, M3, with slight modifications. Each mechanism is a double screw assembly which is secured at its upper end to the gun yoke by the elevating mechanism adapter bolt and at its lower end to the traversing bar through the traversing slide.

a. Description.—(1) *Upper elevating screw.*—This screw (30) is threaded on its outside diameter with a right-hand Acme triple thread to fit the threaded inside diameter of the lower elevating screw (32). The upper screw is hollow and closed at the top by a plug with a light drive fit. Assembled inside the hollow screw and at its lower end is the upper elevating screw stop pin and washer which stops against a shoulder on the inside of the lower elevating screw (32) and thereby prevents the disengagement of the upper and lower elevating screw past maximum elevation. A keyway in the upper screw carries the elevating scale plate (39) with 50 mil divisions, each division representing one complete revolution of the elevating handwheel (34).

(2) *Lower elevating mechanism.*—This screw (32) is threaded on its outside diameter with a left-hand Acme triple thread to fit the threaded inside diameter of the elevating mechanism sleeve (33). The upper end of the screw is provided with a head which assembles the handwheel (34).

(3) *Elevating mechanism sleeve.*—Provision against disengaging the lower elevating screw and the elevating sleeve (33) is afforded by means of the rectangular lower elevating screw stop pin riveted to the stop spring. This spring is assembled in a dovetailed seat on the outside of the sleeve. The pin rides on top of the lower elevat-

ing screw thread until it snaps into a notch at the lower end of the thread. A finger grip is provided on the upper end of the spring to disengage the stop pin from the notch. The sleeve is closed on its lower end by the plug.

(4) *Elevating handwheel.*—The handwheel (34) is graduated into 50 divisions, each division representing 1-mil change in elevation. The handwheel is locked to the lower screw by the elevating handwheel lock screw (37). The retaining screw (38) is provided for manufacturing purposes only and is used to synchronize the graduations in the handwheel with the divisions of the elevating scale plate (39) inserted in the slot of the upper screw.

(5) *Click mechanism.*—The handwheel is equipped with a spring actuated indexing device consisting of an indexing pawl and the indexing pawl spring held in place by the handwheel plug. When the handwheel is turned, this device produces a perceptible click resulting from the indexing pawl engaging notches cut in the elevating handwheel click ring. The latter is housed in and moves vertically with the handwheel, but is kept from rotating by a projection which slides in the longitudinal keyway of the stationary upper screw. Fifty notches are spaced equally around the circumference of the click ring to correspond with the handwheel graduations; each click movement indicates 1-mil change in elevation. An elevating mechanism indicator is assembled to the top of the click ring.

(6) *Traversing slide.*—The traversing slide (31) is locked to the elevating sleeve and clamped in position on the traversing bar of the tripod by the traversing slide lock lever (42). The slide has a limited pivoting movement, controlled by the stop screw (40) which insures full contact of the slide on the traversing bar in all positions of traverse. The slide is clamped on the traversing bar by a lock lever which is assembled on the traversing slide locking screw (43) by a serrated joint held in place with a screw (44). This construction permits the handle to be set at any desired angle. The traversing slide lock spring (45) serves to hold the handle at any set position and enables the gunner to set the handle so that the free and clamped positions are constant and most convenient for thumb operation.

b. Functioning.—The upper elevating screw, being attached to the gun yoke, does not revolve but is free to move up and down in the lower screw. The lower screw is rotated by the elevating handwheel and moves up and down in the thread of the stationary sleeve. One turn of the handwheel clockwise raises the lower screw in the left-hand thread of the sleeve and at the same time raises the upper screw in the right-hand inside thread of the lower screw, thereby raising the gun connection. Anticlockwise movement of the handwheel will lower the gun.

109. Tripod mount, M1917A1.—The tripod mount shown in figures 51 and 52 is a variable height, folding tripod, with tubular legs, based on the M1917 machine-gun tripod design but incorporating a new cradle assembly. The mount is primarily intended for the Browning machine gun, caliber .30, M1917 (water-cooled), and its subcaliber training weapon. The cradle is designed so that the gun is mounted in the approximate line of recoil, thereby increasing stability. The slots in the cradle arc permit of elevation to provide for both ground and antiaircraft fire.

a. Description.—Referring to figure 51, the tripod mount consists of the pintle socket (1) which connects the left (2) and right (3) front legs, and the rear leg (4); an elevating and traversing mechanism (5), and a cradle assembly (6). In actual service with the scout cars, however, the elevating and traversing mechanism is incorporated with the cradle assembly and the latter in turn is mounted and dismounted as a semipermanent part of the gun.

(1) *Pintle socket.*—The central member of the tripod consists of a socket with three projecting serrated lugs. It is identical with the M1917 type except for an enlargement of the seat for the pintle clamping block.

(2) *Pintle.*—The gun pintle (13) rests in the gun pintle support assembled in the forward part of the cradle frame, and is held in detachable position by the quick release gun pintle lock. The pintle is semipermanently attached to the gun at the trunnion block by a pintle bolt assembly which permits the gun with its pintle to be dismounted if necessary.

(3) *Tripod legs.*—The tripod legs are made from seamless steel tubing, assembled with welded spades. Jam handles (7) are assembled to the serrated leg ends by inserting a pin (8) into the respective lugs of the pintle socket. If the jamming handles are unscrewed about one-fourth turn, the height of the legs can be varied or they can be folded back along the rear leg or trail for convenience in transporting the tripod.

(4) *Cradle.*—The D7431 cradle assembly (6) is offset to provide for 1,156 mils (65°) elevation in the cradle slots and designed to rotate in the cradle pintle socket. The cradle frame is of boxlike construction, consisting of two side plates (9) and (10) rigidly assembled and alined by bolts and spacers, and is assembled to the pintle yoke by two trunnion studs. The rear end houses the elevating and traversing mechanism assembly. The ammunition chest support (11) is attached

to the left-side plate. A mil-graduated scale reading 500 to 0 to 400 in increments of 100 each, subdivided by lines equaling 25 mils, is etched on the right-side plate. The frame is adjusted for elevation by a cradle clamping handle (12) adjacent to the right-side plate.

(5) *Elevating and traversing mechanism.*—The D31559 (superseding C59815) elevating and traversing assembly (5) is housed in the rear of the cradle frame. The head of the elevating screw is connected to the gun elevating bracket with an elevating screw joint pin. Slow-motion elevation and traverse within the cradle in increments of one mil are provided through elevating and traversing screws. The motion may be noted from the scale or by the conventional click method. Details of this mechanism are described further in paragraph 111 and shown in figure 54.

b. Mounting.—(1) Remove tripod from vehicle; spread and adjust the tripod legs until the pintle socket assembly is approximately level.

(2) Remove gun, with cradle and elevating mechanism, from carriage mount and secure in the cradle pintle socket with the cradle pintle clamping screw handle.

(3) Adjust the cradle assembly to zero by means of the mil-graduated elevating scale on the right-side plate of the cradle frame, and the index.

110. Pedestal mount, T34.—*a. Description.*—The mount shown in figure 53 is composed of the pedestal assembly (1), cradle (2) with pintle (3) attached, and mounts the Browning machine gun, caliber .30, M1919A4, flexible, with gun pintle (29) attached.

(1) *Pedestal.*—The Pedestal (1) is mounted on the running board (4) of the vehicle and is secured to the side of the vehicle by pedestal bracket (5). The pedestal is machined to seat the cradle pintle which rotates 360° and is adjustable vertically for travel and firing position. Both positions are controlled by the spring loaded cradle pintle lock (6) engaging the upper groove (7) for travel position (shown) and the lower groove (8) for firing position of the mount. The weight of the cradle assembly and gun is supported by the pintle buffer spring (9). Pintle clamp locking screw assembly (10) is provided to lock the pintle in any position of traverse.

(2) *Cradle.*—The cradle is the standard type cradle adopted for machine guns (par. 109a (4)). Swing of the cradle for elevating the gun within the range of the cradle slots is controlled by the clamp handle (12).

(3) *Elevating and traversing mechanism.*—The elevating and traversing mechanism (11) is provided to control fire accuracy. (See par. 109a (5)).

(4) *Gun pintle.*—The machine gun is assembled to the cradle by the gun pintle (13) which is seated in a housing secured to the cradle plates. The pintle is locked to the cradle by the spring-loaded pintle lock (14) which engages a groove in the gun pintle. The rear end of the gun is secured to the cradle by a pin (15), connecting the end of the elevating screw of the elevating mechanism with the gun bracket.

b. Dismounting.—To dismount the gun from the pedestal for ground fire from the tripod, dismount the cradle (2) with the cradle pintle (3) attached by releasing the pintle clamp locking screw (10) withdrawing cradle pintle lock (6) and lifting the gun with its cradle and control mechanism (11) attached.

111. Elevating and traversing mechanism.—The earlier type C59815 mechanism employed for the Browning machine guns, caliber .30, M1917A1 and M1919A4 (pedestal mount, T34), was redesigned according to drawing D31559 and is shown in figure 54. The mechanism is assembled in body (1), which is mounted on the traversing screw (2) and guide (3). Screw (2) is supported at the ends by bearing (4) and click plate (5), and is actuated by traversing knob (6).

a. Description.—At right angles to the traversing screw (2), the body assembles the elevating screw (7) which is actuated by elevating knob (8). The upper end of the elevating screw is machined to seat bushing (9) which in turn forms the seat for pin (10). The bushing construction permits a slight motion in the direction of the line of recoil controlled by a retaining screw which engages a slot milled in the top of the bushing. The elevating screw stop (11) is provided to stop the elevating screw at maximum elevation. The adjustable scales (12 and 13), on the elevating and traversing knobs respectively, are secured in position by the knurled nuts (15).

b. Click mechanism.—A click mechanism is provided for the elevating and traversing mechanisms which indicates a perceptible click to the hand of the gunner for each 1-mil change in elevation or traverse of the machine gun.

112. 4.2 chemical mortar mount.—*a. Description.*—(1) The 4.2 inch chemical mortar for motor mount is shown in figure 55. It consists of a barrel (1) which is mounted on the carriage frame (2) and adjusted in elevation by means of the elevating mechanism, (3). The latter pivots on the traversing screw (4) and is connected with the coupling (5), which is attached to the barrel by the pin assembly (6) passing through the elevating screw (7). Traverse of the weapon is by means of the traversing screw (4) engaging a nut integral with the elevating screw housing. The traversing screw is rotated by means of the handle attached to the inner side of the frame.

(2) The frame (2) is assembled to the base plate (8), swings at pin (9), and is connected to the vehicle by the carriage frame support or slide (10) through pin (11).

(3) The drag bars (12) which are provided to support the rear end of the vehicle and stabilize the mortar are attached to the vehicle by means of trunnions and are connected with the base plate (8) by chains.

(4) Pin assembly (6) is provided with a locking hook and is withdrawn by pressing down on the cap and then turning the cap 180° until the hook clears the bore of the pinhole, when the pin can be withdrawn the length of the slot as controlled by the screw stop.

b. Travel position.—The barrel is secured by the travel lock (13) and base plate (8) in vertical position, chained to the vehicle by chain (14) which in turn is attached to the adjustable hook (15). The elevating mechanism is shown secured in travel position by clamp (16).

c. Firing positions.—(1) With the mortar attached to the vehicle, the carriage frame (2) and barrel (1) are connected by the elevating mechanism (3), and the carriage frame and drag bars (12) are connected to slides (10). A firing angle of 60° is obtainable.

(2) With the mortar emplaced on the ground independent of the vehicle, the carriage frame (2) is stabilized by the supports and tie bars. A firing angle of from 60° to 45° is obtainable.

113. Carriage mount, M22.—The machine-gun mount shown in figures 56 and 57 is assembled on a carriage which travels on a continuous track extending around the inner side of the vehicle body, and it can be locked for firing at any position on the track. An elevating mechanism can be utilized to provide accurate adjustment of the machine gun in elevation.

a. Purpose.—This mount is designed to mount the Browning machine gun, caliber .30, M1919A4, flexible, for ground and antiaircraft fire from inside scout car, M3.

b. Description.—Referring to figure 56, the mount is composed of a carriage assembly (1), a pintle assembly (2), a frame consisting of plates (3) and (4), and the elevating mechanism (5).

(1) *Carriage assembly.*—The carriage travels on the track (6) and assembles the pintle (2) which is fitted to permit 360° traverse of the gun and is secured to the carriage by a nut (7). Clamp bolt (8) is provided to lock the pintle in any position of traverse. The ammunition box support (18) is attached as indicated.

(*a*) The mechanism shown in figure 58 represents the rolling carriage used for all the machine guns track-mounted in scout cars, M3.

It is composed of a body or pintle assembly (2) assembled with two top bearings (3), two bottom bearings (4), four outer rollers (5), and four inner rollers (6). While the side bearings are solid rollers, antifriction bearings are used on the top and bottom.

(*b*) The carriage is locked to the track (1) by lever (7) assembled with right and left cam screws (8) and (9), which in turn mount the clamps (10) and (11). The cam screws are threaded right and left hand respectively and supported by a center bearing (12). The screws are assembled to the lever on serrated bearings to permit adjustment of the lever position to compensate for clamp wear and secured by nuts (13) and (14). Springs (15) are provided to retain the lever in a locked position to prevent accidental moving of the carriage on the track. The carriage clamps are wedge-shaped, and as the lever (7) is released, force outward to wedge the four inner rollers against the track. To unlock the carriage, raise lever.

(*c*) The pintle of the machine-gun mount rotates in the bushing (16) and is clamped in position by handle (17) which actuates the jaws (18) and (19). The jaw (18) is threaded to fit the screw (20), while the jaw (19) is made a slide fit on the screw body. Both jaws are machined to fit the contour of the pintle and are kept in alinement by pins (21) which engage mating slots in the rear portion of the jaws.

(2) *Pintle assembly.*—The pintle assembly (2) mounts a frame composed of plates (3) and (4), which are assembled into a rigid unit by means of the shouldered spacer (9) and the box type construction of the pintle support (10). The frame assembly pivots on the pintle on trunnions (11) which form the fulcrum for the movement of the machine gun in elevation. The frame is locked to the pintle in any position of elevation within the range of the frame by the handle assembly (12). This handle is assembled to a screw which fits the threaded jaw (13) and permits clamping by turning the handle in either direction. The machine gun (19) is assembled to the mount by the gun pintle (14) which is seated in pintle support (10) and is secured by pintle lock assembly (15) on the front end of the machine gun. The rear end of the gun is secured by the slide (16) of the elevating mechanism attached to spacer (9) of the mount.

(3) *Pintle lock.*—The pintle lock assembly (15) consists of a spring slide which engages a mating groove in the pintle (14) and thereby locks the latter to the mount. The slide is actuated by a cam (17) shown in position with the pintle lock engaged. To disengage the lock, place the cam horizontally when a flat on the end of the cam seats on the body of the pintle lock and retains the lock in the disengaged position.

TM 9-705

SCOUT CARS AND MORTAR MOTOR CARRIAGE   113–115

(4) *Elevating mechanism.*—See paragraph 108 and figure 50. One modification concerns the provision of a hinged, spring-actuating trigger (41) to retain the slide on the traversing bar in addition to the locking lever (42).

c. Dismounting.—(1) To remove the machine gun from the carriage mount, release the gun pintle latch (15), disconnect the elevating mechanism by pulling on its trigger, and lift gun with elevating mechanism and gun pintle attached.

(2) To remove the pintle assembly from the carriage, release clamp handle (8), remove nut (7), and lift pintle and frame from carriage.

(3) To remove carriage from track, remove four outer rollers.

d. Lubrication.—Excessive wear and consequent high maintenance costs can be prevented only by keeping the matériel clean and well lubricated. Lubricating oil (Navy contract 2110, equivalent to viscosity of 90 to 120 at 130° F.) should be used. The trunnion bearings, clamping devices, elevating screw, carriage rollers, and other bearing surfaces subject to wear should be lubricated every 8 hours of firing.

114. Carriage mount, M21.—The machine-gun mount (fig. 59) is assembled in a manner similar to that described in paragraph 113, utilizing the same carriage assembly as the carriage mount, M22. This mount is designed for the Browning machine gun, caliber .50, M2, heavy barrel, for ground fire from inside scout car, M3, and antiaircraft fire from outside the vehicle.

115. Carriage mount, D36961.—Machine gun mounts for scout car, M3A1, are shown in figures 60 and 61. The carriage shown in figure 62 assembles either mount and provides for travel on a continuous track extending around the inner side of the vehicle; it can be locked for firing at any position of the track and canted for any position of the vehicle. The usual elevating mechanisms provided with the guns are employed for accurate adjustment.

a. Purpose.—This mount is designed to mount Browning machine gun, caliber .30, M1917A1, and Browning machine gun, caliber .50, M2, heavy barrel, flexible, for ground and antiaircraft fire from inside scout car, M3A1.

b. Description.—The general details of the various mechanisms involved in mounting the guns indicated have been discussed in preceding paragraphs. The major change in the carriage itself from that already described concerns the addition of an anticanting device for the pintle retainer to compensate for the displacement of the track from a horizontal plane. By turning the control wheel clockwise, the vertical centerline of the gun mount will be displaced to the left and vice versa. Sighting and aiming may thus be executed properly regardless of the side slope of the vehicle. The pintle clamp, which prevents the pintle from revolving, is independent of the anticanting control.

Appendix

LIST OF REFERENCES

1. Standard Nomenclature Lists.

Gun, machine, caliber .30, Browning, M1917A1, and mount, tripod, M1917A1	SNL A-5
Gun, machine, caliber .30, Browning, M1919A4, and mount, tripod, M2	SNL A-6
Gun, submachine, caliber .45, Thompson, M1928A1	SNL A-32
Gun, machine, caliber .50, Browning, M2, HB, flexible, and mount, tripod, M3	SNL A-39
Cars, scout, M3 and M3A1, and carriage, motor, 4.2 mortar, M2	SNL G-67
Cleaning and preserving materials	SNL K-1
Chemical Warfare Service Storage Catalog	
Current Standard Nomenclature Lists are as tabulated here. An up-to-date list of SNL's is maintained as the "Ordnance Publications for Supply Index"	(OPSI)

2. Technical Manual.

Cleaning and preserving materials _____ TM 9-850
  (Now published as TR 1395-A)

3. Field Manuals.

Mechanized Cavalry	FM 2-10
Employment of Cavalry	FM 2-15
Thompson submachine gun, caliber .45, M1928A1	FM 23-40
Browning machine gun, caliber .30, M1919A4	FM 23-45
Browning machine gun, caliber .30, M1917A1	FM 23-55
Browning machine gun, caliber .50, M2, HB, flexible	FM 23-60
Motor Transport	FM 25-10

4. Army Regulations.

Transportation of supplies	AR 30-955
Storage of motor vehicle equipment	AR 30-1055
Allowances, fuels, and lubricants for motor vehicles and equipment used for training purposes	AR 730-10
Marking of clothing, equipment, vehicles, and property	AR 850-5
Registration and inventory of motor vehicles	AR 850-10
Military motor vehicles	AR 850-15

5. Other publications.

Motor transport technical service bulletins, Quartermaster Corps.
Circular 1-10, Motor transportation, Quartermaster Corps.

TM 9-705

ORDNANCE DEPARTMENT

RA FSD 651

RA FSD 653

RA FSD 652

Left rear.

FIGURE 1.—Scout car, M3.

SCOUT CARS AND MORTAR MOTOR CARRIAGE

RA FSD 654

④ Right rear.

FIGURE 1.—Scout car, M3—Continued

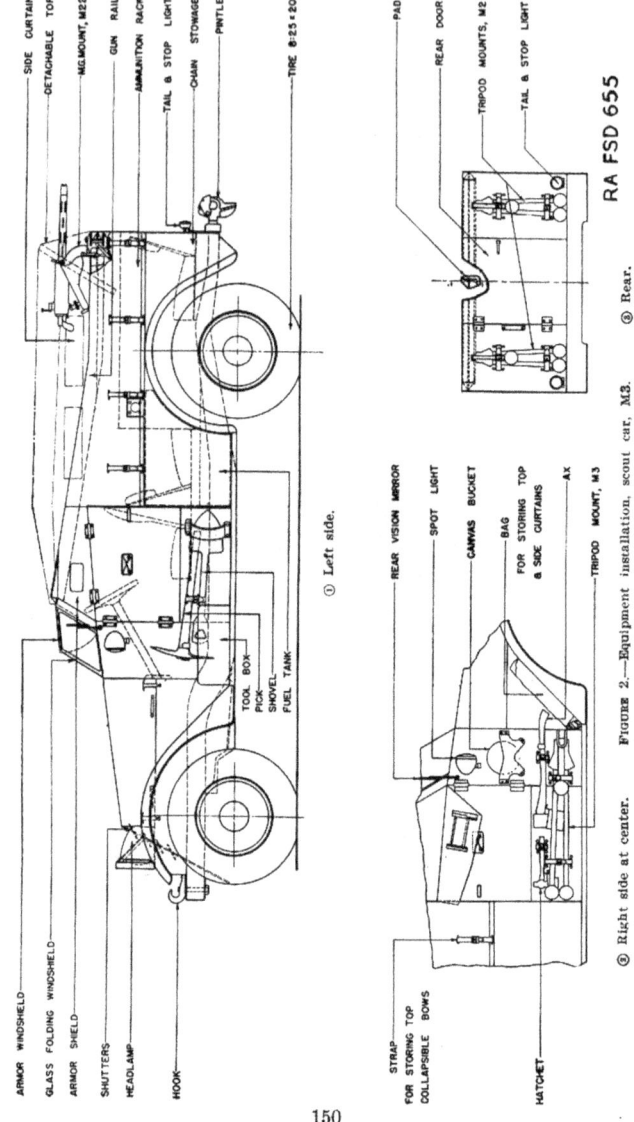

FIGURE 2.—Equipment installation, scout car, M3.

TM 9-705

SCOUT CARS AND MORTAR MOTOR CARRIAGE

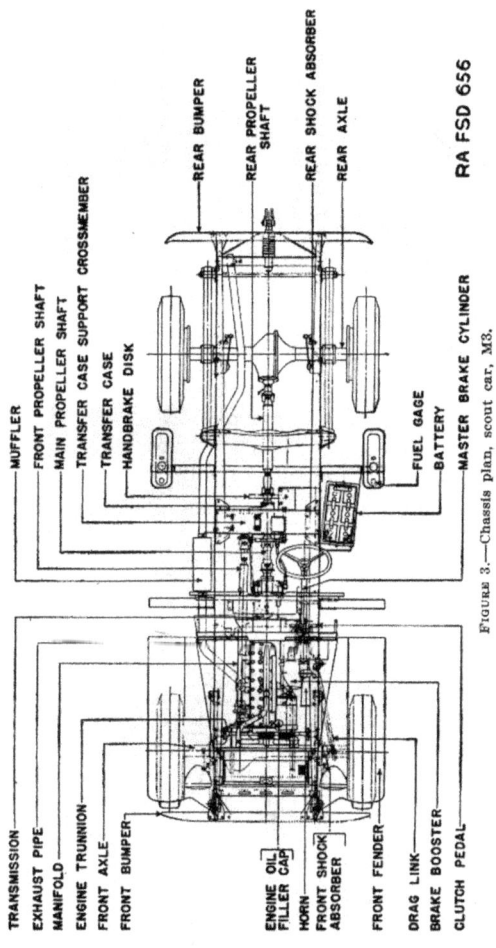

FIGURE 3.—Chassis plan, scout car, M3.

TM 9-705

ORDNANCE DEPARTMENT

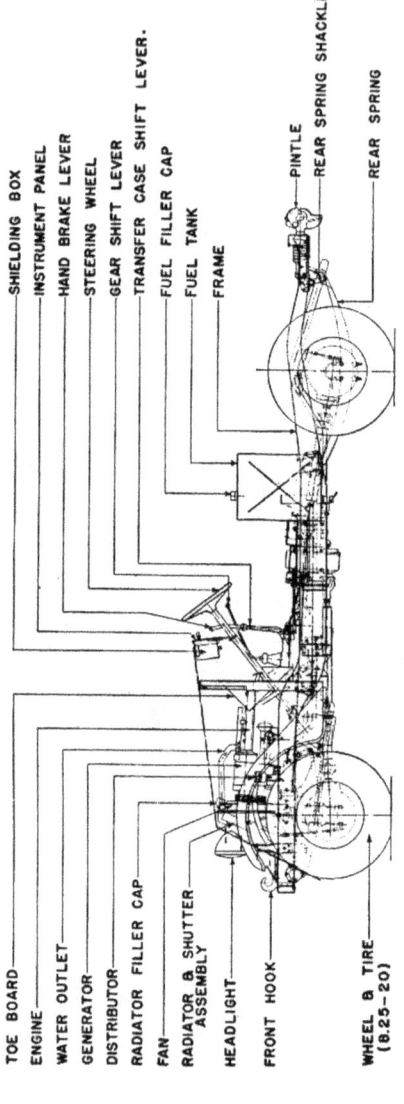

FIGURE 4.—Chassis elevation, scout car, M3.

SCOUT CARS AND MORTAR MOTOR CARRIAGE

RA FSD 663

① Left front.

RA FSD 665

RA FSD 664

② Left rear.

FIGURE 5.—Mortar motor carriage, M2.

TM 9-705

ORDNANCE DEPARTMENT

① Tonneau.

FIGURE 5—Mortar motor carriage, M2—Continued

TM 9-705

SCOUT CARS AND MORTAR MOTOR CARRIAGE

RA FSD 660

①

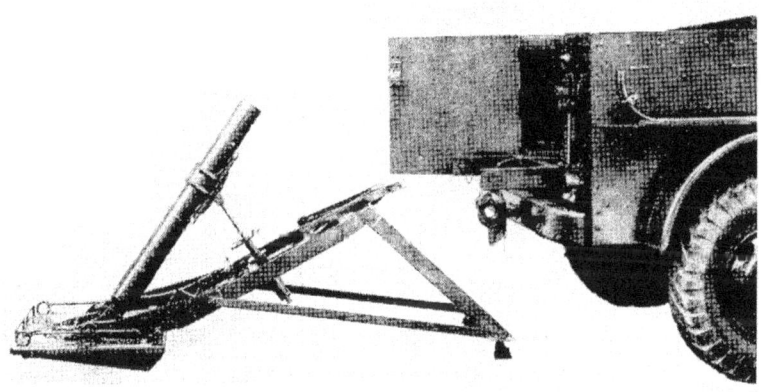

RA FSD 661

②

FIGURE 6.—Mortar motor carriage, M2.

TM 9-705

ORDNANCE DEPARTMENT

RA FSD 667

① Left front.

RA FSD 669

② Right front.

RA FSD 668
③ Rear.

FIGURE 7.—Scout car, M3A1.

SCOUT CARS AND MORTAR MOTOR CARRIAGE

④ Front.

FIGURE 7—Scout car, M3A1—Continued

TM 9-705

ORDNANCE DEPARTMENT

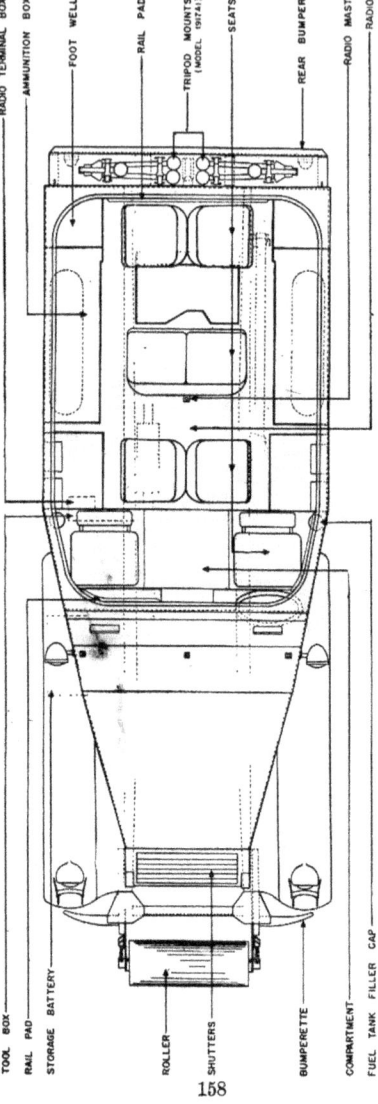

Figure 8.—Equipment installation, scout car, M3A1.

SCOUT CARS AND MORTAR MOTOR CARRIAGE

TM 9-705

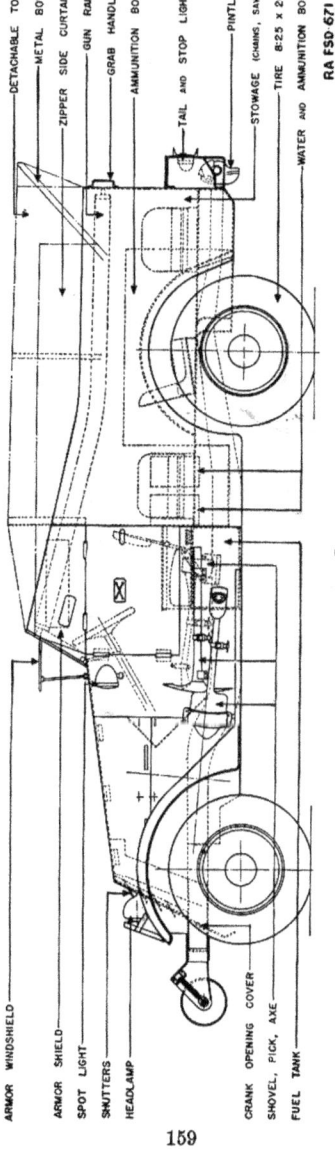

Figure 8.—Equipment installation, scout car, M3A1—Continued

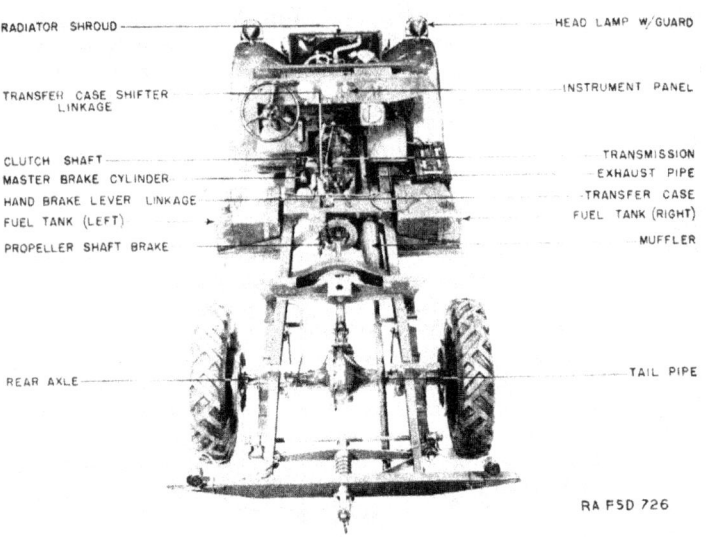

FIGURE 9.—Chassis plan, scout car, M3A1.

SCOUT CARS AND MORTAR MOTOR CARRIAGE

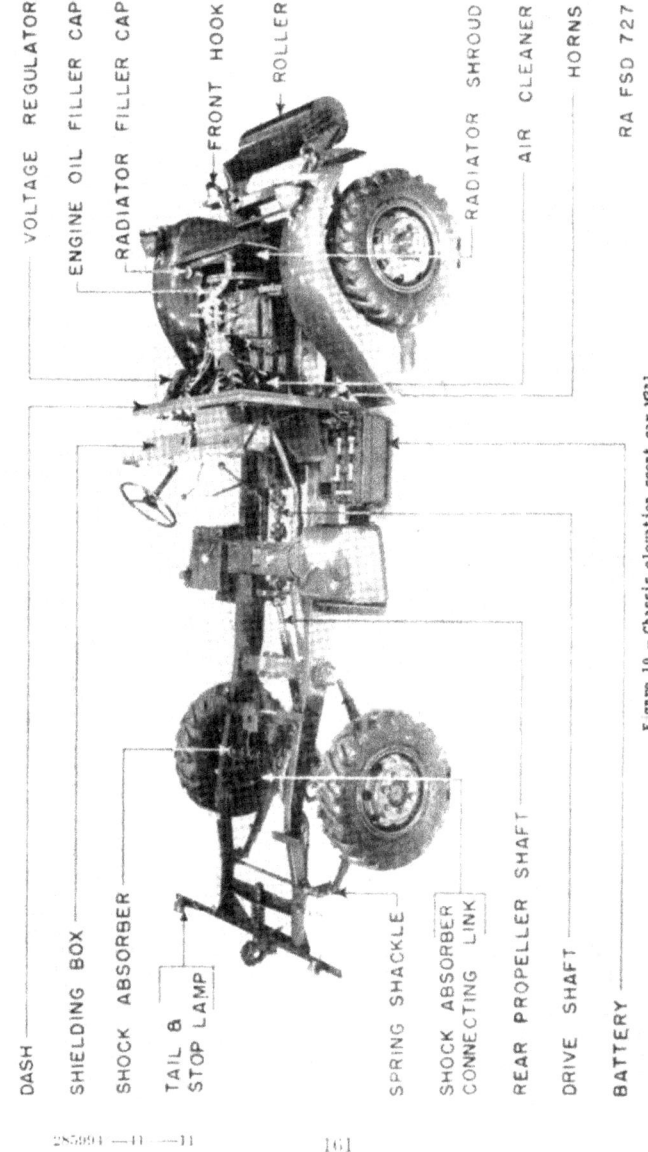

Figure 10 - Chassis elevation scout car M3A1

TM 9–705

ORDNANCE DEPARTMENT

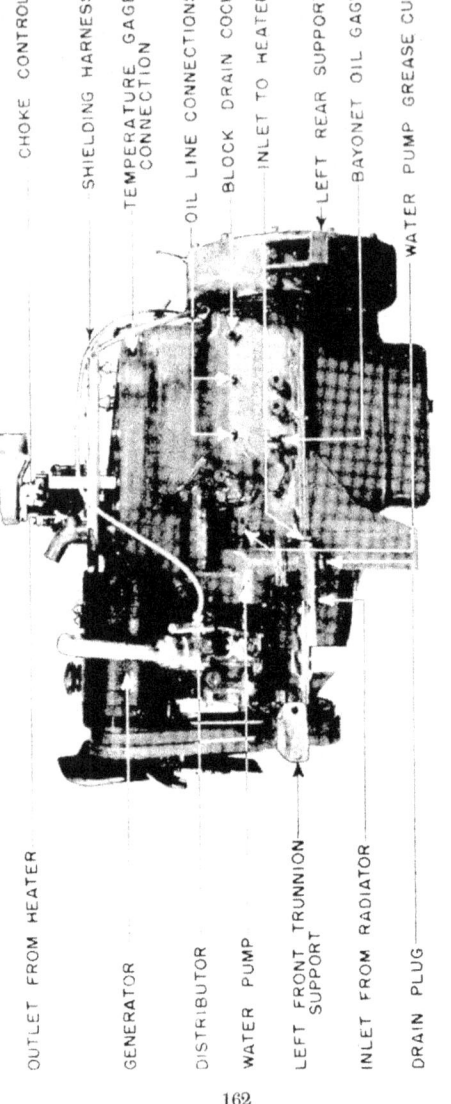

① Left side.

Figure 11.—Hercules engine.

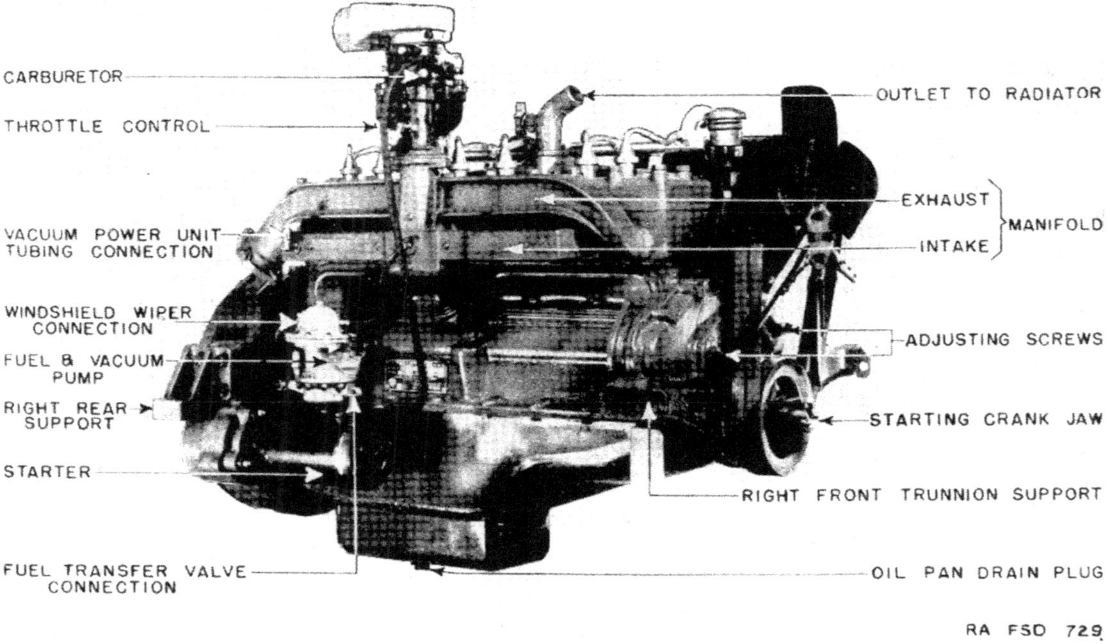

Figure 11.—Hercules engine—Continued.

② Right front.

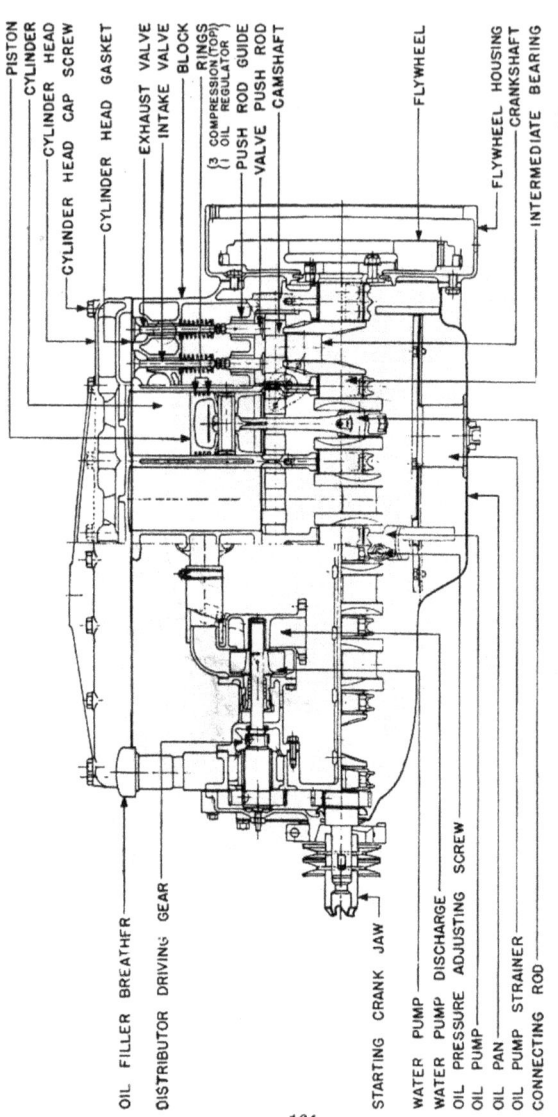

Figure 11.—② Hercules engine—Continued.

SCOUT CARS AND MORTAR MOTOR CARRIAGE

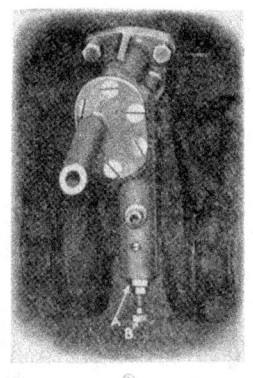

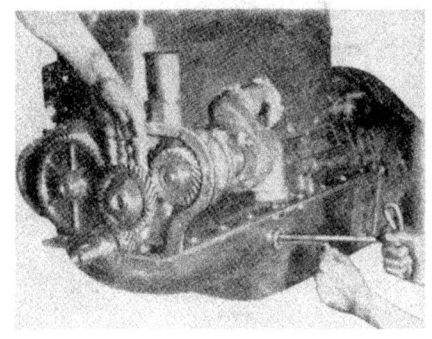

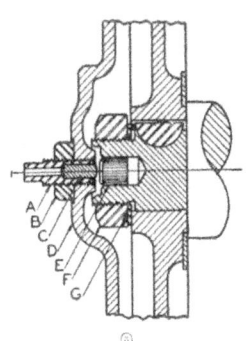

FIGURE 12.—Oil pump; timing gears.

④

FIGURE 12.—Oil pump; timing gears—Continued

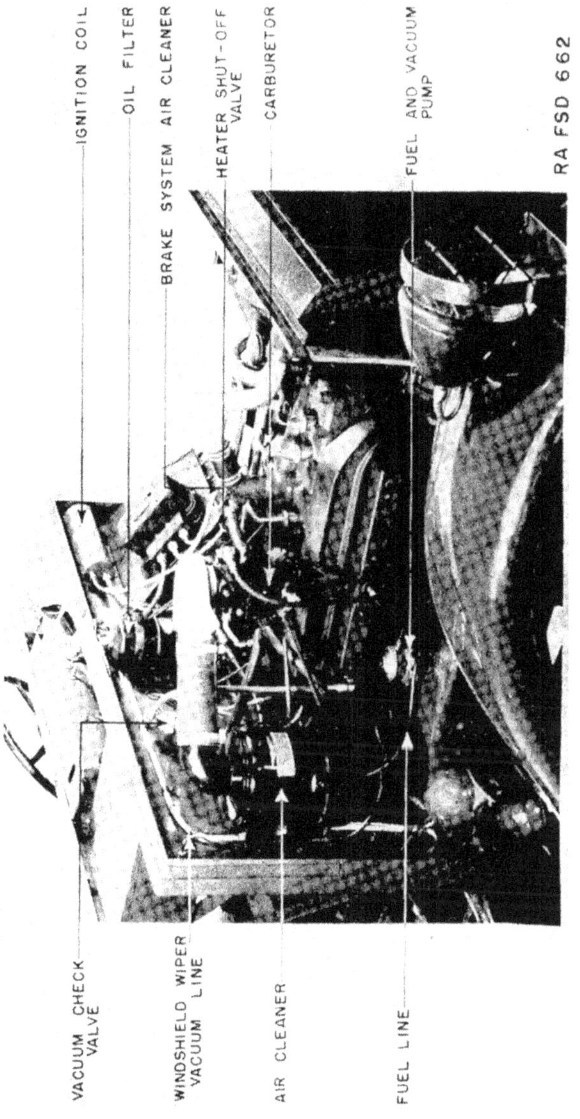

TM 9–705
SCOUT CARS AND MORTAR MOTOR CARRIAGE

FIGURE 13.—Air-fuel system, scout car, M3A1.

RA FSD 662

TM 9-705

ORDNANCE DEPARTMENT

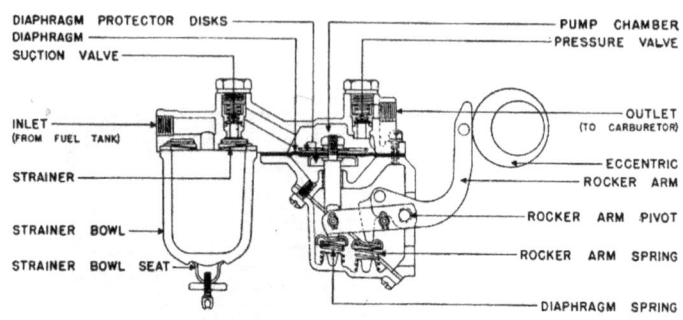

① Series "B" pump.

② Series "AV" pump.

FIGURE 14.—A. C. fuel pumps.

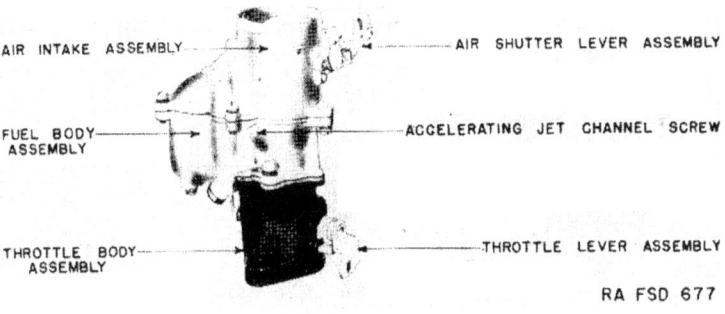

① Model 20-B-10.

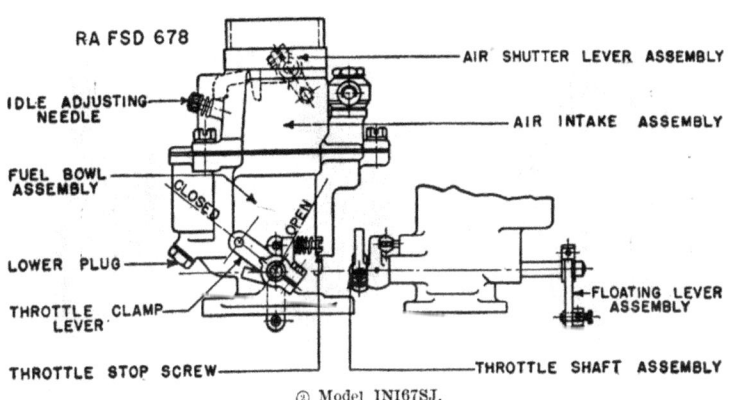

② Model 1N167SJ.

FIGURE 15.—Zenith carburetors.

TM 9-705
ORDNANCE DEPARTMENT

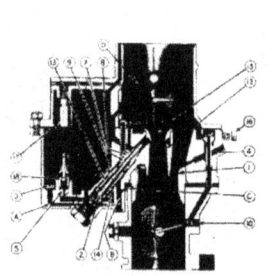
FUEL AND IDLING SYSTEM

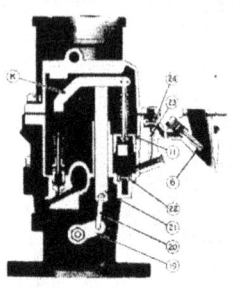
ACCELERATING SYSTEM

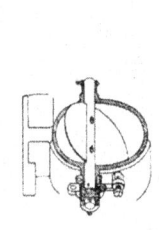
STRANGLER SHAFT

RA FSD 679

① Model 20–B–10.

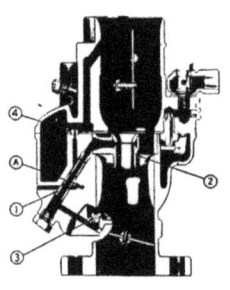
COMPENSATING SYSTEM

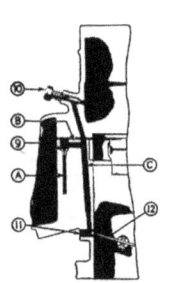
IDLING SYSTEM

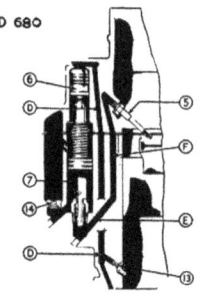
ACCELERATING SYSTEM

RA FSD 680

② Model IN167SJ.

FIGURE 16.—Carburetor systems.

FIGURE 17.—Ignition system, scout car, M3A1.

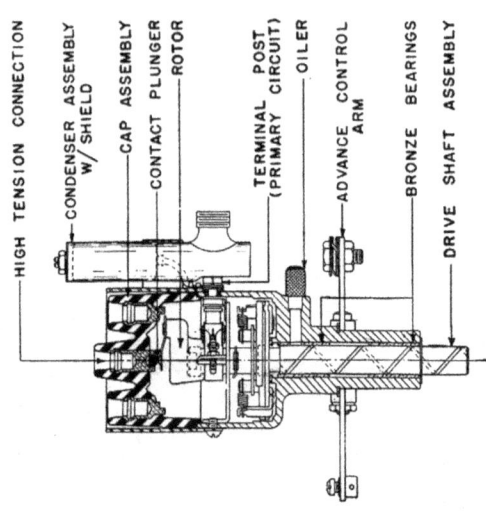

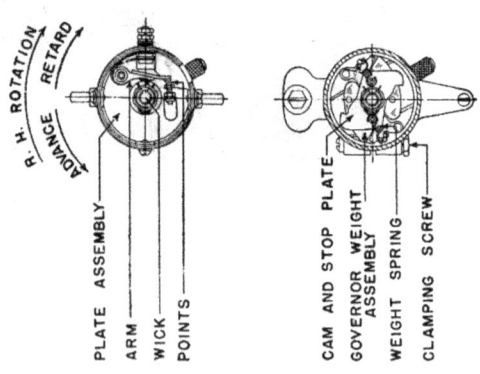

Figure 18.—Distributor.

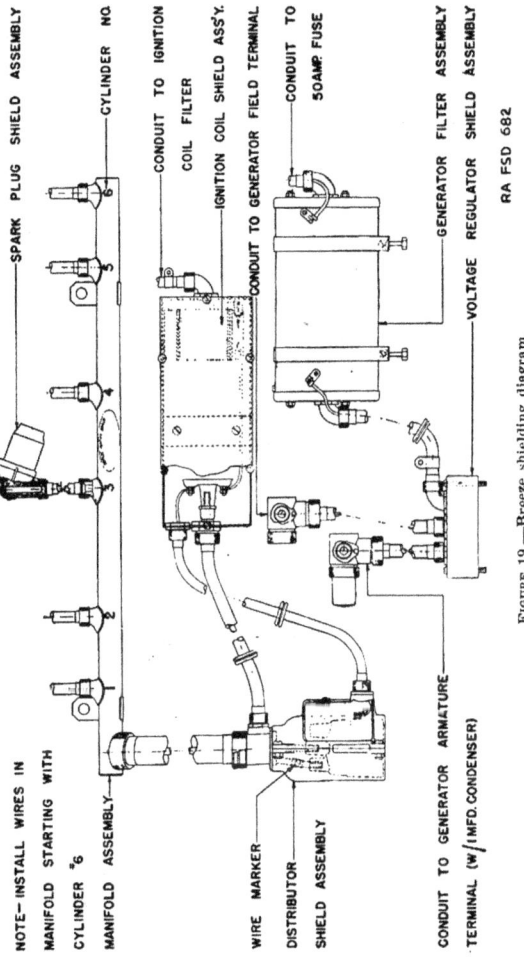

Figure 19.—Breeze shielding diagram.

TM 9-705

ORDNANCE DEPARTMENT

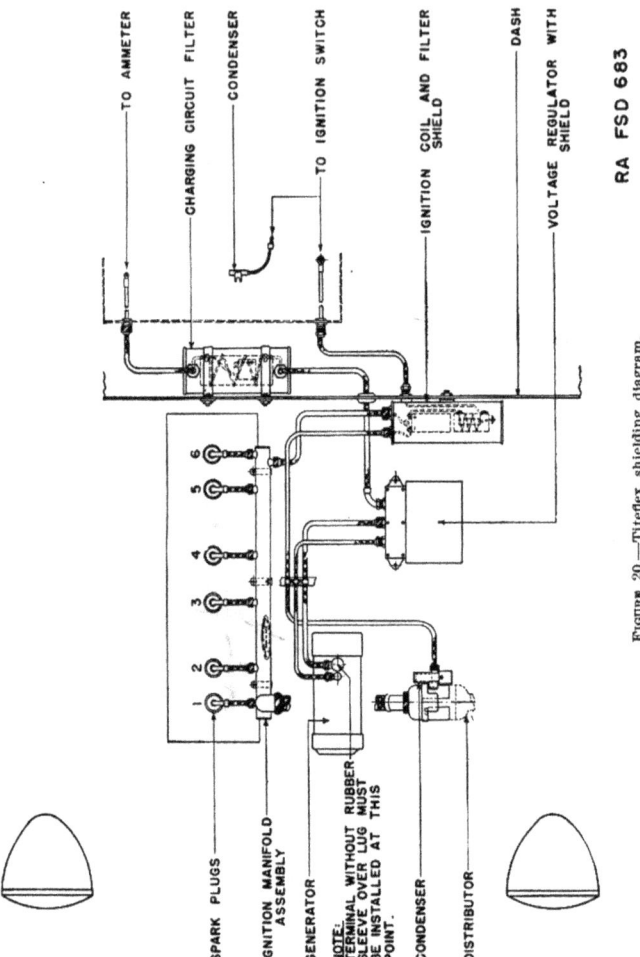

Figure 20.—Titeflex shielding diagram.

SCOUT CARS AND MORTAR MOTOR CARRIAGE

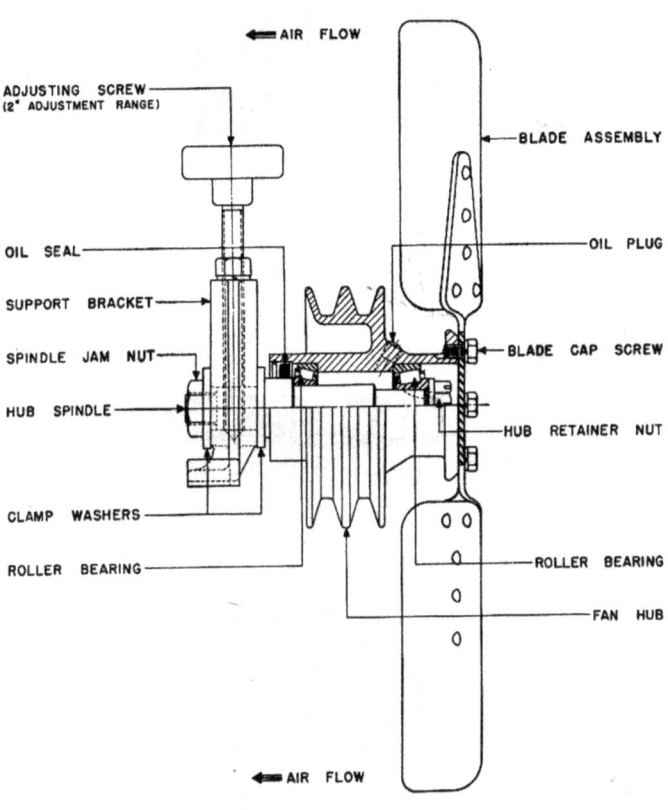

Figure 21.—Fan and pulley.

TM 9-705

ORDNANCE DEPARTMENT

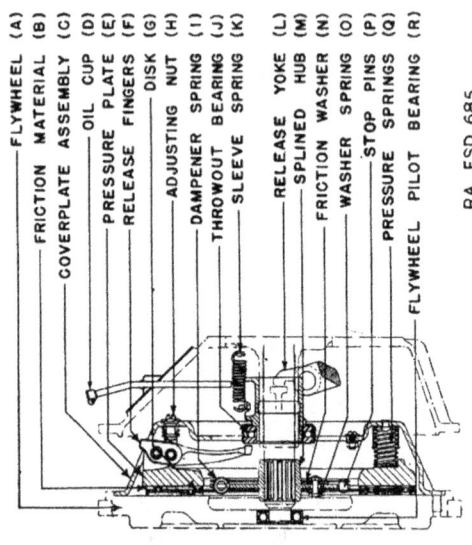

FIGURE 22.—Clutch.

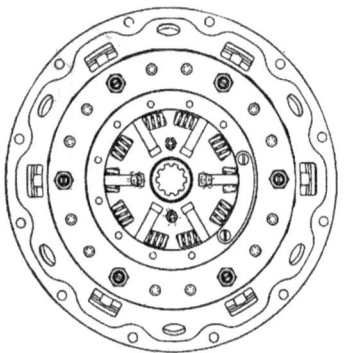

TM 9-705

SCOUT CARS AND MORTAR MOTOR CARRIAGE

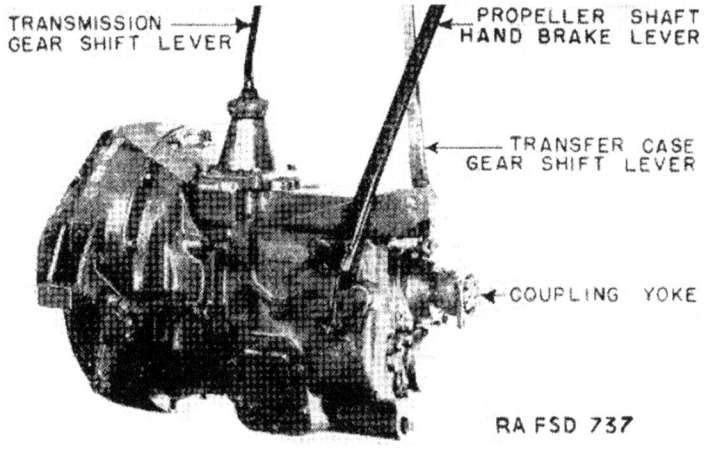

① Left side.

② Right side.

FIGURE 23.—Transmission.

TM 9-705

ORDNANCE DEPARTMENT

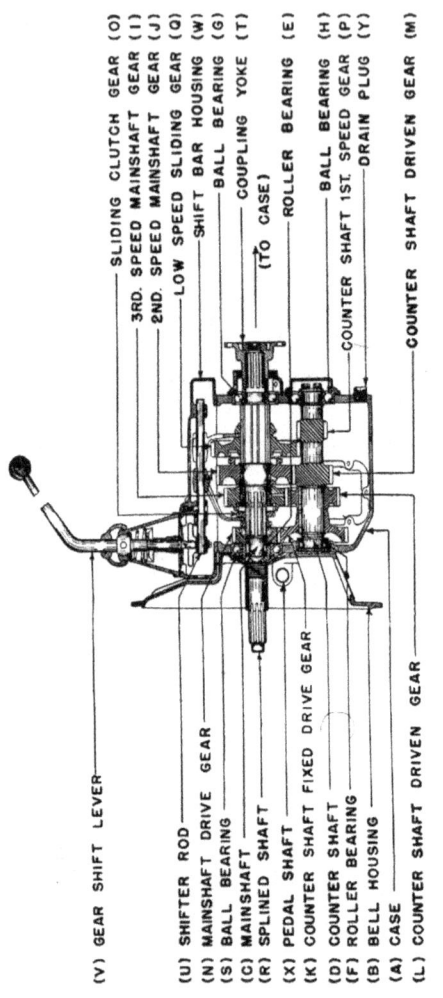

FIGURE 23.—Transmission—Continued

③ Sectionalized.

RA FSD 686

(V) GEAR SHIFT LEVER
(U) SHIFTER ROD
(N) MAINSHAFT DRIVE GEAR
(S) BALL BEARING
(C) MAINSHAFT
(R) SPLINED SHAFT
(X) PEDAL SHAFT
(K) COUNTER SHAFT FIXED DRIVE GEAR
(D) COUNTER SHAFT
(F) ROLLER BEARING
(B) BELL HOUSING
(A) CASE
(L) COUNTER SHAFT DRIVEN GEAR

(O) SLIDING CLUTCH GEAR
(I) 3RD. SPEED MAINSHAFT GEAR
(J) 2ND. SPEED MAINSHAFT GEAR
(Q) LOW SPEED SLIDING GEAR
(W) SHIFT BAR HOUSING
(G) BALL BEARING
(T) COUPLING YOKE
(TO CASE)
(E) ROLLER BEARING
(H) BALL BEARING
(P) COUNTER SHAFT 1ST SPEED GEAR
(Y) DRAIN PLUG
(M) COUNTER SHAFT DRIVEN GEAR

178

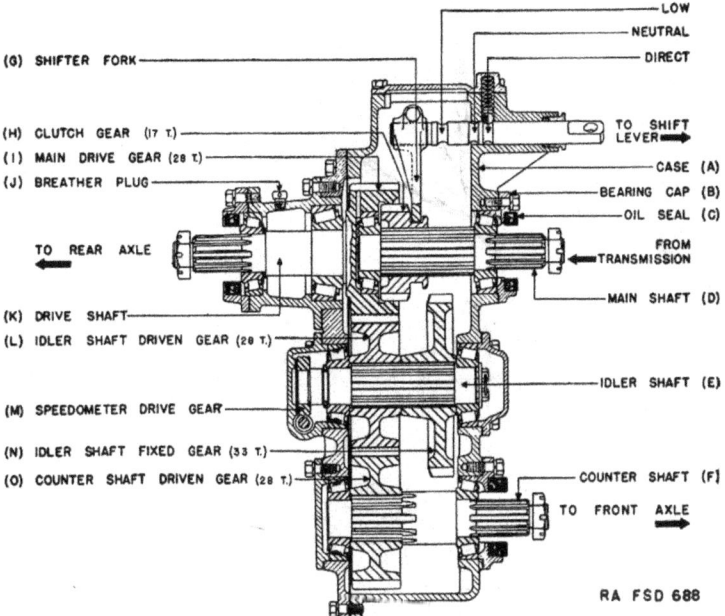

FIGURE 24.—Transfer case, scout car, M3.

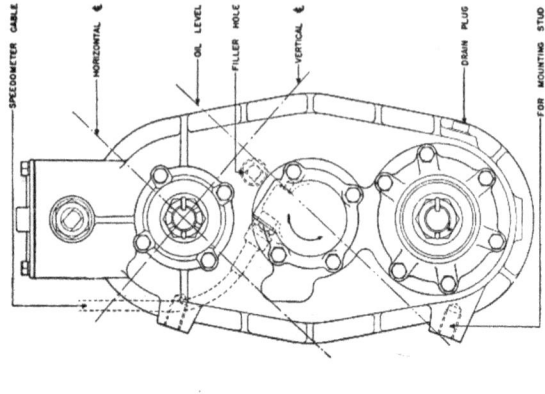

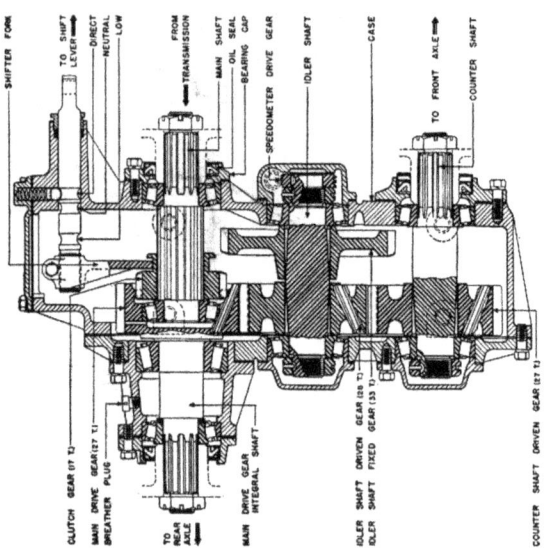

FIGURE 25.—Transfer case, scout car, M3A1.

TM 9-705

SCOUT CARS AND MORTAR MOTOR CARRIAGE

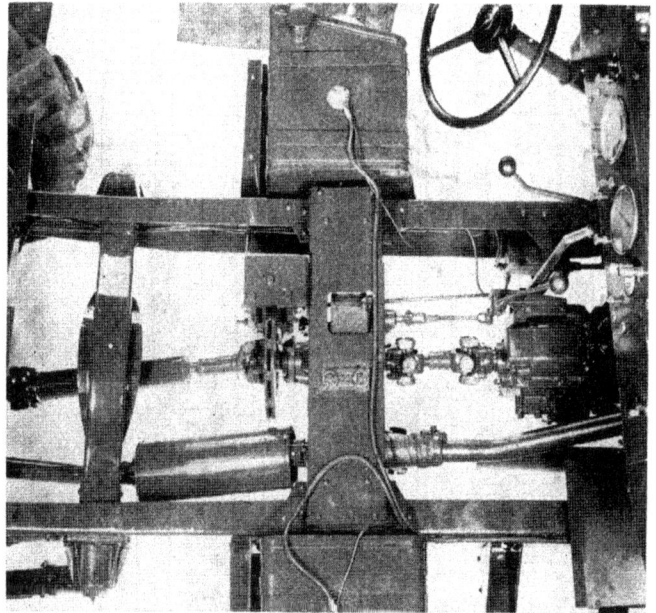

FIGURE 26.—Propeller shafts and shaft brake, scout car, M3A1.

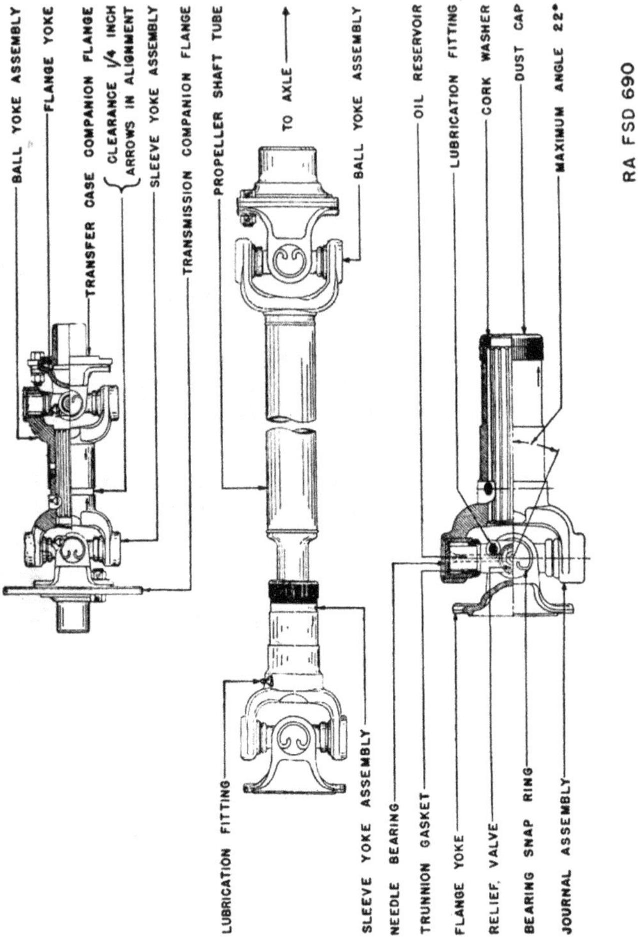

FIGURE 27.—Propeller shafts.

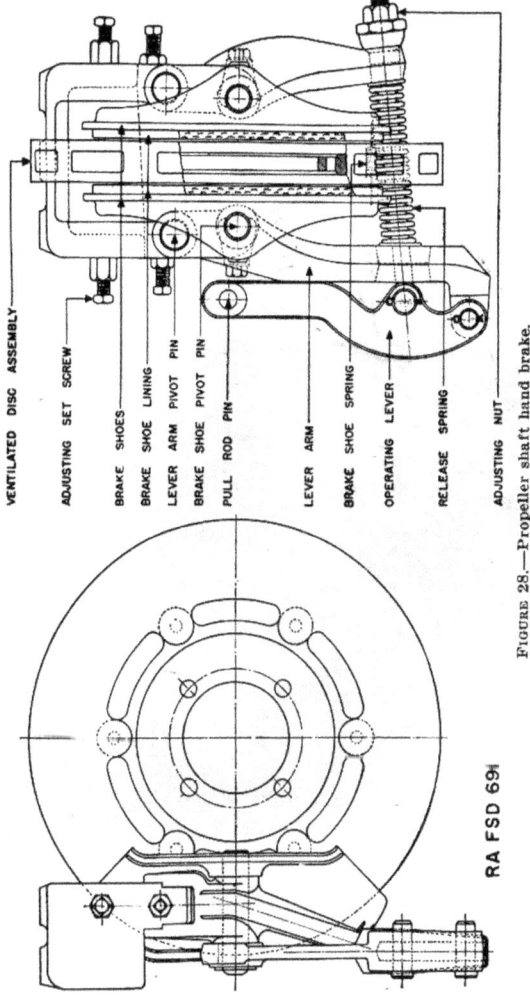

Figure 28.—Propeller shaft hand brake.

TM 9-705

ORDNANCE DEPARTMENT

Figure 29.—Front axle, scout car, M3A1.

SCOUT CARS AND MORTAR MOTOR CARRIAGE

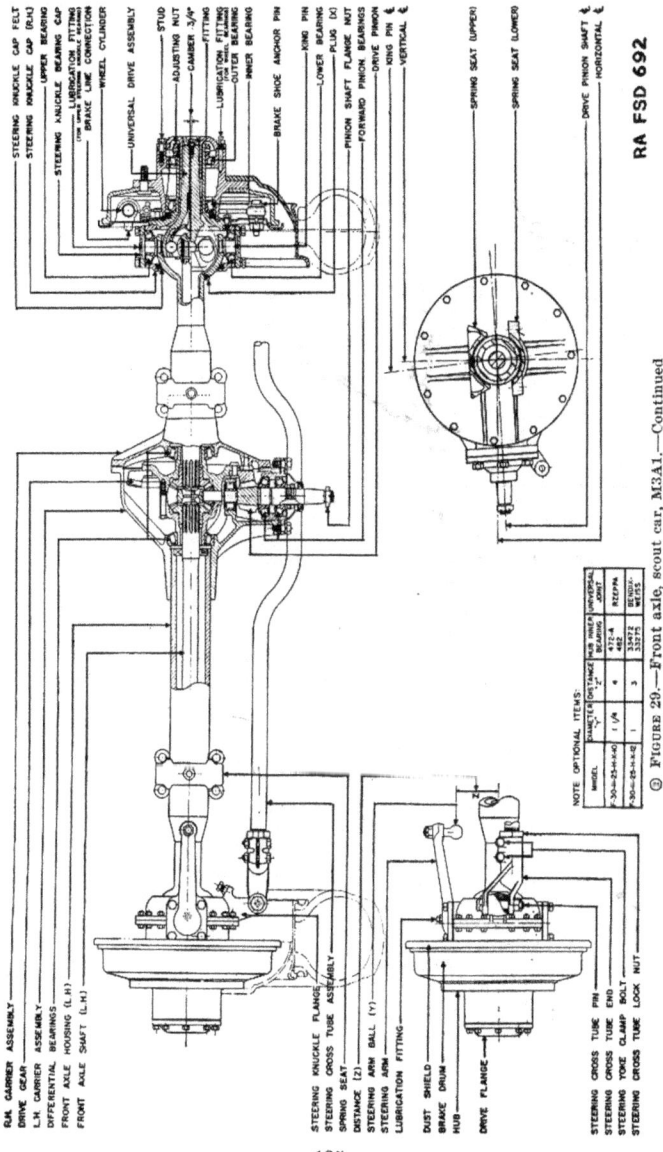

© FIGURE 29.—Front axle, scout car, M3A1.—Continued

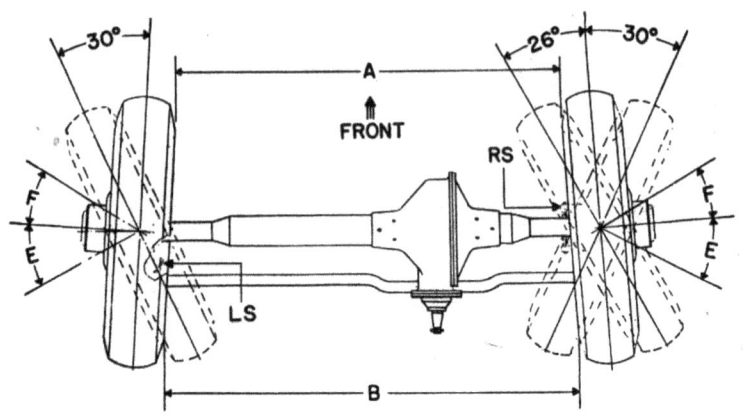

FRONT WHEEL ALIGNMENT CHART

B MINUS A —TOE-IN OF 1/8" ± 1/16"   **C**—CAMBER OF 3/4°   **D**—CASTOR OF 5° TO 7°
E—STEERING ANGLE OF 30° MAXIMUM AT INNER WHEEL
F—STEERING ANGLE OF 26° APPROXIMATELY AT OUTER WHEEL
LS—WITH STOPS IN REAR, ADJUST TO GET 30° ANGLE AT INNER WHEEL
RS—WITH STOPS IN FRONT, ADJUST TO GET 30° ANGLE AT LEFT WHEEL
YY—VERTICAL CENTER LINE   **ZZ**—KING PIN CENTER LINE

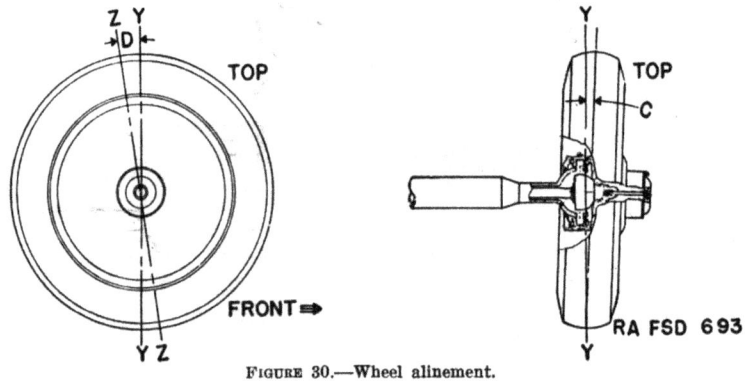

FIGURE 30.—Wheel alinement.

TM 9-705

SCOUT CARS AND MORTAR MOTOR CARRIAGE

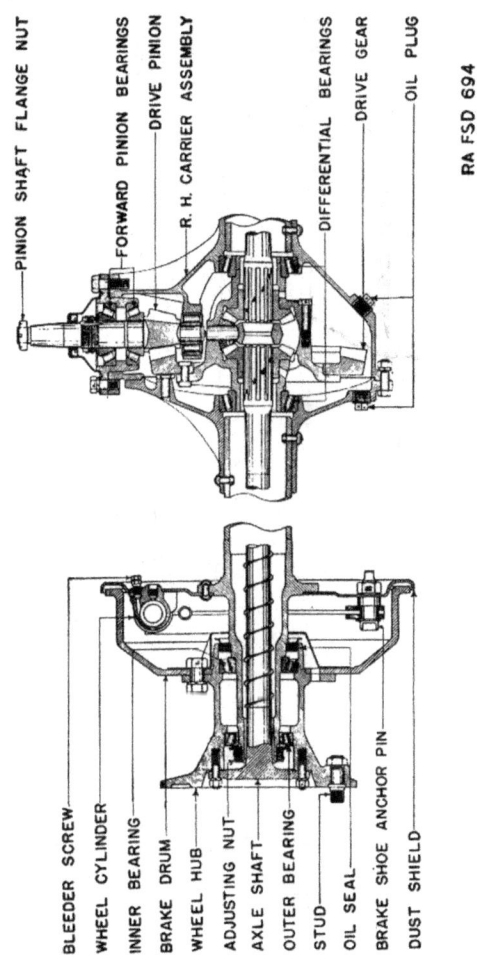

① Rear wheel hub and brake drum.   ② Rear axle differential housing.

FIGURE 31.—Rear axle.

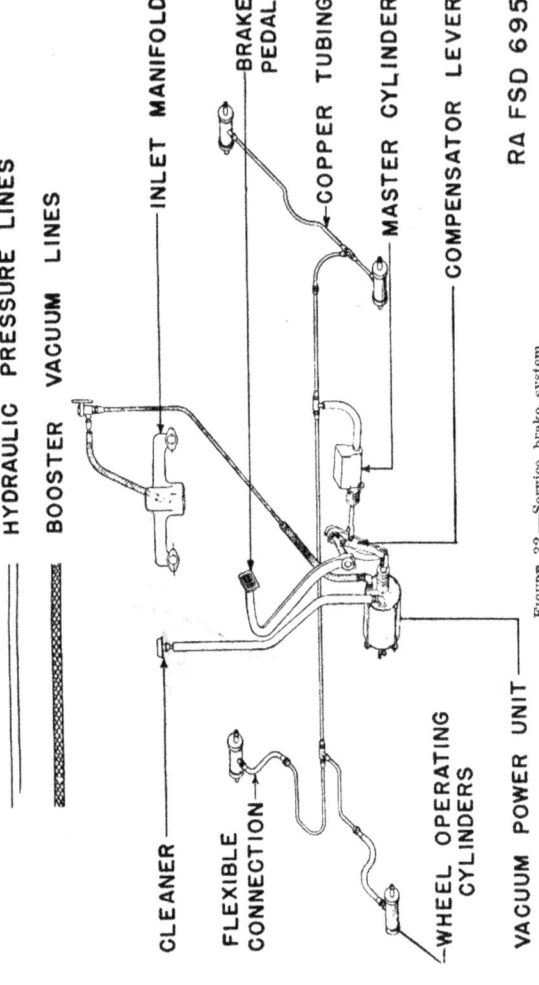

Figure 32.—Service brake system.

SCOUT CARS AND MORTAR MOTOR CARRIAGE　　TM 9–705

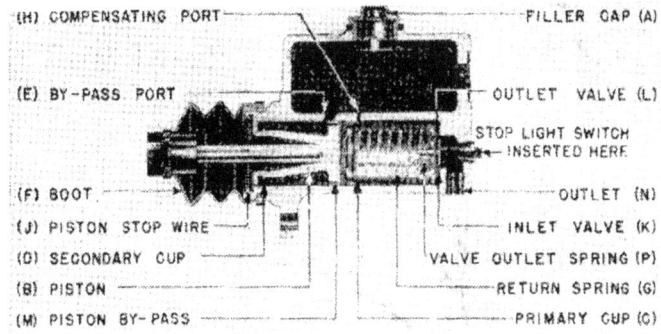

① Master cylinder.

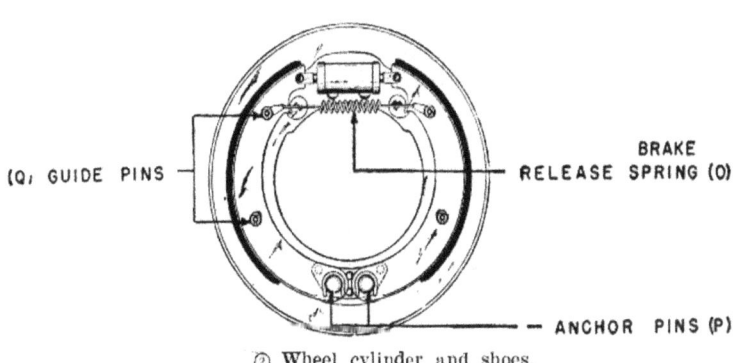

② Wheel cylinder and shoes.

③ Cylinder and adjusting cams.　　RA FSD 696

FIGURE 33.—Brake cylinders.

TM 9-705

ORDNANCE DEPARTMENT

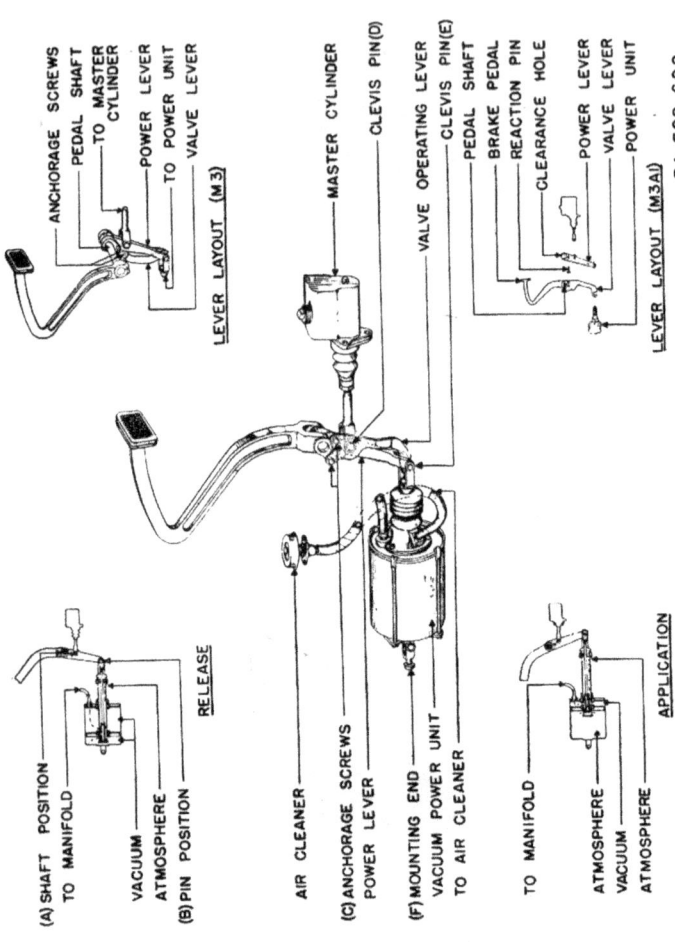

Figure 34.—Service brake linkage.

SCOUT CARS AND MORTAR MOTOR CARRIAGE

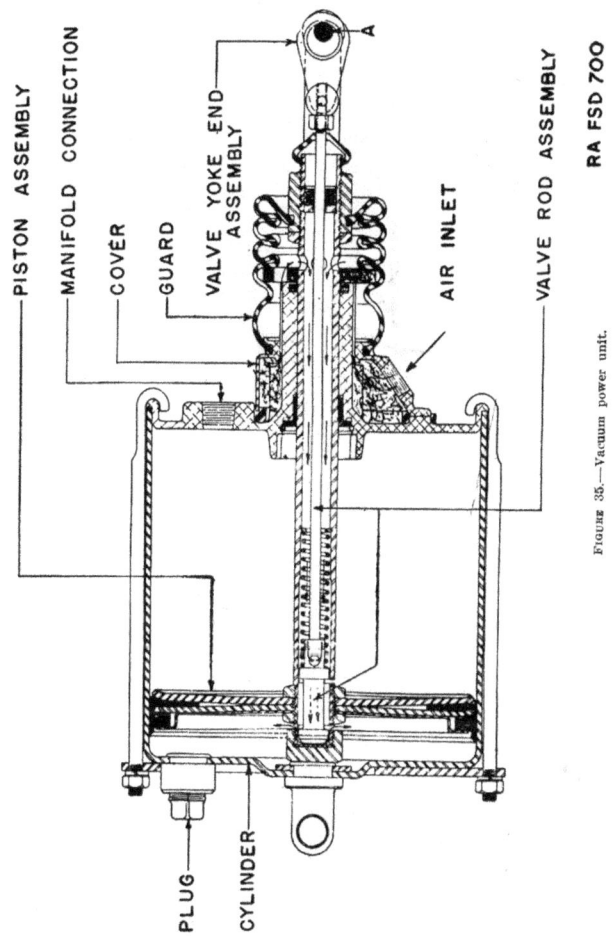

Figure 35.—Vacuum power unit.

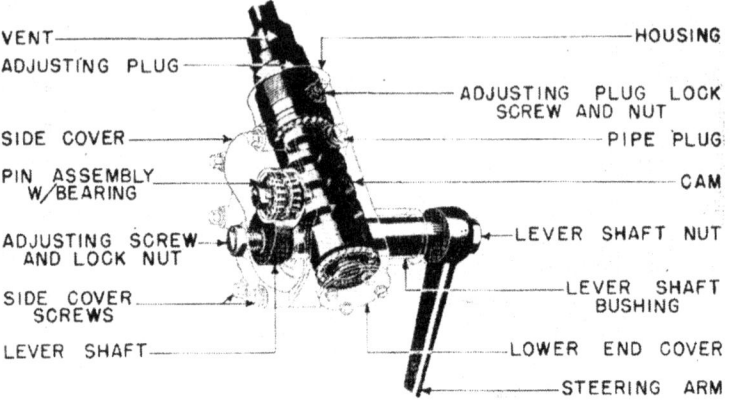

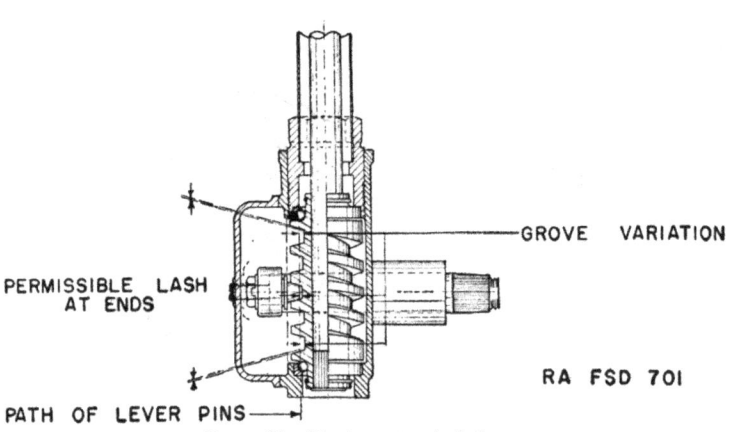

Figure 36.—Steering gear, single lever.

SCOUT CARS AND MORTAR MOTOR CARRIAGE

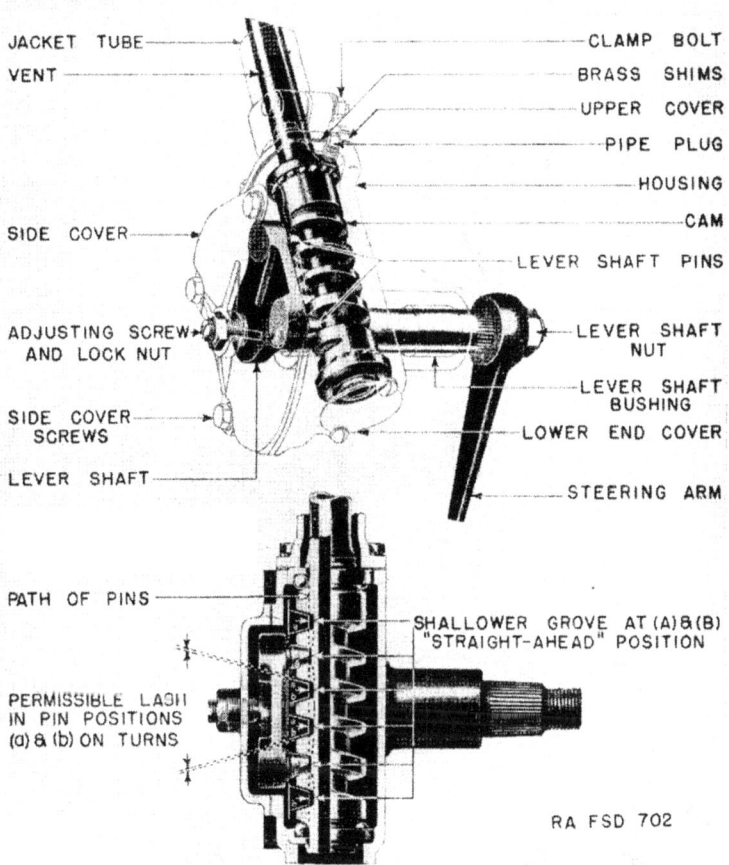

FIGURE 37.—Steering gear, twin lever.

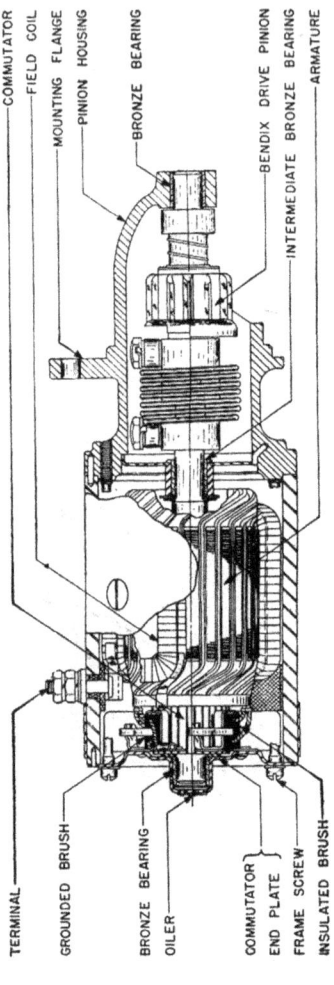

Figure 38.—Starting motor.

TM 9-705

SCOUT CARS AND MORTAR MOTOR CARRIAGE

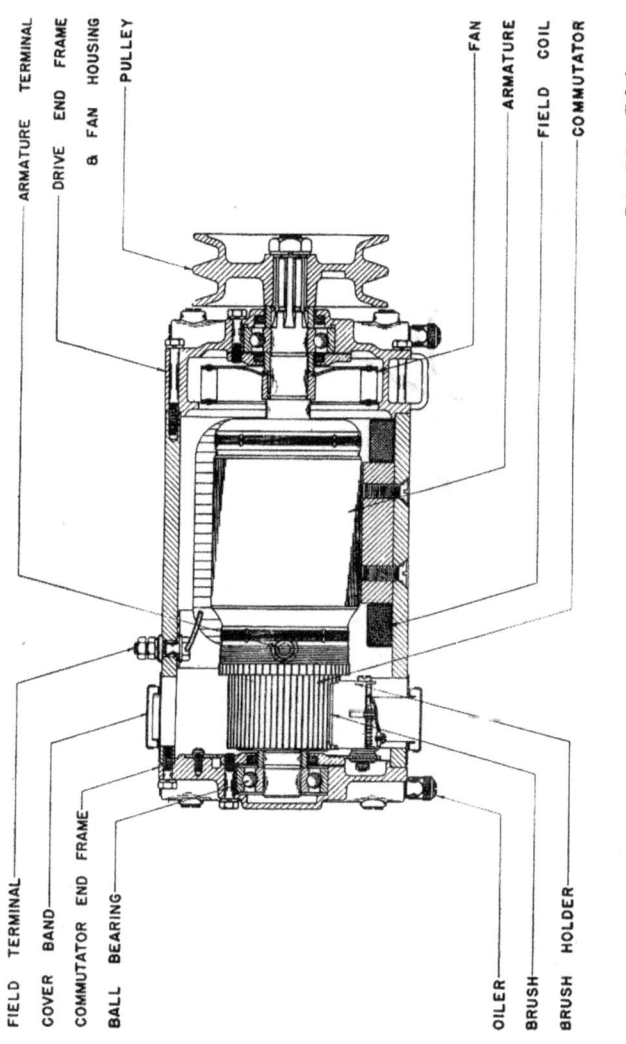

FIGURE 39.—Delco-Remy generator.

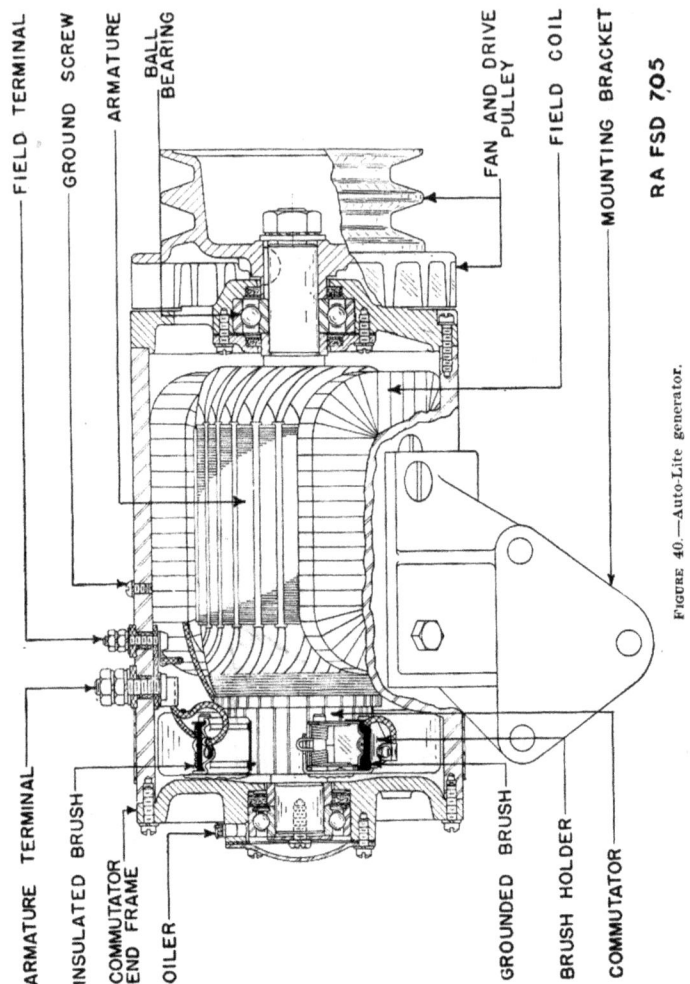

Figure 40.—Auto-Lite generator.

SCOUT CARS AND MORTAR MOTOR CARRIAGE

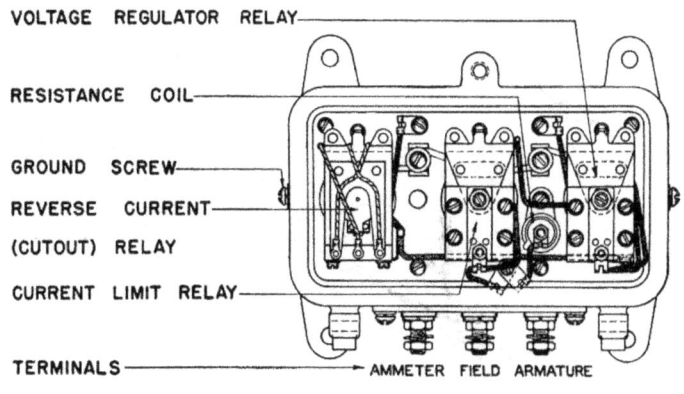

① Delco-Remy.

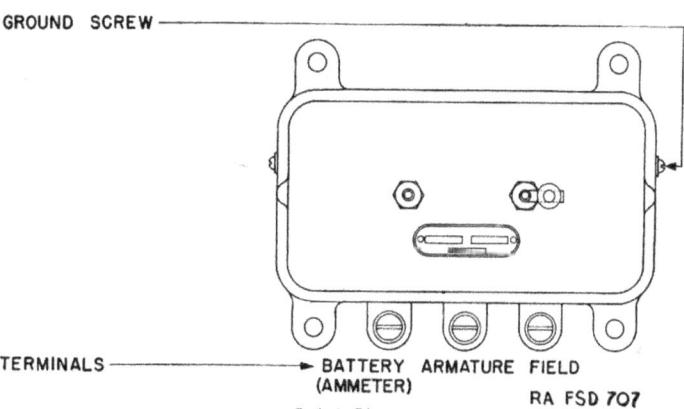

② Auto-Lite.

FIGURE 41.—Voltage regulators.

TM 9-705

ORDNANCE DEPARTMENT

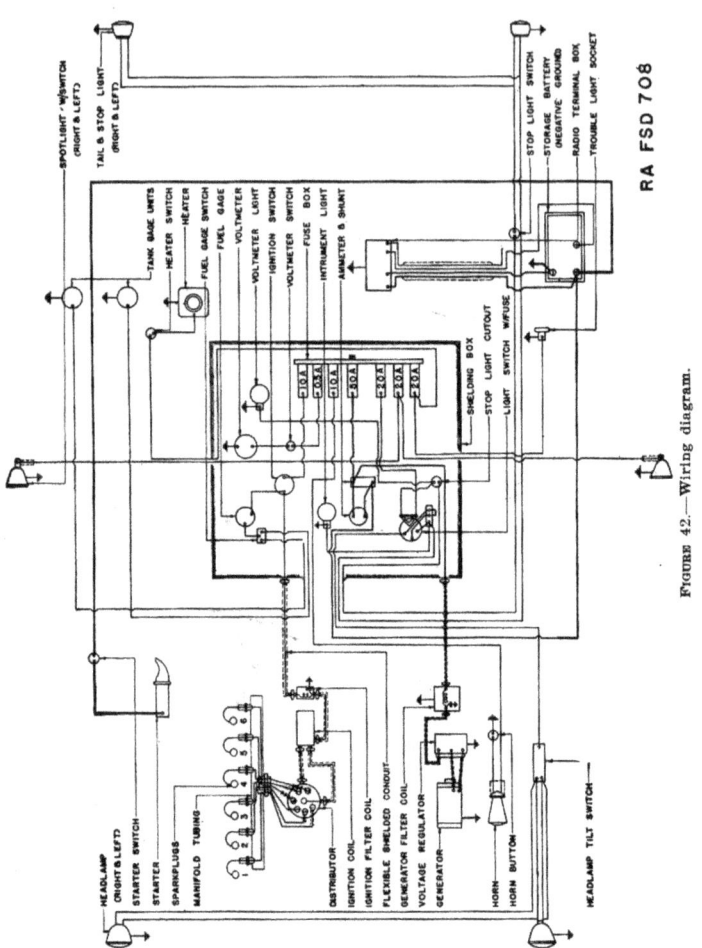

Figure 42.—Wiring diagram.

198

TM 9-705

SCOUT CARS AND MORTAR MOTOR CARRIAGE

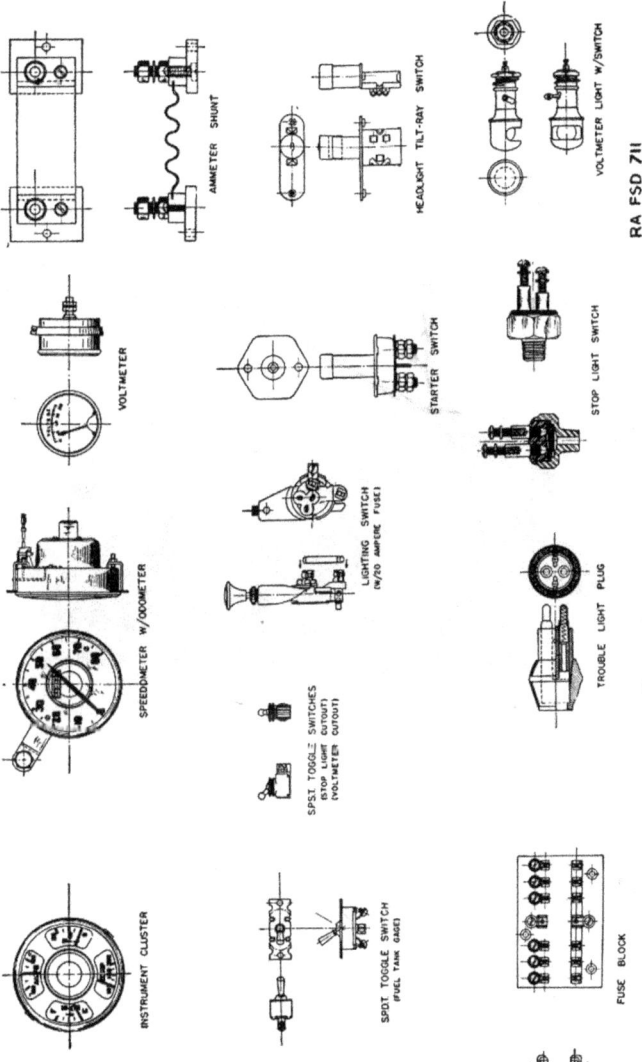

FIGURE 48.—Instrument panel details.

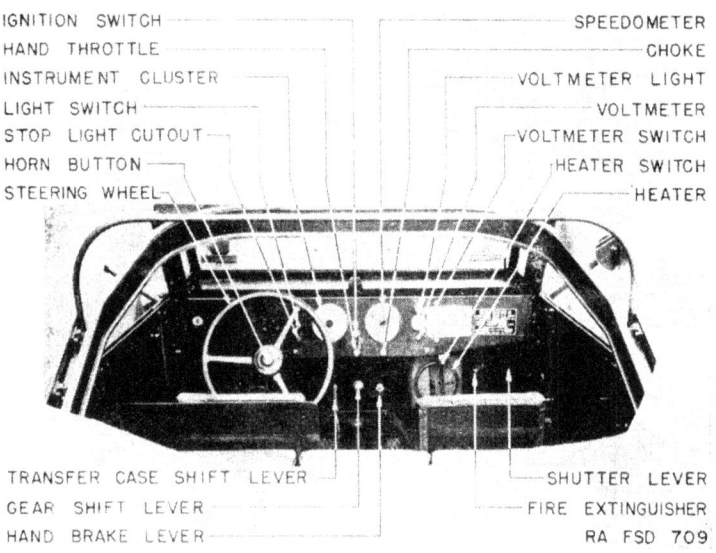

FIGURE 44.—Instrument panel and controls, scout car, M3.

SCOUT CARS AND MORTAR MOTOR CARRIAGE

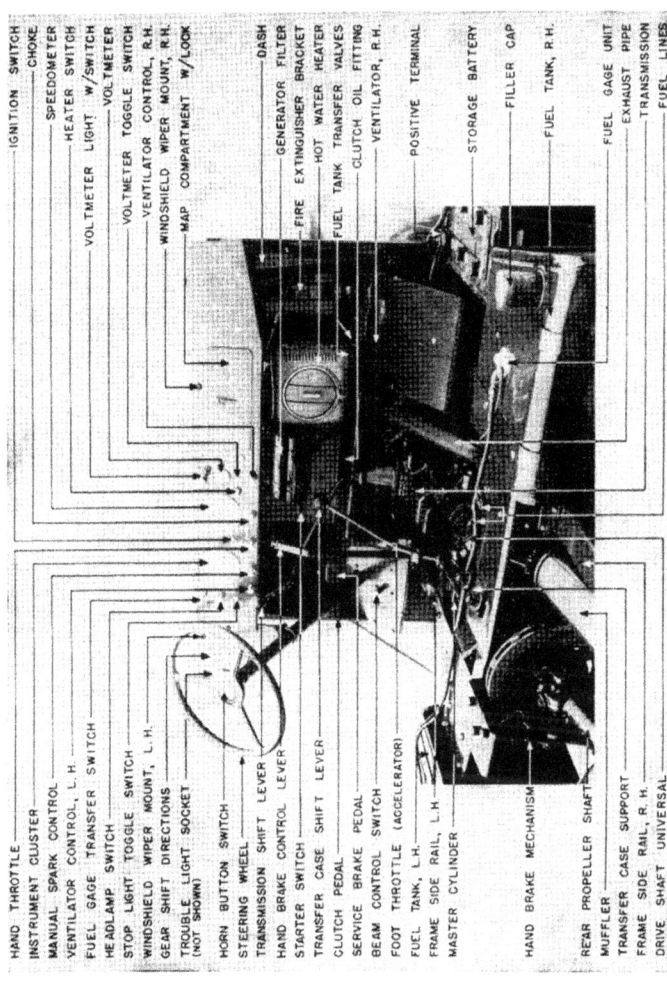

FIGURE 45.—Instrument panel and controls, scout car, M3A1.

TM 9-705

ORDNANCE DEPARTMENT

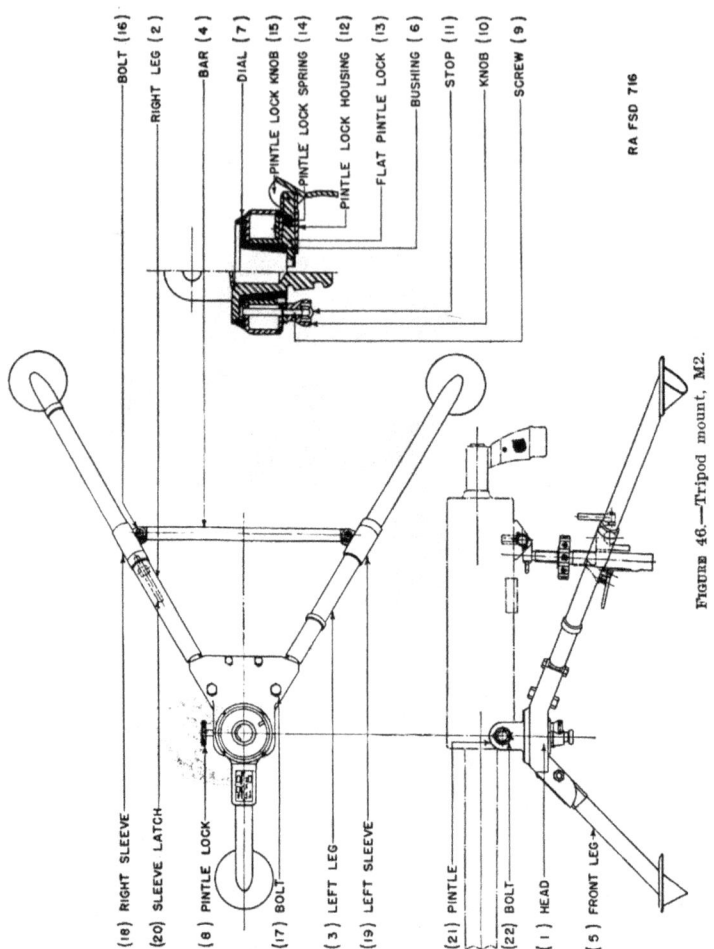

Figure 46.—Tripod mount, M2.

TM 9-705

SCOUT CARS AND MORTAR MOTOR CARRIAGE

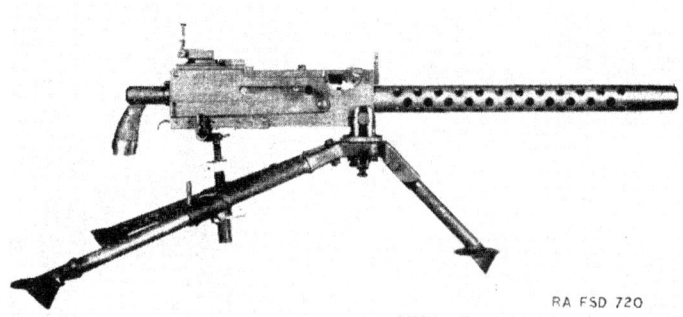

RA FSD 720

FIGURE 47.—Tripod mount, M2, with gun.

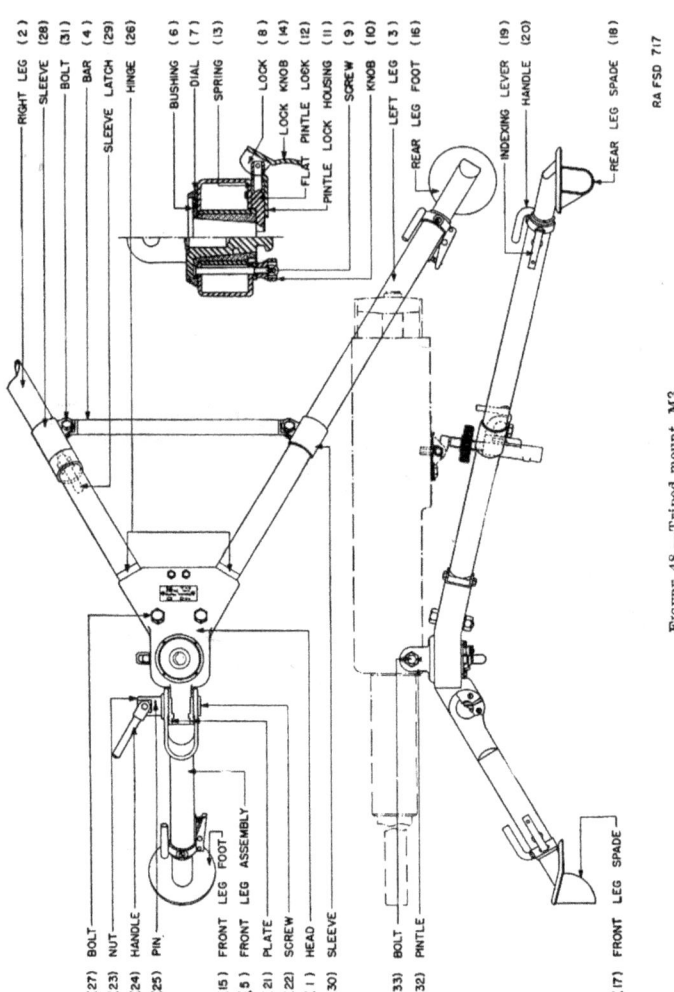

Figure 48.—Tripod mount, M3.

TM 9-705

SCOUT CARS AND MORTAR MOTOR CARRIAGE

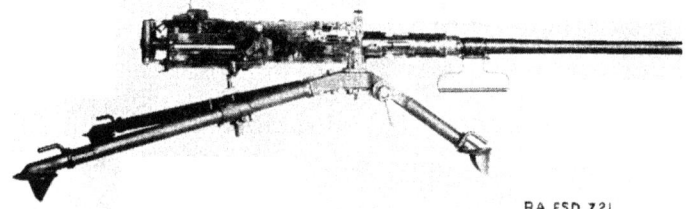

RA FSD 721

FIGURE 49.—Tripod mount, M3, with gun.

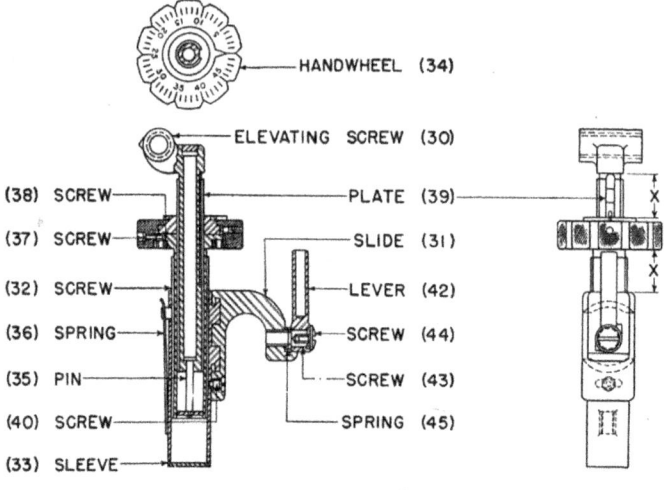

① Elevating mechanism tripod mount, caliber .50.

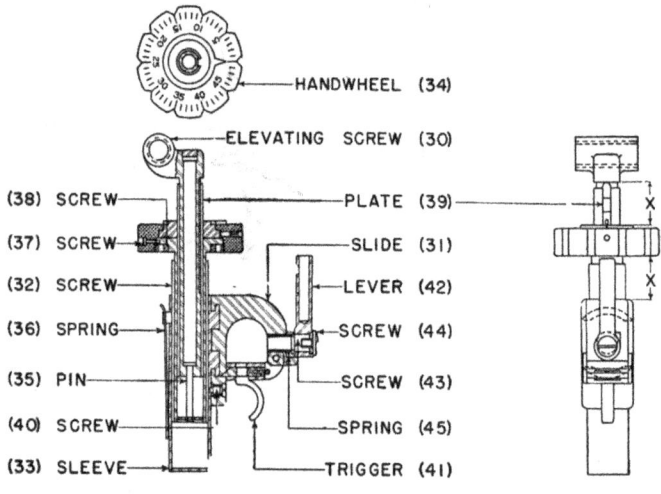

② Elevating mechanism mount, M21, caliber .50.
FIGURE 50.—Elevating mechanisms.

SCOUT CARS AND MORTAR MOTOR CARRIAGE

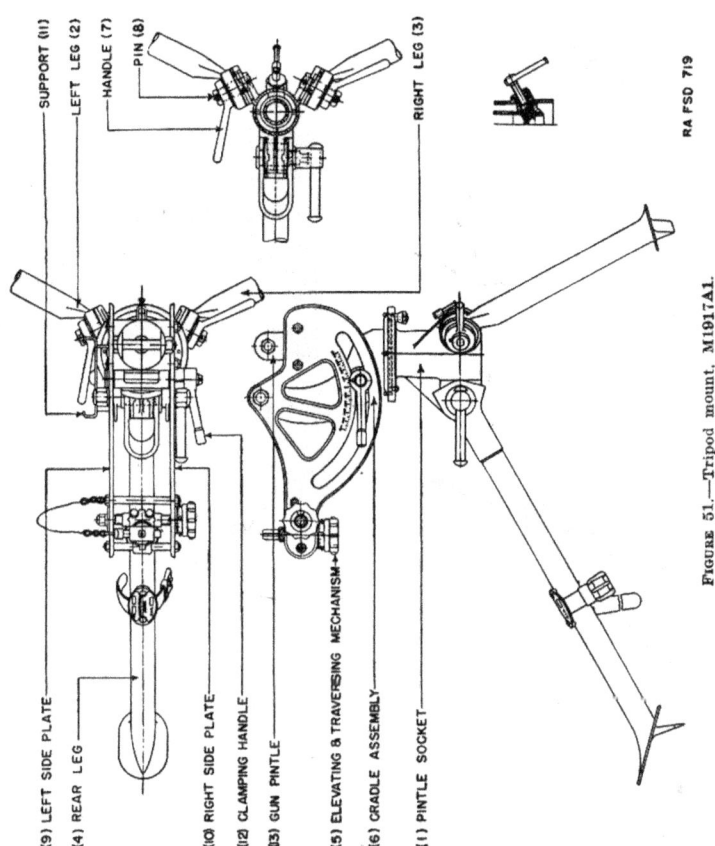

Figure 51.—Tripod mount, M1917A1.

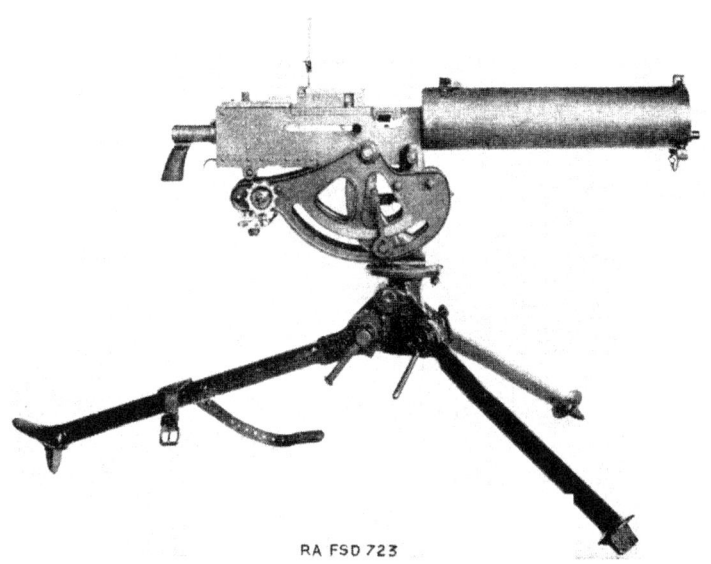

FIGURE 52.—Tripod mount, M1917A1, with gun.

SCOUT CARS AND MORTAR MOTOR CARRIAGE

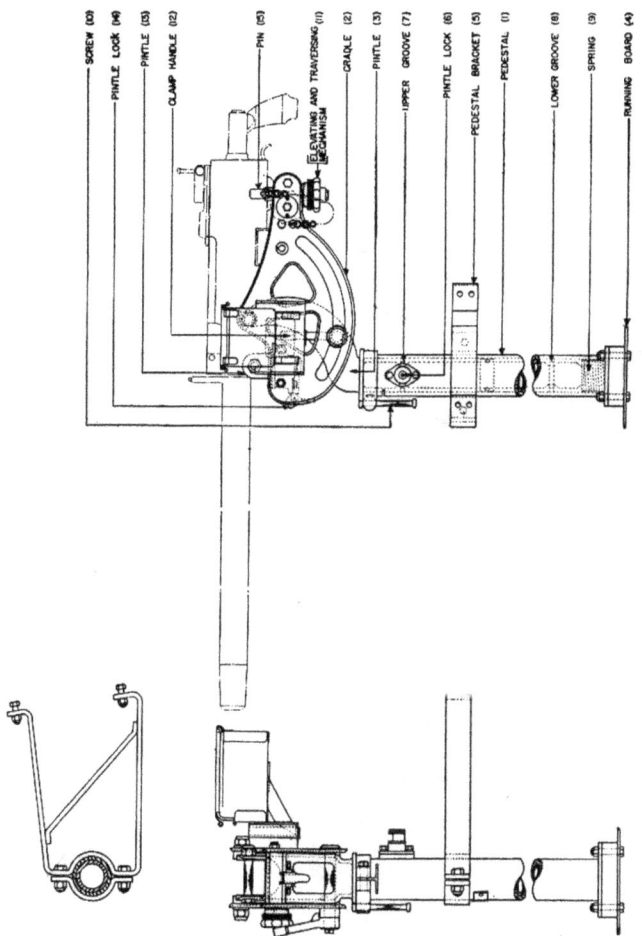

FIGURE 53.—Pedestal mount, T34.

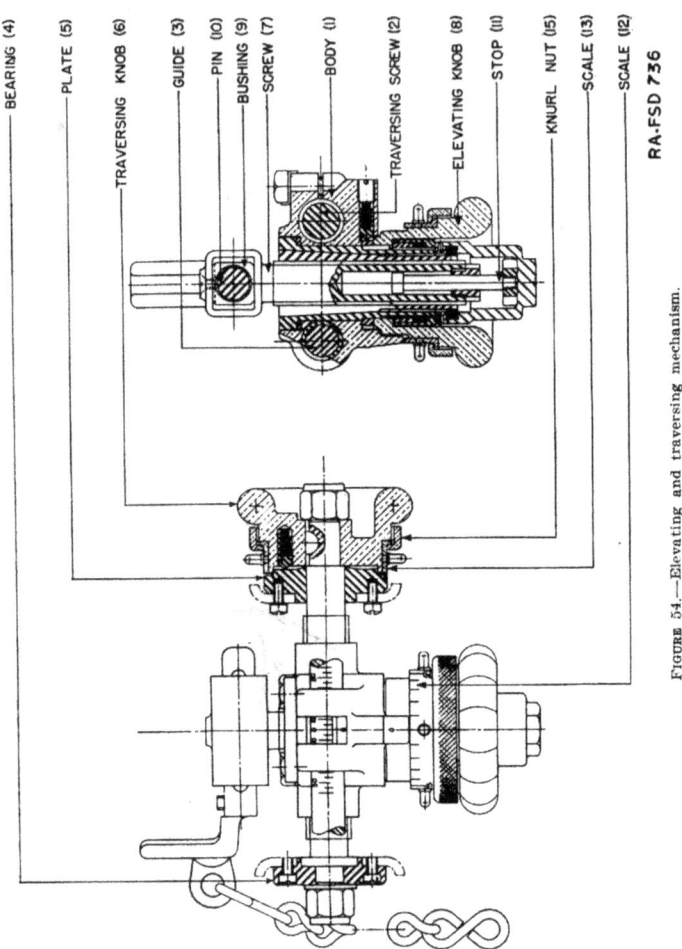

FIGURE 54.—Elevating and traversing mechanism.

TM 9-705

SCOUT CARS AND MORTAR MOTOR CARRIAGE

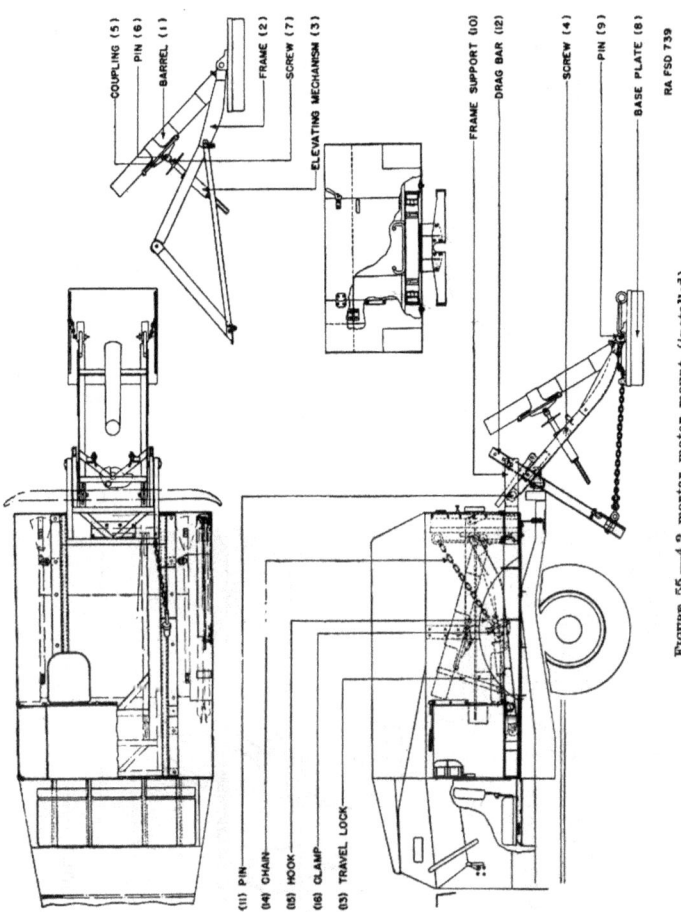

FIGURE 55.—4.2 mortar motor mount (installed).

TM 9-705

ORDNANCE DEPARTMENT

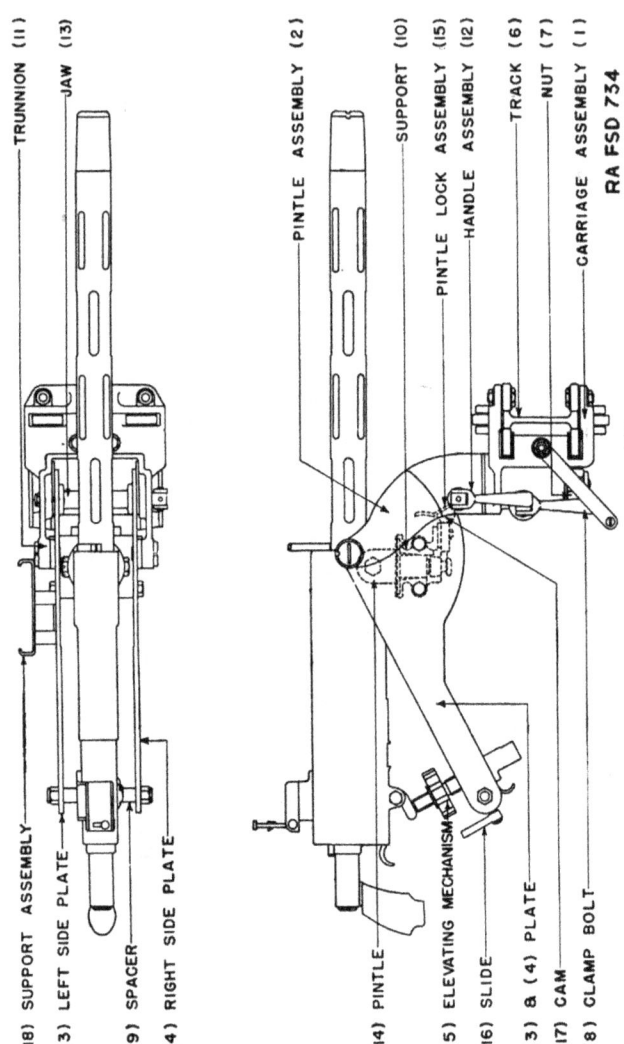

FIGURE 56.—Carriage mount, M22.

TM 9-705

SCOUT CARS AND MORTAR MOTOR CARRIAGE

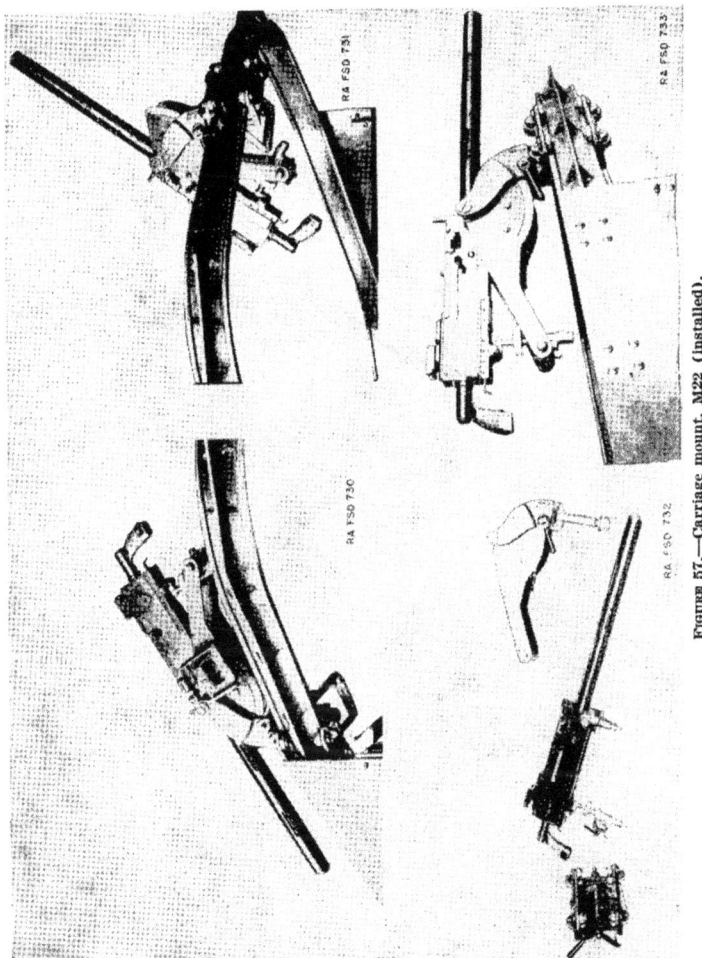

FIGURE 57.—Carriage mount, M22 (installed).

TM 9-705
ORDNANCE DEPARTMENT

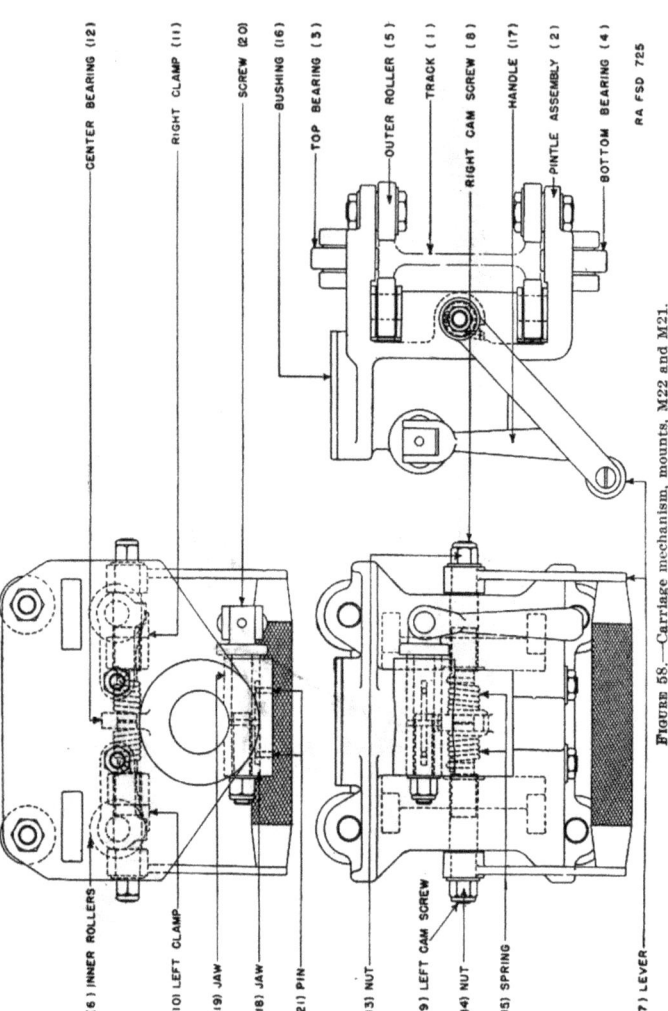

Figure 58.—Carriage mechanism, mounts, M22 and M21.

SCOUT CARS AND MORTAR MOTOR CARRIAGE

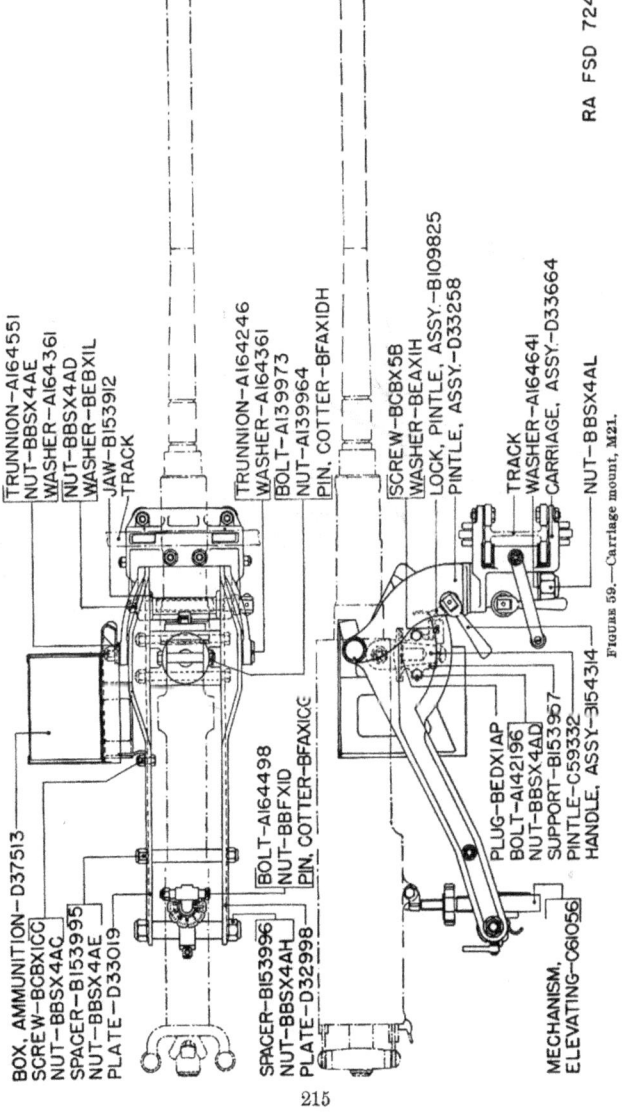

Figure 59.—Carriage mount, M21.

TM 9-705

ORDNANCE DEPARTMENT

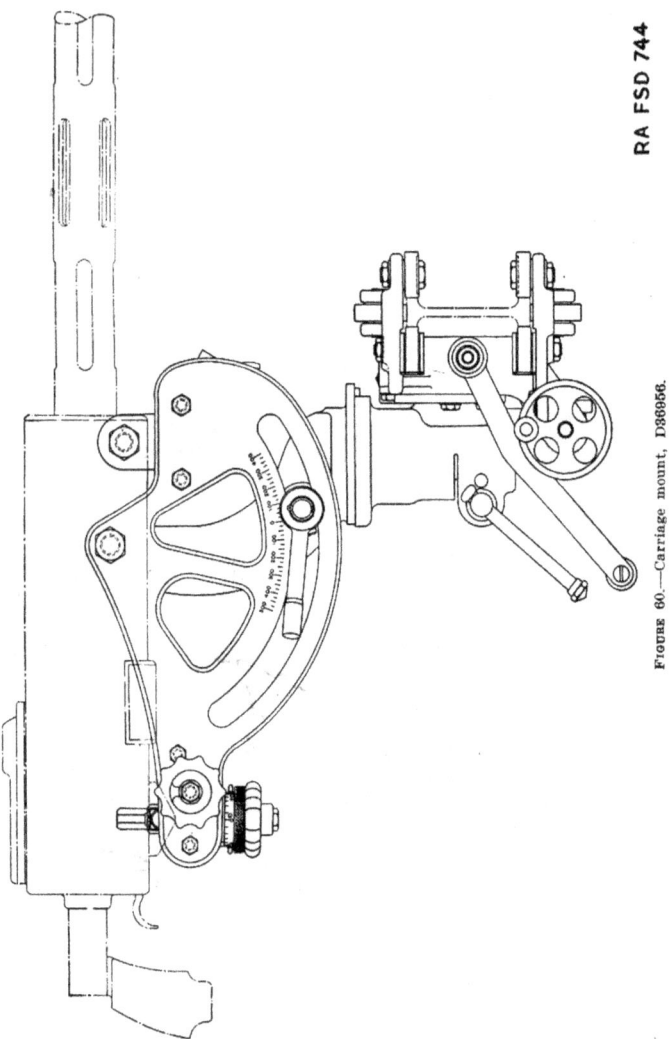

FIGURE 60.—Carriage mount, D38956.

RA FSD 744

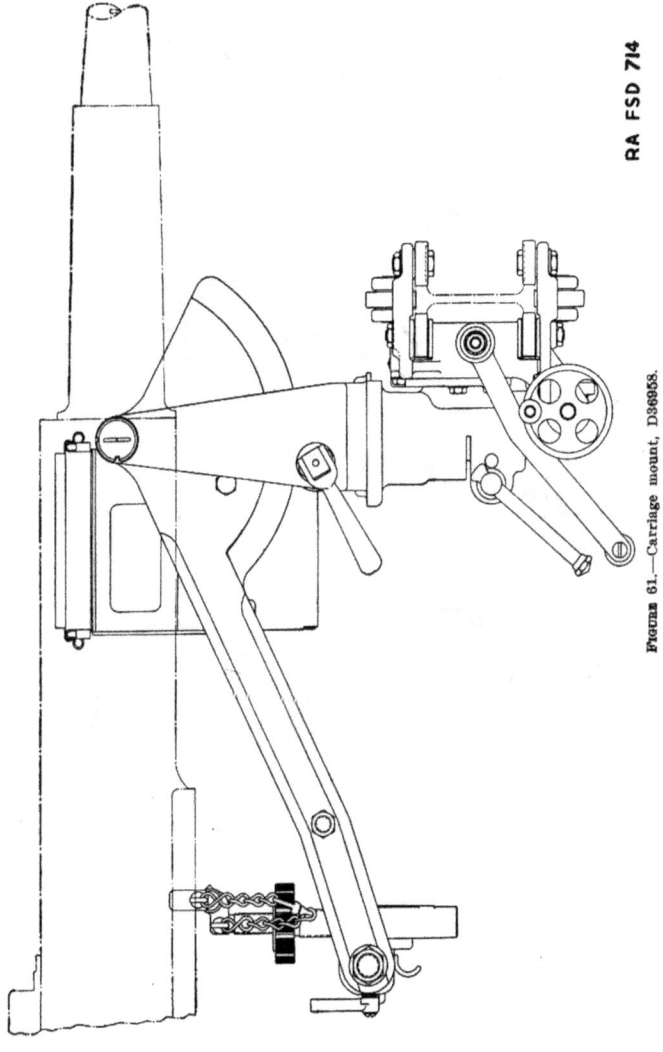

Figure 61.—Carriage mount, D36958.

TM 9-705

ORDNANCE DEPARTMENT

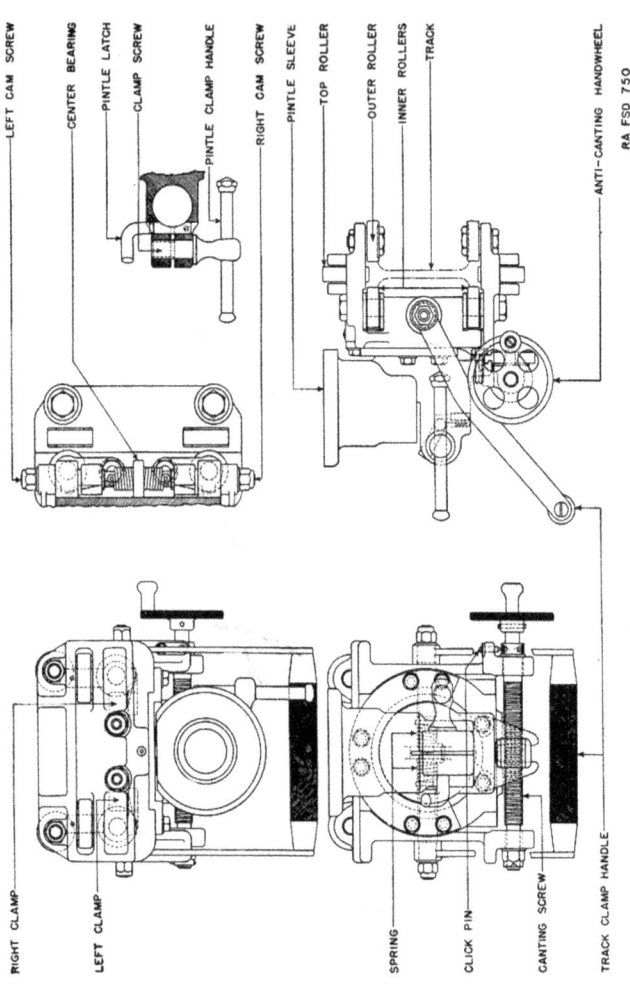

FIGURE 62.—Carriage mechanism, mounts D36956 and D36958.

218

INDEX

	Paragraphs	Pages
Accessories	104	133
Electrical	58	73
Air cleaners	15	21
Armament and mounts	105–115	134
Axles:		
Front	44	47
Rear	45	50
Battery, storage	54	66
Brakes:		
Hand	43	46
Hydraulic	47	52
Servicing	48	55
Carburetor	14	18
Carriage, motor, 4.2 mortar, M2:		
Characteristics	4	5
Description	3	2
Operation	61–76	78
Carriage mount:		
D36961	115	145
M21	114	145
M22	113	143
Chemical mortar mount, 4.2	112	142
Circuits, ignition system	18	24
Cleaning of vehicle	98	129
Clutch:		
Adjustment	30	40
Construction	29	39
Lubrication	31	40
Coil, ignition	19	26
Control devices	63	80
Electrical	58	73
Cooling system:		
Fan	25	35
Operation and maintenance	27	36
Water pump	26	36
Distributor, ignition system	20	26
Driver:		
Inspections by	65	82
Maintenance by	73	90
Reports by	74	93
Signals for	69	87
Driving handicaps	68	87
Echelons, maintenance	84–86	103
Electrical system	53	65
Wiring	59	76

INDEX

	Paragraphs	Pages
Elevating mechanism	108	138
Elevating and traversing mechanism	111	142
Engine:		
Group	5–11	8
Characteristics	6	8
Components:		
Electrical	8	13
Mechanical	7	9
Lubrication	10	13
Timing	9	13
Troubles and remedies	11	15
Starting and warming up	66	83
Equipment, electrical:		
Accessories	58	73
Battery, storage	54	66
Control	58	73
Generator	56	71
Lighting	58	73
Starting motor	55	70
Voltage regulator	57	72
Examination for operator's permit	75	94
Fan, cooling system	25	35
Fuel system:		
Air cleaners	15	21
Carburetor	14	18
Pump	13	17
Troubles and remedies	16	22
Gages	60	76
Gears, ratios and shifts	34	41
Auxiliary	38	43
Generators	56	71
Ignition system:		
Circuits	18	24
Coil	19	26
Distributor	20	26
Spark plugs	21	28
Timing	22	30
Troubles and remedies	23	32
Inspections:		
By driver	65	82
Command	95	128
Maintenance	96	128
Technical	97	129
Instructions, operation	61–76	78
Instruments and gages	60	76
Joints, universal	41	45
Lighting equipment	58	73
Lubricants, application	92, 93	112, 123

TM 9-705

INDEX

	Paragraphs	Pages
Lubrication	89-93	110
Clutch	31	40
Engine group	10	13
Methods	90	111
Propeller shaft	42	45
Schedules for	91	111
Transfer case	39	44
Transmission	35	42
Maintenance	83-88	102
By driver	73	90
Cooling system	27	36
Echelons:		
First (driver, assistant, and crew)	84	103
Second (troop or battery)	85	103
Third and fourth	86	103
Inspections	96	128
On marches	88	109
Operations	87	105
Marching, operating instructions for	71	88
Motor, starter	55	70
Mounts:		
Carriage:		
D36961	115	145
M21	114	145
M22	113	143
Chemical mortar, 4.2	112	142
Pedestal, T34	110	141
Tripod:		
M2	106	135
M3	107	137
M1917A1	109	140
Operation:		
Cooling system	27	36
Instructions	61-76	78
Maintenance	87	105
Requirements	61	78
Vehicle	67	84
Controls	63	80
Expedients:		
Camp	82	101
Field	77-82	96
Pioneer work	80	100
Traction aids	79	100
Repair	81	101
Handicaps in	68	87
Inspections of	72	89
By driver	65	82
Instructions in	61-72	78
On marches	71	88
Permit for, examination	75	94
Placing in service	64	81

221

INDEX

	Paragraphs	Pages
Operation —Continued.		
Vehicle—Continued.		
Road rules	70	87
Signals for driver	69	87
Starting and warming up engine	66	83
Troubles and remedies	76	94
Ordnance Motor Book	101	132
Painting vehicles	99	130
Parts, spare	103	133
Pedestal mount, T34	110	141
Propeller shaft:		
Brakes, hand	43	46
Lubrication	42	45
Universal joints	41	45
Power unit, vacuum	49	58
Pump:		
Fuel	13	17
Water, cooling system	26	36
References, list	2, App.	2, 147
Repair expedients	81	101
Reports by driver	74	93
Road rules	70	87
Scout car, M3 and M3A1:		
Accessories	104	133
Armament and mounts	105–115	134
Axle assemblies and steering gear	44–52	47
Care and preservation	98–100	129
Characteristics	4	5
Clutch	28–31	39
Cooling system	24–27	35
Description	3	2
Engine group	5–11	8
Equipment, electrical	53–59	65
Fuel system	12–16	16
Ignition system	17–23	24
Inspections	65, 94–97	82, 125
Instruments and gages	60	76
Lubrication	89–93	110
Maintenance	83–88	102
Operation	61–76	78
Expedients, field	77–82	96
Propeller shafts	40–43	45
Records	101, 102	132, 133
Spare parts	103	133
Transfer case	36–39	43
Transmission	32–35	40
Servicing hydraulic brakes	48	55
Shafts, propeller	40–43	45
Shock absorbers	51	61
Signals for driver	69	87
Spark plugs	21	28

INDEX

	Paragraphs	Pages
Springs	50	60
Starter motor	55	70
Steering mechanism	52	63
Storage of vehicles	100	131
Timing:		
Engine group	9	13
Ignition system	22	30
Tires	46	51
Traction aids	79	100
Transfer case:		
Auxiliary gear ratios and shifts	38	43
Construction	37	43
Lubrication	39	44
Transfer of vehicles, record	102	133
Transmission:		
Construction	33	40
Gear ratio and shifts	34	41
Lubrication	35	42
Transversing mechanism	111	142
Tripod mounts:		
M2	106	135
M3	107	137
M1917A1	109	140
Troubles and remedies:		
Engine group	11	15
Fuel system	16	22
Ignition system	23	32
Operation	76	94
Units, power, vacuum	49	58
Universal joints	44	47
Voltage regulator	57	72
Water pump, cooling system	26	36
Wheels	46	51
Wiring, electrical	59	76

[A. G. 062.11 (11-20-40).]

By ORDER OF THE SECRETARY OF WAR:

G. C. MARSHALL,
Chief of Staff.

OFFICIAL:

E. S. ADAMS,
    Major General,
        The Adjutant General.

DISTRIBUTION:

    D(3); B(3); R 2, 6, 7, 10, 17 (5); Bn 17 (3); IBn 2, 6 (3); C 17 (5); IC 2, 6, 7, 9, 10 (5).

©2012 Periscope Film LLC
All Rights Reserved
ISBN#978-1-937684-71-6